James Merrill

The End of Religion

Also by Dom Aelred Graham

THE LOVE OF GOD
An Essay in Analysis

THE FINAL VICTORY
A War-Time Meditation

THE CHRIST OF CATHOLICISM
A Meditative Study

CATHOLICISM AND THE WORLD TODAY

CHRISTIAN THOUGHT AND ACTION
The Role of Catholicism in Our Time

ZEN CATHOLICISM
A Suggestion

CONVERSATIONS: CHRISTIAN AND BUDDHIST
Encounters in Japan

The End of Religion

Autobiographical Explorations

DOM AELRED GRAHAM

Better is the end of a thing than its beginning
—ECCLESIASTES 7:8

Harcourt Brace Jovanovich, Inc., *New York & London*

The lines by T. S. Eliot quoted in the epigraph are from "The Dry
Salvages" in *Four Quartets,* copyright, 1943, by T. S. Eliot. Reprinted
by permission of Harcourt Brace Jovanovich, Inc. The lines by
James Henry Breasted are from "Hymn to Aton" in *The Dawn of
Conscience.* Reprinted by permission of Charles Scribner's Sons from
The Dawn of Conscience, page 281, by James H. Breasted. Copyright
1933 James Henry Breasted; renewal copyright © 1961 Charles Breasted,
James Breasted, Jr., and Astrid Breasted Hormann. The lines by W. H. Auden
are from "The Cave of Making: Postscript," in *About the House.* Reprinted
by permission of Faber and Faber, Ltd. The excerpts from *Sufism,* by
A. J. Arberry, are reprinted by permission of the publisher, George
Allen & Unwin, Ltd. The material quoted from *From Primitives to Zen,*
by Mircea Eliade, is reprinted by permission of the publisher, Harper
& Row. The excerpts from *The Masks of God: Creative Mythology,* by
Joseph Campbell, are reprinted by permission of The Viking Press,
Incorporated, Publishers.

ISBN 0-15-128795-3
Library of Congress Catalog Card Number: 77-139461
Printed in the United States of America
A B C D E

We shall not cease from exploration
And the end of all our exploring
Will be to arrive where we started
And know the place for the first time.

—T. S. ELIOT, *Little Gidding*

Preface

Few preliminaries are needed to this book. Its title, subtitle, and table of contents indicate pretty accurately what it is about. "Autobiographical explorations," intended as a limitation, to emphasize that a large theme is being mediated through a single, only moderately well-qualified personality, may have led to self-disclosure being carried to the point of self-indulgence. On the other hand, the rather philosophical debate with myself occupying the first half-dozen pages (so I have been advised on high authority) gives no hint of the liveliness and general interest of the book as a whole. This counsel should be taken to heart, by way of a little judicious skipping, on the part of those who have no taste for abstractions. However, it must in fairness be said that the author is concerned throughout, or so he believes, with his avowed subject in preference to himself.

Institutional religion is in difficulties these days—partly, I think, because the possibility is not widely enough recognized of people being deeply concerned about religion and yet tired of listening to "the churches." That, at any rate, is one of the positions allowed for in this essay. Inevitably, the Christian churches will come in; but so will Hinduism, Buddhism, Judaism, and Islam—not as parts of the overworked topic of "comparative religion," or with an eye to some future "universal church," but for the purpose of trying to discover what religion basically is, what it is all about. There is even mention of a "religion of no religion," which may not prove quite so disconcerting as it sounds. At the end of our inquiry we could find that religion is at once simpler, more inviting, and better attuned to the realities of this world than is often supposed.

The need for an investigation like the one here attempted, I believe, is among the many factors underlying the unrest, now startlingly apparent, within the Roman Church—to which all my life I have happily and gratefully belonged. Ecumenism, today so fashionable in official quarters, is in itself an admission that the Christian communions, each in its own way, have something to learn, perhaps also not a little to unlearn. Religion, in the form of rigid and distinctive ecclesiastical structures, may well be nearing its end, only to raise the much more fundamental question: What is the end, the abiding goal, of religion itself? When one considers, for example, the wealth of religious inspiration deriving from India, how odd appears the standpoint of those who take it for granted that Christianity alone can provide the answer. It is this assumption, implicitly at least, that will come up for review in the following pages. The Christian Church, like its individual members, may gain rather than lose by becoming fully aware of its limitations—envisaging the prospect that it could have a long, painful, and as yet unsuspected pilgrimage to make before it is guided "into all the truth" (John 16:13).

Experience and observation, rather than any notable professional scholarship, are the resources on which we shall draw. Though I speak from the Catholic tradition, it is without any sense of hindrance in following the argument wherever it may lead. If the conclusions are sometimes only hinted at, leaving the field open to further investigation, I hesitate to press logic to extremes from personal uncertainty, not as curtailed by any outside authority. As the book is concerned with religion in its essence (or, to be more accurate, in its "dynamism"), seen from a confessedly personal viewpoint, printing the ecclesiastical imprimatur, with its deceptive suggestion of specific Church endorsement, would seem out of place. Nevertheless, any reader interested in such matters may rest assured that this essay is published with the appropriate ecclesiastical permission and *permissu superiorum ordinis,* while at the same time neither the English Benedictine Congregation, of which I am privileged to be a member, nor anyone other than the author can be held responsible for any statement made or any opinion expressed in this book. Finally, I should like to thank the Abbot and community at Ampleforth, my own brethren in religion, who with their kind co-operation and genuine interest provided the ideal conditions under which this book was written. Whatever its defects, the circumstances of authorship cannot be blamed for them.

AELRED GRAHAM

Ampleforth Abbey
York

Contents

The End of Religion

1. Viewpoint of an Author Attempting To Be Honest

It seems to me—let that be the determining phrase, the general rubric, governing all that is said in this book. The first person singular and its derivatives are likely to abound; but this should lessen rather than otherwise any latent dogmatism in the opinions here expressed. "I think," after all, is decidedly more modest than "it is." For a writer striving to reach the heart of religion the obligation to be open and self-revealing—to let it be seen how fallible and even vulnerable he can be—appears bound up with his whole project. John Henry Newman, unfolding so persuasively to the England of the 1860's, with all the refinements of which his acute mind was capable, how he understood the Christian Church, saw no alternative but to weave into the account of his intellectual development a disclosure of his own personality. And yet how difficult he found it: "For who can know himself, and the multitude of subtle influences which act upon him? But now, in the 1970's, when the focus of interest is no longer Catholicism versus Protestantism, or even Christianity, but simply religion itself, and where the reticence that marked the Victorian age would today be considered lack of candor, how much more demanding is the challenge to hide nothing in one's life that could bear upon what one says and why one says it. Though the present essay be comparable to the future Cardinal's *Apologia Pro Vita Sua* only in the coincidence that I now happen to be roughly the age he was when he wrote that celebrated history of his religious opinions, one sentence in it finds its fitting context here: "I have done various bold things in my life: this is the boldest."

First, by way of parenthesis, a mildly academic word touching the mental climate in which these pages are likely to be judged—at least in the learned circles for which they are no more than incidentally intended. When we think about the world around us—external reality—is it *that* we are thinking of, or merely our ideas about that? The philosopher Descartes raised this problem with his famous *Cogito, ergo sum* ("I think, therefore I am"), and on the whole favored our ideas about the world over the world itself. Kant—taking his cue from Hume, who held that "reason is the slave of passion"—went further and posited that our mental categories, the style of our own thinking, was what gave substance to the whole conscious content of our minds. Freud was to press forward with the suggestion that self-knowledge, based on normal consciousness, is totally inadequate. If we wish to be honest, or even sane, we must bring into the field of awareness our unconscious motivations and conflicts, which in fact determine a great deal of what we think and do. Today, both phenomenologists and existentialists would have us avoid all questions that cannot be answered merely by describing appearances carefully. Martin Heidegger and Jean-Paul Sartre, though differing from each other in much, appear to agree that the world of man, "brute existence," is in itself meaningless; what meaning it seems to have we impose upon it. The world I know is my personal interpretation. An uninterpreted world is a contradiction in terms, like a square circle.

These positions have all been criticized, particularly by orthodox theologians, and their weaknesses exposed; but they have permanently modified the living tradition of Western thought. It would be hard to refute Edmund Husserl's thesis that philosophy cannot return to a pre-Cartesian point of view, i.e., to a merely objective way of looking at, or trying to look at, reality; the subjective element cannot be evaded. Were we to proceed as if these deeply significant contributions to our understanding of the human condition had never been made, we should be wasting our time. When the intellectual climate has changed so perceptibly, almost within living memory, those concerned to propagate an older Christian ideology are faced with a familiar dilemma. Are they to join or oppose the trend of the times? There is plenty of evidence to show that both courses are being adopted, and in some cases a little of each, according to taste. The conservative-minded strive to stand fast by the old ways, employing techniques of varying degrees of subtlety; the progressives, eager to be in the vanguard of modern thought, are ready to reinterpret the Gospel message and to show its relevance in the most unpromising situations.

With the external fabric of organized Christianity being desperately shored up, showing signs of eventual collapse, and the livelier of the younger generation alienated from most forms of institutional religion, it is not surprising that many of the Church authorities are dismayed. Few of them, however, show any inclination to face, much less to answer, the fundamental questions. What is the purpose of religion? What is its relation to truth, as attested by evidence and experience? Can Christianity validate its claim to be an all-sufficing way of life in today's world? Do the time-honored externals of the Christian religion look perhaps too superficial, a little tired and archaic, its creed and ritual (even though recently revised) too weighted with a literal historicism to command lasting notice from a generation that expects religion to throw light on its most urgent concerns, to touch the deepest level of the human spirit, and to do so not with reference to the past or future but now.

"The believer," wrote Nietzsche in his *Umwertung aller Werthe*, "is not free to have any conscience at all for the question 'true or untrue': to have integrity on *this* point would be his end." [1] Here is a challenge, it seems to me, that the professing Christian has ultimately to face.

> There lives more faith in honest doubt,
> Believe me, than in half the creeds.

These well-known lines from Tennyson's *In Memoriam* have their point today, particularly for Catholics, since the upheavals and confusion following upon the Second Vatican Council. The area of doubt for the trained theologian may remain at the verbal and conceptual level; that is to say, he could be uncertain about which of a variety of statements most nearly represents a fundamental Christian position. With the faithful in general—for whom words, concepts, and the realities they represent are often inextricably interlinked—the crisis of belief could be traumatic indeed. It can lead to a sickness of heart, a sense that religion does not matter very much, since its spokesmen appear unable either to uphold convincingly the traditional creeds or to develop their implications in a realistic manner. More hopefully, such a testing moment can be one of unaccountable enlightenment, a virtual breakthrough, by which the individual believer pierces to the very heart of religion. Grateful for the traditional influences that have permeated his life, repudiating nothing

1. Quoted from Joseph Campbell, *The Masks of God: Creative Mythology* (New York: Viking Press, 1968), p. 584.

that holds a possibility of truth, contemptuous of no authority, holding glad communion with his brethren and with any who would have it so, he must above all be faithful to his own insight, persuaded that, however precariously, he stands (in the phrase of T. S. Eliot) "at the still point of the turning world."

"Nor is it at all apparent . . ." writes a perceptive reviewer in *The Times Literary Supplement*, commenting, fairly enough, on some published "conversations" of mine with Buddhists in Japan. "Nor is it at all apparent what kind of Catholic Dom Aelred is." Clarification on this point is clearly called for in any attempt to be simply truthful. To bring to light what is partly hidden, from myself not least, is one of the motives for embarking on this essay. Though unhappy with the label "Thomist" (creative thought, as already touched on, has been vastly augmented since Aquinas wrote), or for that matter with any other label, I still find—as was the case more than thirty years ago—St. Thomas's conception of the nature of faith by far the most satisfying. Whether it tallies with what emerges from the Gospels, or St. Paul, or what is nowadays called "biblical theology," is, of course, another question. Thomas's basically contemplative position, centered in the first place on God under the aspect of "Ultimate Truth" (*Veritas Prima*) rather than on the redemptive work of Christ, differs sharply from that of Martin Luther and the reformers generally.

Thomas treats of faith *ex professo* at the beginning of the second part (its second part) of his *Summa Theologica*. Partly from the habit of his times, partly no doubt from personal inclination, he explains faith not in historical or even biblical terms but with reference to a sixth-century treatise on "The Divine Names" by a Christian Neoplatonist, Pseudo-Dionysius the Areopagite (whom Thomas mistakenly regarded as the contemporary of St. Paul, and as thus having almost apostolic authority). "Faith is focused upon simple and eternally existing Truth." [2] Admittedly, Thomas is here considering di-

---

2. "*Fides est circa simplicem, et semper existentem veritatem.*" *Summa Theologica*, II–II, 1, i, *sed contra*. Here, whatever St. Thomas himself may have meant, I now understand "eternally existing truth" not as a timeless Platonic essence but as a revelation that transcends the antithesis between essence and existence, static and dynamic, carrying over into the area of what I shall call "pure Existence." This thought will be developed later (see pp. 263 ff.).

vine truth as it is revealed by God (Truth itself); but his position becomes more interesting when we consider the idea—or rather, the non-idea—he holds of God. God's essence cannot be grasped conceptually at all (*Summa*, I, 12, ii). No descriptive classification applies to God; he is not in any genus (*Summa*, I, 3, v). God is the sole Reality of which it can be said that existence constitutes its essence (*Summa*, I, 3, iv). In other words, God is quintessential *Existence* (*Ipsum esse subsistens*).

A metaphysical, seemingly abstract approach such as this—which I have no intention at this point of pursuing further—is doubtless unsatisfactory to biblical scholars and historians; it appears far removed from the style of "salvation history," which has recently come into vogue. But I think it could be shown that these lines of investigation converge rather than separate. We need not follow St. Thomas through the intricacies of his deductive logic; they are forbiddingly unattractive to the average mind of today. When, however, we speak of God as unqualified *Existence*, we are not back in the thirteenth century but in today's climate of thought with the later work of Heidegger and Paul Tillich. Relatively few people can become attuned to the dynamic of biblical history, so that it enters significantly into their lives; but everyone knows, or rather experiences in varying degrees of awareness, what it is to exist—to *have*, if not to be, existence. Clearing the mind so that we see the situation in these terms, we are, so to speak, on the divine wave length; we awake to the sense that we ourselves, in Boris Pasternak's felicitous phrase, are the "guests of existence."

This having been said, we must at once take account of the fact that though God may be unique he appears differently to everyone who approaches or thinks about him. Even those who adhere to the same creed will be found to have in their thinking and devotional life their own private God. "What is accepted by the mind," runs a scholastic adage, "is received according to the measure of that mind." The point may be illustrated by a personal encounter.

As these pages were being drafted a young man of twenty-one came to see me. His Christianity proved to be vestigial, and he had become seriously interested in Taoism, since, according to his view, it provided a framework within which to live a life in harmony with nature. At the same time, he wanted to experience something of the Benedictine way of living; hence his visit to our monastery. He spent several days in active discussion with various members of the community, sharing in our prayer life, work, and recreation. Then he came to say good-bye. He had enjoyed his visit immensely, was deeply impressed with the obvious unity, the manifest spirit of charity among the brethren. Only one thing puzzled him: he had made a point of asking everyone he talked with about his notion of God. To his astonishment, although all had much the same background and training, revered the same religious tradition, professed the same faith, no two accounts of what God meant to the individual were even approximately identical. Subjectivity controlled the experience of each.

To return to the author's attempt to be honest. "The chief duty of man," Rudolf Bultmann has written, "is to achieve clarity in thinking and speaking about his own situation." [3] Coming from perhaps the most influential Protestant theologian of our time, to whose work I confess myself greatly indebted, this is an interesting pronouncement in a number of ways. In the first place, it is doubtful whether the duty as described is incumbent on, or capable of observance by, mankind as a whole. Secondly, it appears in a context that shows the early Bultmann to have greater confidence in the potentialities of reason and speech than he could have learned from his philosophical mentor, Heidegger. "The irrational has no significance for him [i.e., man] and the unutterable for him is really a nothing." Both these statements are highly questionable; they would, I think, be repudiated by exponents of the Hindu-Buddhist tradition, for which religious insight only attains its goal when the mind has reached beyond "name and form." Nevertheless, Bultmann's point is valuable in that it stresses one of the requirements of the Western cultivated mind, for which such pearls of Eastern wisdom as the Taoist, Lao Tzu's— "Those who know do not speak; those who speak do not know"—lack luster. A religious position must be spelled out in words to the fullest degree possible. Those who nowadays make such an attempt are rightly expected not to hide behind impersonal generalities but to bear witness from a clearly revealed consciousness of their own situation.

There are a good many factors working against anybody who is

3. *Faith and Understanding*, trans. Louise Pettibone Smith (London: S.C.M. Press, 1969), p. 115.

concerned to say what he really thinks about religion. High on the list are those stemming from his own personality. We all have an "image" we strive to present to the world at large, behind which lies our true character, of whose nature we are but partly aware. The external image and the underlying character may be only remotely connected with each other. But it is the character that we reveal, perhaps despite ourselves, in a life dedicated to religion. At least this is so in the area of everyday conduct. When we come to speak or write on some religious theme, all the problems involved in making an acceptable public appearance present themselves. Consider the scriptural stereotypes, the spiritual clichés, the hollow rhetoric, the moralistic denunciations, the would-be dramatic touches that can often do service for a disclosure of that in which the business of being saved, the attainment of final freedom and enlightenment, actually consist.

The flaw and the difficulty lie partly in the phrase "religious theme," of which use has just been made. As long as religion is regarded as a separate department of life, offering themes for appropriate discourse when we and our audience are in the mood, we are still at one or two removes from reality. Religious insight is imparted only superficially by words; what moves and stimulates others is a *presence*. Not an appearance on the stage of a strong, self-confident "personality," but a human embodiment, an actualization in flesh and blood, of existential truth, demanding attention for the sufficient reason that under given conditions of space and time it happens to be there. Thus the Buddha, Socrates, and Jesus—to take the historical order—wrote down no verbal message; they made their impression by direct contact with their contemporaries. So deep was this impression that it inspired their disciples in varying ways to make some record of it. From such an account posterity might learn of these master spirits—who they were, what they said and did. Fortunately, the resulting literature, in part at least, is itself of such a quality that it conveys something of the "presence" by which it was inspired.

Today any such presence is rarely found; we are left, for the most part, with intermediaries. Their modest function is to capture what they can of the original insight, strive to identify themselves with it, and transmit it to others by means of words. The religious monologue is happily no longer in fashion. Could it be that the days of the formal sermon in church are slowly being numbered? Dialogue may not be the total answer; experts and specialists must still be given time and space to have their say. But in matters religious who, it may fairly be asked, are the experts? The gulf between clergy and laity is rapidly being closed; the layman is exercising his right to talk back. Nowadays teachers and preachers are liable to be asked, usually by the young, about their intimate personal lives. To what extent do you practice what you preach? Why do you lay down ethical rules in areas of life of which you have no experience—an unmarried clergy, for instance, dealing with marriage and clerical celibacy? How do you, a monk and priest, compensate for a lack of normal sex life? Tell us more.

Questions of this kind, in my experience, are asked with no hostile intent. On the contrary, they are often touchingly expressed, as from one faltering human being to another. Their intent—mixed, no doubt, with an element of personal interest—is to try to elucidate a genuine problem. The quest is for "authenticity," to discover and pay heed to the imperatives of one's own being, not to be satisfied with living by the often dubious standards supplied by the "establishment." The authentic person is not content to operate in an area of tension, between the pull of the ideal and the possibilities of the real; he must act in "obedience to the voice of being"; that is, the *existence* in which his own life situation is immersed, or more accurately, which it creates. The light by which he acts does not come from some Platonic ideal order; it arises right there on the spot where he is, from the total situation in which he finds himself. And it may involve him in greater personal sacrifice than an "unauthentic" program for action, an ethical code, to which he has been taught to pay lip service. What then, in such a context, is to be said of a religious position that seems to have a built-in structure, where theory is one thing and actual practice another? Candor, obviously, is the only possible response.

On and off throughout these pages we shall be concerned with this problem. My own attempts to achieve authenticity may involve me in comment that sounds a little odd, coming from a Catholic priest and monk—particularly one who has no quarrel with his Church or any of its officials. Controversial opinions are offered as topics for discussion, hints of how the Christian mind might develop in the future, not as from one who speaks with authority. By way of indicating how certain lines of thought have come about, I shall venture to strike quite often an autobiographical note. It may not resound so loudly as to tell all, in the manner of a true-confession story, but perhaps clearly enough to reveal to the reader, especially one who seeks grounds for disagreement, why it is I happen to think the way I do. How far I shall succeed in this paradoxical exercise and keep loyal to the conviction that truth-telling may never be separated from compassion and that egoism mars them both, remains problematical indeed.

The doubtful enterprise of a religious autobiography was begun, as is well known, by St. Augustine. As his *Confessions* have been extravagantly praised, it is worth recalling that Hilaire Belloc thought it the most boring of books. A modern historian has described it as "that strange mixture of vanity and humility, of rant and eloquence, of superstition and common sense." [4] But no one who risks saying anything about himself in the context of religion can forget Augustine, the Church Father who, for better or worse, more than any other has formed the mind of Western Christendom. Absurd as the comparison is, and embarrassing as the technique of publicly addressing the Deity on matters so relatively trivial would be today, Augustine strikes me as a model of honesty, though perhaps one should qualify this statement by adding that he was as honest as his own psychology and experience permitted him to be. Feelings of guilt and sinfulness apart, one wonders how well he understood the depth and permanence of his infection by Manichaeism—that heresy according to which man's bodily functions pertained to the "kingdom of darkness." Converted to orthodoxy though he was, of him at least—and who would deny its application to himself?—Nietzsche's memorable intuition holds true: "The degree and kind of a man's sexuality reach up into the ultimate pinnacle of his spirit." [5]

Apart from the variety of motives arising from human vanity, tempting an author to be less than candid, there are others that press particularly on a Catholic writer. He often appears to be so conscious of the Church's official position that he becomes merely its exponent

4. E. E. Kellett, *A Short History of Religions* (Baltimore: Penguin Books, 1962), p. 233.
5. Friedrich Nietzsche, *Beyond Good and Evil*, trans. Walter Kaufmann (New York: Random House, 1966), p. 81.

and loses any capacity for original thought. However, as official positions are today becoming more and more fluid, he may soon be left with no alternative but to think for himself. One knows from experience how strong is the urge to operate in any religious investigation with the whole panoply of Catholic assumptions, forgetful that some of them, to say the least, may be open to question. This state of affairs appears conspicuously when Catholics well equipped in terms of scholarship are dealing with the religions of India and the Far East. The approach is frequently sympathetic and appreciative but rarely is there any attempt to view, say, Hinduism or Buddhism on their own terms. Implicitly, the point of interest is where and how they can finally be assimilated by the Church. The superiority complex of Western Christianity—made up, it may prove to be, of cultural and political rather than intrinsically religious elements—has still to be resolved.

We have only to open the morning newspaper to become aware that many of the Catholic assumptions just alluded to are being openly challenged. The result is that almost any thoughtful person is likely to be found, like Lord Acton, wearing his Catholicism "with a difference." Whenever anything I shall have to say in the following pages is related to Church doctrine, the latter will be placed, so to speak, in brackets, by a kind of epoche[6]—so prescinding from, without ignoring or challenging, currently accepted Catholic positions. Thus we are led to certain factors that could favor, in this instance, the attempt to be quite honest. First among these is the conviction that to discern the truth and then tell it as one sees it is both more important and more interesting than to plead even the highest cause. Truth is reached not only by insight and experience but from a sense of balance, seeing life steadily and seeing it whole, and this is easier to achieve in one's sixties than in one's thirties. "To grow old," says Albert Camus, "is to pass from passion to compassion." When one's ambitions, such as they were, have been fulfilled, and when one is relieved of the struggle for existence, surrounded and well understood by congenial companions, having carried responsibility for the welfare of others, been given the opportunity to travel widely, and generally to have "seen the scene," one has little excuse for allowing the faults that often go with authorship—jealousy of one's peers, or

6. Without using this term precisely in the specialized sense in which it appears in Edmund Husserl's phenomenology.

an itch for controversy—to mar this essay with even a tincture of special pleading.

More equivocal, no doubt, is a conscious tendency to skepticism and to prefer the radical to the conventional approach. The same might be said of a distaste for being involved in the "generation gap," and where the generations conflict, to prefer the intuitions of youth to the experience of age. Again, I confess to being faintly weary of "commitment"—both the word and the thing—and hankering after what the Zen masters call "the position of no position," while acknowledging that every position in the last analysis is a personal one. Hence arises the final test of honesty. I believe that in an enterprise such as this, modest in length but significant in its substance, an author should do two things: he should let his positive qualifications for the task speak for themselves, while at the same time indicating the factors in his approach or his personal life that might distort the picture, that is, so far as he is aware of these. Thus the reader can assess on his own account the author's effort to speak truly: first, by how candidly he relates the limiting personal factors, and secondly, by how apparent to the reader are other such factors of which the author has failed to take note. After giving some thought to what strikes me as the ambiguities in the religious position of most people, I shall try to be more explicit about my own. Governing the whole discussion, however, is an admirably expressed thought by my favorite living poet:

> At lucky moment we seem on the brink
> Of really saying what we think we think:
> But, even then, an honest eye should wink.[7]

7. W. H. Auden, Postscript to "The Cave of Making," in *About the House* (London: Faber and Faber, 1966), p. 22.

2. Ambiguities of Being Religious

The Christian religion today, it seems to me, has lost much of its power to stimulate the mind. It appears dull and uninteresting, especially to the young. Watch an undergraduate thumbing through religious paperbacks: the chances are that he will ignore the Gospel commentaries, the portentous tractates on theology (however up-to-date and "existential"), linger for a while over Teilhard de Chardin or the latest Bultmann, then take to the pay desk a volume or two on Hinduism or Zen. He shows good judgment if he is concerned with enriching the imagination, expanding his mental vision.

When I was young, popular Sunday newspapers would sometimes bring out a series of articles on "What Religion Means to Me" by well-known politicians, film stars, footballers, jockeys, and the like. With youthful superciliousness I used to think this all a mistake; the people who should have been consulted were theologians and philosophers, the brighter bishops, and so as not to neglect the laity, one or two reformed criminals who had seen the light. Now I am not so sure. Anyone who writes sincerely about religion reveals in some way what it means to him. And if religion touches life in its totality, why should the revelations of "religionists" (not a term of ridicule, at least in the United States) command any more attention than the honest thoughts of the technically inexpert?

Among the whole range of human interests, it can plausibly be argued, religion suffers more damage from handling by professional and academic experts than any other. The reason is partly linguistic. The wellsprings of the historic religions are buried in poetry: highly metaphysical, as in the Vedas and the Upanishads; resonant and dramatic, as in parts of Hebrew scripture; often sensuously beautiful and evocative, as in certain Homeric hymns. Modern expositors of religion, however, are seldom endowed with an ear for the poetic, or even pleasingly lucid, use of language. With few exceptions, language is not for them an instrument of music, whose notes reverberate within the attentive consciousness; rather it is a verbal mechanism to be utilized for hammering out mental concepts.

A more serious difficulty attending any form of religious professionalism is its nonpreoccupation with truth for its own sake. This need not imply the least element of conscious dishonesty; the obstacle lies in a mind filled with largely unexamined assumptions. Academic professors of religion are curiously prone to take in each other's theological washing, often in the form of more or less thinly disguised doctoral theses. Their disquisitions are addressed, by implication, to their colleagues or rivals rather than to ordinary human beings. Hence, their pages tend to be sprinkled with names of which the average reader has never heard, their arguments often focused on abstruse intramural controversies that lead even one with some inside knowledge to nod drowsily as the tome tumbles incontinently from his hands.

One of the more recent attempts to enliven religious discussion has been to take at its face value Nietzsche's pronouncement: "God is dead. God remains dead. And we have killed him. How shall we, the murderers of all murderers, comfort ourselves? What was holiest and most powerful of all that the world has yet owned has bled to death under our knives." [1] Much ink has been poured out, in the divinity schools and philosophical circles generally, by way of elucidating this theme. For Heidegger it appears to mean that "God is absent," for Martin Buber that "God is in eclipse," but for Sartre, apparently, that God is dead only in the sense that he has never been alive. What does not emerge clearly is the kind of God who is supposed to have died. If it is the tribal God, as portrayed in much of the Old Testament, then perhaps we need not grieve too much. Few will deny that Nietzsche's announcement "gave vividness to the spiritual crisis of Western thought. The issue is the erosion and bankruptcy of religious sensitivity." [2] Meanwhile, mankind as a whole doubtless goes on its way, worshiping its various Gods as much or as little as in centuries past.

1. Friedrich Nietzsche, "The Gay Science," in *Existentialism from Dostoyevsky to Sartre,* ed. Walter Kaufmann (New York: Meridian, 1956), p. 105. Quoted from F. Thomas Trotter, "Variations on the 'Death of God' Theme in Recent Theology," in *The Meaning of the Death of God,* edited with an introduction by Bernard Murchland (New York: Random House, 1967), p. 15.

2. Trotter, "Variations on the 'Death of God' Theme," p. 15.

It must be admitted that that role of the priest and minister is scarcely less ambiguous than that of the university professor. "Fewer and fewer people accept his authority, care what he thinks, or listen to what he says. Even when he tries to be interesting, he is ignored. (The death of God has barely created a stir outside theological circles.) So . . . many a clergyman is trying to be 'relevant.' He is seeking out popular causes that can be given a Christian content." [3] The most embarrassing situation of all may eventually turn out to be that of those who regard themselves as the recipients and authoritative exponents of some allegedly divine tradition, at least insofar as this is claimed to be satisfactorily documented and formulated in words. Official religious persons, for all their sense of responsibility and dedication, are seen to be caught in an inescapable dilemma. They must attempt to impose a traditional system of belief that they have in no way originated, and at the same time face the truth that authentic religious witness can only originate in the mind and heart of each individual. The three originators of the great world religions, Jesus, the Buddha, Muhammad, apart from the status later accorded them by their followers, were the antithesis of official religious persons. Instead of upholding an existing tradition and declaring it sacrosanct, they criticized radically the established customs of their time and offered something more inward in their place. Each in his own life situation could make his own the words: "You have heard that it was said to the men of old. . . . But I say to you . . ." (Matthew 5: 21-22).

Thus a person who is professedly religious is to some extent suspect; he is suspect of inauthenticity. He needs to prove himself, not so much to others, though they are included, as to his own self-judgment. How is he to proceed? One test of the believer's religious insight, as well as of his honesty, is the extent to which he is prepared to re-examine and where necessary criticize constructively his own position. To undertake this task in the calm light of the available evidence appears to be the challenge that the climate of the times and the pressure of events are forcing upon us. Usually, in an inquiry of this kind, we begin with some definition of religion, most often in terms of a relationship with God. For us in the West, wherever reli-

3. Holmes Welch, "Chinese Omens for the Christian Clergy," *UUA NOW— The Magazine of the Unitarian Universalist Association*, 150, No. 12, (Spring, 1969), p. 24.

gious indoctrination still prevails, God is often proclaimed in terms
of what is sometimes called the Judaeo-Christian tradition. But on
examination this may well prove to be an inaccurate, question-
begging phrase. It would be hard to establish any continuity
(though the attempt has been made) between the picture of the
God intervening in history, as disclosed in the Jewish Torah, and the
timeless Deity, whose concept is unfolded, for example, in Thomas's
Summa Theologica.

When we look into the non-Semitic religions—beyond the boundaries of Judaism, Christianity, and Islam—we are confronted with
religious beliefs and practices that do not presuppose God, or at any
rate a "personal God," without which many orthodox Christians
would hold genuine religion to be unthinkable. Such is the case with
Buddhism, Jainism, and some forms of Hinduism, though it would
be the grossest mistake to apply the description "atheistic," as the
term is commonly understood in the West, to these beliefs. From a
sojourn of only a few months in India, one quickly learns that the
devotees of Vishnu and Shiva have little interest in exploring the
question: Do these divinities really exist? It is enough that they exist
in the minds of believers. The heroes of the two great Indian epics,
the Mahabharata and the Ramayana, Krishna and Rama respectively, have some shadowy basis in historic fact; yet few Hindus
think it worthwhile to seek to detach what is history from what is
poetic invention. It suffices that these stories inspire, encourage, and
delight the Indian religious mind to a degree, it seems safe to say, at
last equal to the impact of the New Testament on the average
Western Christian today.

A distinction may obviously be drawn between a man who
merely practices religion and one who is truly religious. External
worship—vocal prayer, hymn singing, reverential postures, votive
offerings—has always accompanied belief in the gods. Modern
churchgoing involves all these practices, and though it may sometimes indicate no more than social habit and a wish to conform, it
can also be the expression of a deeply religious attitude to life. Many
definitions or descriptions of religion have been offered, not all of
them complimentary. We recall Lucretius: "Religion can be produc-
tive of boundless evils"; or Marx: "Religion is the opiate of the
people"—and we may acknowledge that both, so far as they go, are
valid points. Less one-sidedly, we remember Schleiermacher on reli-

gion: "It is a feeling of absolute dependence"; or Newman: "The essence of religion is authority and obedience"; or, more generally, Max Müller: "Anything that lifts man above the realities of this material life is religion." Matthew Arnold's attempt is perhaps best known: religion, in his view, was "morality touched with emotion." "Unfortunately," as Ernest Kellett points out in his stimulating *A Short History of Religions,* "in almost all nations, till comparatively recent times, that which all agreed to call religion had little or nothing to do with morality: and often the first step in the construction of ethical systems was to denounce the current religion as at best nonmoral." [4]

Well known in modern theological circles is the late Paul Tillich's description of religion as that which focuses man's attention on his "ultimate concern." To me this is not notably significant, if only because for practical purposes whatever one's theoretical beliefs, the ultimate concern might be the nation, a political party, one's family, a beloved person, or even acquiring power or making money. An important question arises at this point: What is the man who adheres to a religion seeking? Adjustment to present existence? Salvation hereafter? Or both? Or neither? Raising the inquiry for a moment to the ideal order, I offer my own view of what religion is, or rather what it should be. It seems to me to be an attitude, or life style, based on the conviction that one's individual ego needs to undergo a transformation, whereby we become our authentic selves by being brought into harmony with pure Existence—"pure" in this context being understood, let it be stressed, not in its minimal sense of mere existence but in what might be called its full existential dynamism. If this sounds too metaphysical, even mystical, I shall make every effort to elucidate it in the course of what follows. As it may turn out to be the fundamental article of a personal *credo,* it could just possibly lend these pages whatever consistency may be claimed for them.

Apart from pointing out the familiar antinomies involved in all organized religion—cultic observance as against genuine holiness, churchgoing as against enlightened and compassionate conduct in everyday life—how far is criticism of a religious institution compatible with the loyalty required of its members? The answer depends on various factors. We have already noticed that charismatic personalities, founders and reformers of a given religion, are ready to break

4. Kellett, *A Short History of Religions,* p. 9.

with traditions accepted unquestioningly by their co-religionists. But the case is different with one who is no more than an interested student, a modest practitioner of, let us say, the Christian way of life. Religious institutions are by their nature uniquely vulnerable to the shafts of conscientious objectors. Administrators and spokesmen for such institutions have little intrinsic authority and are often without a popular constituency to which they can look for support. It is true that they are ready to claim that they speak and act in the name of God and to demand a hearing, or rather more than a hearing, on that account. Unfortunately, or perhaps fortunately, God is equally accessible to the ordinary layman, whose conscience he can enlighten directly without benefit of any human intermediary.

The possibilities of conflict in such a situation clearly underlie the confusions following upon the Second Vatican Council. This assembly has been described on the one hand as a "second Pentecost" and on the other as "an overpublicized fiasco." The truth, as usual, may lie somewhere between the extremes. The Council evolved from its debates certain norms, or guidelines, concerning Christian belief, ethical conduct and public worship. These are to be received with appropriate respect by all who acknowledge the Council's jurisdiction. If the sequel has proved disappointing to many, that may merely show what an imperfect instrument the Council was for achieving its intended purpose, a "renewal" of religion. Vernacular liturgy, to state only its advantages, may make public worship better understood; ecumenism can help to promote interdenominational good will; declarations in favor of a spirit of service, as distinct from authoritarianism, point to the heart of Christianity. But these achievements, as juridical acts, are no more than verbal; they lend color, though not substance, to the legal fiction that if the formula is found, the problem has been solved.

Without prejudice to the traditional constitution of the Church, it may be suggested that what is now becoming apparent to all is the theological truism that any ecclesiastical system as such cannot fully meet the aspirations of those who desire to be authentically religious. In other words, spiritual renewal lies beyond the scope of administrative acts. The most these can do is point the way, help to provide the atmosphere in which each individual may undergo, by an actual experience as well as symbolically, a rebirth, lose his egocentricity and become an enlightened, free, and loving human being. To what extent Vatican II has been successful in attaining these objectives it is still too early to say. My own view is that the Council has been the occasion, rather than the direct cause, of a healthy sense of liberation springing up among the faithful. For those who prefer to live under the pressure of authority this experience can be troubling. To those for whom freedom pertains to the essence of religion the Council and its aftermath call for gratitude and rejoicing.

A further ambiguity surrounding religion, at least as it has hitherto been regarded in the West, is that it is an approach to the *unknown*. Faith is in things "not seen" (Hebrews 11:1). Here we are at once faced with questions concerning the nature of knowledge. Is the substance of Christian faith really unknown? Or is it rather that we cannot reduce it to rational concepts? Perhaps, under certain conditions, it can become a matter of inner experience, and that, in its own way, is a form of knowledge. (Let the reader reflect for a moment on his most vital and pleasurable experiences; they cannot be conceptualized by the intellect, but could he pretend that he does not *know* them?) It is true also that Christian tradition is associated with "mysteries," for whose validity divine authority is cited; but there is nothing mysterious about the command to love God above all things and to love our neighbor with the same love as we love ourselves. This twofold imperative, according to Christianity's founder, makes up the sum total of religion. "On these two commandments depend all the law and the prophets" (Matthew 22:40). To attempt to fulfill these requirements, it goes without saying, is not to take refuge in mystery. Rather the opposite; we enter the path of a self-authenticating sanity, which I take to be, at least in part, the goal of every religious concern. The call to liberation and enlightenment of the Hindu-Buddhist tradition, for example, though within a different context and discipline, is but another expression of the same ultimate need—to be in some way identified with pure Existence, both in itself and as embodied in each of its manifestations.

If there is such a thing as progress in religious insight, for which there is plenty of evidence, then the emphases in Catholicism a century hence could well be very different from what they are today. Not that progress, which is a development from a less to a more enlightened state of affairs, is inevitable. The latest news from the Vatican need not be the best news. What may come to be recognized more and more is that with respect to an assured knowledge of the historical content of the various religious traditions, many of the laity are better informed than the clergy. Official declarations *de haut en bas* are likely to be scrutinized in the light of the supporting evidence, instead of being unquestioningly accepted. The official status of those professionally concerned with religion will be weighed against their personal integrity and manifest sense of fellowship with those to whom they address themselves. The effective Church leader will appear less as an authoritative figure and more as a beneficent presence among those he wishes to influence.

These truisms point to the possibility that the institutional fabric of religion may need, from time to time, to be reshaped under pressure from its inner spirit. The removal of what is in fact ignorance—that is to say, unawareness of all that true religion implies—creates problems for those whose chief preoccupation is to maintain intact a traditional religious framework. Anyone who has had official responsibility in the Church, on however small a scale, knows how attractive normal routine can become and how unwelcome some suggested innovation. So it is that those interested in exploring the deeper potentialities of the spiritual life are apt—to their great loss, it may often be—to keep a respectful distance from persons in ecclesiastical high places. "If you wish to sail comfortably in the barque of Peter," the late Ronald Knox used to remark, "keep as far away as possible from the engine room."

The progressive removal of ignorance (in the sense just described), a process inseparable from any religious advance, cannot fail to benefit all parties in the Church. In particular, it should largely obviate the need for head-on collisions between those who wield authority and their subordinates. The latter might well be less challenging and more compassionate toward responsible officials than often appears to be the case. In today's world, where democracy tinges religious as well as secular institutions, the arbitrary use of Church authority brings its own penalties in terms of isolation, ineffectiveness, and general disregard. This sad situation need not be aggravated by individual rebellion. When an insoluble conflict of conscience arises the common good and right order normally require that personal integrity be safeguarded by quiet words and unobtrusive actions rather than openly demonstrated in the press and before television cameras.

Catholicism, it seems to me, is both an ideology and a way of life. Responsible authorities could help both themselves and others by considering more carefully these two quite distinct aspects of the Christian heritage. The assumption hitherto, at least from the time of the early Church councils, has been that in order to preserve the way of life you must concentrate on the ideology. But this has always been a very dubious assumption, and in the skeptical climate of to-day it is less plausible than ever. Anyone who has had lengthy experience in unfolding Catholic doctrine to both teen-agers and mature theological students may have observed that those most concerned to take Christ for their model often have little interest in the niceties of dogma. Implicitly, the questions they ask are: What ought I to do? What should my attitude be? What kind of person can I become? Whereas the enthusiastic student, the theologian of tomorrow, eager to evaluate sources and engage in dialectic, sometimes conveys the impression that he is lacking in religious sensitivity, which is an affair of the heart as much as of the head. At any rate, events may persuade Church authorities to give more of their attention to fostering the Christian way of life in terms of the love of God and our neighbor and to be less anxious about Catholicism's rational superstructure. The *Summa Theologica*, for all its immense value, is still highly favored in Rome; yet it owes more to Plato, Aristotle, and the Stoic philosophy than it does to the recorded words of Jesus.

By the same token, the products of science and technology, the results of physiological, biological, and psychological research, are obviously so complex, so pregnant with potentially beneficial consequences, and their investigation so highly specialized, that professional churchmen might wisely be the last, rather than the first, to pronounce upon their compatibility with true religion. Their verdict would thus finally come not as a stubborn appeal to the standards of a bygone age but as an enlightened and judicious comment on a consensus of experts, reached in the light of all the available evidence.

Another question arises: To what extent is religion bound up with its cultural and national setting? At the institutional level the links have always been close. Where, in a variety of places, the official creed is the same its outward expression differs considerably: the Catholicism of the United States, for example, but faintly reproduces that of Italy or Spain. If religion is to be a unifying rather than a divisive force, we must reach beyond its external structure. Religion, at least in the West, has up to now combined more or less happily theoretical universalism with practical exclusivism—which is not as inconsistent as it appears. All the highly developed religions are prepared to be universalist, provided it be on their own terms. Thus Vatican II revealed the Roman Church, in the midst of its ecumenical endeavors, highlighting and appropriating to itself an Old Testament concept, "the people of God." Paradoxically, the stress was removed from the traditional and universalist title, *Catholic,* and placed upon the exclusivist biblical doctrine of election and predestination. Perhaps the difficulty, if it is one, is apparent rather than real. Since the Church's theology is very much broader in scope than merely biblical, no lengthy reflection is needed to conclude that, on Catholicism's own premises, every human being is in some sense a member of the people of God.

When we look beyond the borders of Christianity, further questions arise. If we take account of the dominant religious tradition of India, Japan, and Southeast Asia, we shall soon be confronted with a basic problem: Is religion best seen in terms of a *relationship* or an *identity* with the pure Existence we call God? Although orthodox Christians subscribe to the view that we are made in God's "image" (Genesis 1:27), that is as far as they will go. Any suggestion that we are ourselves in some way divine—which is a commonplace of Hindu belief—is regarded as blasphemy. In Christ man is substantially one with God, but his case is held to be unique. The best that can be said for the rest of us is that we are children before a heavenly Father, sheep being pastured by a careful Shepherd, as in the Twenty-Third Psalm. Is there any possibility of agreement between this position and a statement in the most famous of the Upanishads? "Whoever worships a deity thinking 'He is another, and I am another,' is in ignorance." [5] Perhaps some reconciliation of these viewpoints, if such is desired, is to be found, not so much in any cosmology or theory of the universe, as in personal experience elucidated by psychology. For the moment, let us say that the ideal situation be-

5. Brihadaranyaka Upanishad, I, IV, 10, quoted from *Religious Hinduism— A Presentation and Appraisal,* by Jesuit scholars (Allahabad: St. Paul Publications, 1964), p. 108. This work is to be commended to those in search of a sympathetic exposition of the Hindu religion, combined with a criticism of it from the Catholic point of view.

tween God and man is best expressed as neither identity nor relationship but as harmony.

Finally, today's ecumenical movement, it will hardly be denied, has its fair share of ambiguities. Insofar as it is a drive toward religious tolerance, interdenominational good will, and general amiability, it is clearly above criticism. It may be questioned, however, whether at present it involves any exploration of religion in depth, or throws much light on the human condition. Its roots are to be found almost entirely in Western European culture, either in Europe itself —particularly in the countries most affected by the Reformation: Germany, Holland, France, and England—or transplanted to North America. As far as the Roman Church is concerned, ecumenism only came alive as a measure of self-defense, when the need became apparent to seek allies against Marxism and the inroads of an irreligious secularism. The persons most influential in the movement are admittedly the most admirable priests and ministers, each deeply committed to his own communion and in many ways a reproach to those who lack their enthusiasm. But whether their efforts lead to an intensifying or lessening of religious conviction is an open question. It is not altogether surprising that the query has been raised: "Ecumenism—triumph or disaster? A sign of strength or of weakness?"

The ecumenical movement of Christians has been on the front page throughout the years of the Second Vatican Council. Is ecumenism "a great leap forward" on the part of religious communities, or does it represent a last grouping of these communities before they come to a quiet death by attrition in a secular world? [6]

Provided we approach the underlying problems at a rather different level, there is no need to accept either of these alternatives. Everything lies, it seems to me, in compassionate insight. Something more, no one will deny, is required than the camaraderie of interdenominational dialogue. To a realistic eye it might appear that beneath the surface of friendly gestures and manifest good will there still remain, standing as solidly as ever, the age-old impediments of hereditary and ethnical prejudices, together with corporate ecclesiastical vested interests, effectively blocking any effort to reunite what

6. Martin E. Marty, Introduction to *The Religious Situation 1968*, ed. Donald R. Cutler (Boston: Beacon Press, 1968), p. xl.

is left of Christendom. In any case, is the right approach really at the organizational level, the meeting of hierarch with hierarch, the search for mutual understanding with respect to doctrine, the finding of the comprehensive formula? If we can reach the deeper level of an ecumenism of the spirit, we shall not expect differences of Church organization and doctrinal formulations to disappear. We might discover that they do not matter very much.

But now I must give some account if not of the genesis of these perhaps too confidently expressed opinions at least of the personality behind them. All self-portraiture, they say, must necessarily be flattering. It may well be so. One can but try, here as elsewhere, to speak truly, so that no one, least of all oneself, is deceived.

3. The Personal Equation

"Personal equation," according to my 1926 edition of Fowler's *Modern English Usage*, "is a phrase of definite meaning." In his mildly pedantic, slightly derisive manner Fowler gives examples of its wrong usage and attributes them to the fact that "the learned sound of *equation* . . . has commended it to those who want some expression or other with *personal* in it." He gives its true meaning as "the correction, quantitatively expressed, that an individual's observation of astronomical or other phenomena is known by experiment to require; minutely accurate assessment is essential to the notion." Broadly, without minute accuracy, qualitatively rather than quantitatively, and as bearing upon "other phenomena," this is the meaning accepted here. All that is actually being offered to the reader is a notched and splintered measuring rod, no more than a chance to evaluate what I say about religion by what I say about myself.

"That past which cannot become a present," said Sören Kierkegaard, "is not worth remembering." What has led to my present state of mind, one of contemplative noncommitment? My earliest recollections of religion are those, I suppose, of the average early-twentieth-century Catholic child. I remember vividly going to my first confession and Communion along with my older brother and younger sister. (We were all born within a space of three years.) How old I was then I can only guess—probably seven or eight. The priest, invisible behind the curtained confessional grill, struck me as very matter-of-fact. This may have been because I had nothing exciting to tell; but he conveyed no awareness of what a tremendous thing it was for a child to go to confession for the first time. Not that I was very afraid—just a few little tremors. But in retrospect I think he was quite right. Confession is not meant to be an emotional affair; it should be handled kindly but coolly. I shall say more about confession later.

On the eve of our first Communion the priest gave us an unconsecrated host by way of practice so that we could receive and swallow it properly and not let it fall off our tongues. The next day, after I had been given the consecrated Host, I felt the experience was completely different. One just *knew* that Jesus was present. I told my mother this. She said that Napoleon, when he was in exile on St. Helena, had written in his memoirs that when he made his first Holy Communion it was the happiest day of his life. I never later troubled to verify whether this was historical fact; but at the time and for years afterward I solemnly believed it.

Today, over half a century afterward, I still think that the priests and nuns who introduced me to the Christian sacraments could not have done it better; they truly represented a "mothering" Church. Perhaps some of the clergy who are most vocal in the present movement for religious "renewal" have forgotten to bring their childhood along with them. Or it may be that the Church has yet to learn how to present her message according to age and the stages of mental development. She does, or did, well with children; not so well with adolescents and grown-ups, especially those who are thoughtful and reflective.

Like many children, I thought Benediction of the Blessed Sacrament much more impressive than the Mass. One could see the Host in the monstrance, enshrined in a golden sunburst, lit up with clusters of glittering candles. Then the clouds of incense—the more the better, I then used to think—floating up to the roof, diffusing their sensuous, prayer-inducing odor. Even the unintelligible Latin seemed to add to the significance of it all: it was ancient and mysterious and led the mind to regions unattainable, so I felt, by common everyday speech.

Not that mine, as I recollect, was an unduly pious childhood. We were warmly cared for by our parents but kept under reasonable discipline. In the early years we had a governess, Miss Bolton. Her first name was Nina, though of course we never called her by it. As she was understanding and kind, I liked her greatly; but once in a fit of anger I bit her hand, so that she cried. This made me very contrite. My father, when he heard of it, obliged me to kneel and apologize to her before the family. All was peace and friendship again, but I felt ashamed for a long time afterward—more, I'm afraid, because of my own humiliation than on account of the pain I had inflicted.

This aggressiveness and concern for my own ego, to the point of being insensitive to other people, was to prove a recurring pattern through future years.

My first significant memory of a public event was while sitting on the breakfast-room floor in front of the fire listening to my father reading from a newspaper about the sinking of the *Titanic*. This world-shaking disaster happened in April, 1912, so that I was then between four and five. What struck me most was the account of the ship's orchestra playing on the open deck and the people singing hymns while the ship went down. Possibly I am projecting later sentiments backward to the earlier date, but it seems to me that even then I underwent a kind of catharsis of pity and terror. Years afterward, in my teens, I used to stand before the memorial plaque hanging in the foyer of the Philharmonic Hall in Liverpool, which listed the names of the members of the ship's band, and my mind would flood once more with the memory of that terrible event.

My father and I were habitually on warm and friendly terms, though, as he had married late, he could not have been less than forty years my senior. He used to take me for walks when I was quite small, and I would ply him with questions about everything we saw. He must have found these ceaseless interrogations something of a trial, until at length he hit upon an effective defense technique. "Now old man," he would say to his seven-year-old son, "before you raise your next point, I think you should ask yourself: Isn't what I'm going to say perhaps a silly question?" This slowed me down considerably, though it did not occur to me at the time that I was being offered anything but a serious piece of advice. Occasionally I got round it by saying, "Please tell me if *this* is a silly question."

In a few years these encounters moved from periods of questions and answers to serious and often humorous conversations. He would tell me about his business and explain some of its problems. It never interested me much except when it touched him personally. He was a Liverpool cotton merchant, like my grandfather, and quite successful, so that we were relatively well off until the depression of the late twenties and early thirties, when he was badly hit. He had a great variety of interests and wanted me to share them. He would take me to watch cricket and football games, to boxing matches and even horse races, where, on his advice, I once backed a winner at eight to one! Cricket I found boring, though as so many people I was later to admire think it the opposite, I gladly acknowledge the blind spot. Football appealed much more, especially soccer—or "Association" as it was then rather pompously called. I thought a good professional game a splendid and exciting spectacle. I still do. In my sixtieth year, I had the chance to watch the favorite team of my boyhood days in the Cup Final at Wembley. It was with a pang of real sorrow that I saw them lose. I never liked boxing; it seemed to me cruel and inhuman, and the sight and sound of the onlookers' reactions even more horrifying than what went on in the ring. This impression, I would think, has not changed.

My father's attitude to religion puzzled me a little. It was from him I learned the agnostic's prayer, which amused rather than shocked us both: "O my God, if there be a God, save my soul, if I have a soul." He always welcomed priests to the house, and he showed a moderate interest in Church affairs; but though he read much, I never saw him reading a religious book, nor did we as a family subscribe to any Catholic periodicals. In my early teens I experienced for a few months a strong religious phase. Before going to school I would get up early each morning and walk about a mile to the parish church to attend seven o'clock Mass and receive Communion. It was in the winter months and dark, and one could not eat or drink before the Eucharist in those days. My mother, on the whole, encouraged these proceedings; but I felt that my father, though he made no comment, did not approve. He had something of the old-time Jansenist attitude to daily Communion: at the most, once a month was all that was appropriate. He would sometimes say with the gentlest irony that the family should go to Holy Communion as often as they pleased, but for his part he did not feel worthy.

On the other hand, he loved a good sermon. At a time when there was no radio or television and theaters and cinemas were closed, Sunday-evening service was fairly popular. He and I would either walk or take a trolley car to St. Francis Xavier Church and listen to a longish discourse by a Jesuit father. At first I found these experiences, as pious people say, something to be "offered up"; but later I would go on my own—sometimes accompanied by an older friend, who had a mildly sardonic, though youthfully overemphatic, turn of wit, which he would employ for my benefit and instruction. The formula for delivering these sermons, he explained, is invariably the same: the priest reads a piece of scripture for two minutes and then murders

it for thirty. This struck me as amusing then, even though I knew
the remark as an extravagant caricature and wildly untrue. A few
years later he became a priest himself, so that he had his own opportunity to vary the formula. He was to prove a loyal and valued
friend for life, his outstanding integrity maturing and mellowing
to a settled wisdom.

My mother's influence on her children's upbringing was in many
ways more incisive than my father's. She was staunchly Catholic but
anxious that we should get on in the world and make the best of our
educational opportunities while young. She wanted to send us boys
away to boarding school but could not persuade my father to agree.
I failed to fulfill her hopes that I become a conspicuously successful
student, at least in the early years, though I think she may have been
unaware of the fact. Having had only a limited formal education
herself, she was perhaps deceived by my mental facility in certain
areas. I could remember what I had read and express myself fluently,
but I lacked energy and the willingness to assimilate material that
did not interest me. To begin with, everything was easy, and for two
or three years I was near the top of the class; but when the subject
matter was not immediately intelligible, and so lost its appeal, I
wanted to give up, and if pressed, became resentful. Everything having to do with the study of the English language absorbed my interest. I cannot remember a time when I was not susceptible to its
beauty. I would sit and learn one of Keats's odes by heart, though it
was not a school assignment, just for the pleasure of reciting it to
myself aloud. Similarly, the elements of abstract thought, as represented by Euclid's geometry, proved equally easy and delightful.
Once I was the only student in the class who volunteered to demon-
strate on the blackboard Pythagoras's theorem. But I would not
apply myself to turning out accurate Latin unprepared translations,
or mastering a list of irregular verbs or a series of chemical formulas.

The inevitable result was that I lost my place in class, grew unhappy at school, and begged my parents to take me away and let me
find a job—which they did in my sixteenth year. It was not until
nearly a decade later, between my twenty-third and twenty-sixth
year that, thanks to the Benedictine fathers at Ampleforth whose
community I had joined, the lost ground was rather more than made
up. With their tutoring and encouragement under most favorable

conditions—for all of which I was to remain deeply grateful—I filled
in the gaps in my secondary schooling, learned solid habits of study,
and so was prepared, now with the strongest motivation, to take up
the more specialized work of theology at Oxford.

Even when at kindergarten, taught by the Sisters of Notre Dame,
with whom I was always happy, instruction in religion, along with its
practice, never failed to interest me. Here there was no lagging behind. The basis of the verbal teaching was the catechism with its
clearly formulated questions and answers. At the age of nine or ten
this particularly struck my mind as much more interesting than our
occasional incursions into Bible history and New Testament stories.
Such a point of view is, I'm afraid, little short of heresy today, when
all Christians are supposed to be historically minded. It was not until
I was able to study the Gospels at close quarters and in detail that
their overriding importance came home to me. But what I was concerned to know at a time when my eyes were opening on the world
was not so much the story of God's revelation to the Jewish people,
or even the life of Jesus, but who God and Jesus were and what they
wanted me to do. The catechism, backed as it was by the authority
and example of the Sisters, clearly and emphatically told me this, or
so I unhesitatingly believed. In other words, it was God and his Son
Jesus, as presented in the teaching of the Church, who claimed my
loyalty and devotion.

The First World War was on its miserable course while I was
making these initial discoveries in religion. After this appalling conflict was over, I learned much about it through reading; but while it
was going on, though I was old enough to take notice, it made curiously little impression on me. No doubt this was because the male
members of the family were either too old or too young to be involved in the fighting, there were no bombing raids where we lived,
and my parents were able to protect us children from the harsher
effects of rationing and the general inconvenience. A small incident,
which happened one afternoon during my kindergarten days, took
its place among the family legends. As the school day was about to
end, a serious item of news was being passed around the convent.
There were signs of sorrow and dismay on the Sisters' faces. At last I
heard the words, not formally announced to the school, but spoken
quietly by one nun to another. "Kitchener is dead; his ship was
sunk." At the time I knew nothing of Kitchener of Khartoum, or who

commanded the British army. On reaching home I informed my
mother with some agitation that the most important person in the
convent kitchen had been drowned.

Since the chief purpose of these autobiographical notes is to indicate something of my mental and spiritual development by way of
background to anything I might have to say about religion, I shall
leave out any specific reference to my six years of contact with business and commerce. "Contact" is the operative word, as nothing in
those areas absorbed my interest, and my personal life lay elsewhere.
The nine-to-five routine I found not unpleasant; my associates, including those in control, were agreeable, and what I earned
amounted to very acceptable pocket money. The experience of the
business world proved an asset in later years when my duties as Prior
of a Benedictine monastery and school in the United States brought
me face to face with everyday practical and financial problems only
obscurely related to the things of the spirit. But how could insurance
policies and sale contracts compete for attention in a youthful mind,
preoccupied with poetry, music, and drama, with a series of intense
emotional experiences, and underlying them all, a felt need to bring
a sense of purpose and dedication into my life?

Of the essence of these emotional experiences I shall try to speak
quite frankly, not because it is particularly agreeable to do so, but
because I think the integrity of this essay in some measure depends
on it. With Nietzsche and Freud, I am inclined to believe that one's
highest ideals, including those of religion, are conditioned, though
not wholly determined, by one's attitude to sex. And not only by the
attitude but by one's individual experience—whether this takes the
form of indulgence, repression, sublimation, or just conceivably, a
blending of the first with the last. Openness on this point seems specially called for in relation to the current controversies surrounding
clerical celibacy. This does not appear to be a matter that can be
argued satisfactorily on abstract principles. All due discretion being
safeguarded, we should perhaps know rather more than we do of the
private lives and fantasies both of those who uphold and those who
oppose the custom of an unmarried clergy.

For one who joins a religious order and reaches stability in such a
life the sexual struggles and escapades of earlier years tend to fade
into the background. They are almost never alluded to in conversa-

tion and are hardly ever, except occasionally with outspoken youngsters, a subject for question. The result is that we are apt to pronounce judgment on the sexual mores of the day not in the light of our total life experience but from the standpoint of the ethical maturity we suppose ourselves to have attained. Our own failures, if such they are to be accounted, become lost in the mists of time. Nietzsche has summed up the psychology of this situation: "'I have done that,' says my memory. 'I cannot have done that,' says my pride, and remains inexorable. Eventually—memory yields." [1]

It has been said that masturbation gives all the pleasures of sexual intercourse without its responsibilities. With those pleasures, regarded as "unlawful" by the Church, I was, like the vast majority of Catholic boys, fully acquainted. The result, needless to say, was a sense of guilt, which I hastened to alleviate by going to confession. The reactions of the priests to these self-accusations varied greatly. Once I was told that if the practice continued my mind would be weakened. This frightened me, but for the time being I don't think it made much difference. Some forty years were to elapse before the well-meaning Father, who so dealt with these matters, could read such an observation as the following:

> In this country we have only recently emerged from an era in which masturbation was not only regarded as unnatural, but actually held responsible for mental illness; and, even now, some adolescents suffer torments of conscience on this account, although masturbation is so universal a practice that ninety-three per cent of males and sixty-two per cent of females have some experience of it.[2]

Eventually there came a quiet but major turning point in my life. I went with the usual tale of woe to a Jesuit priest, who had a reputation for holiness. From him there was no word of reproach: he told me to say for my penance ten times: "O Sacred Heart of Jesus, I put all my trust in Thee." He added that he would pray for me. After this I did not fail again for several years, and when later, in various forms, I occasionally did, it was not as one overwhelmed by habit, but from deliberate self-indulgence, or for the sake of relaxation, or because in some vague sort of way, I thought it appropriate. The

1. Nietzsche, *Beyond Good and Evil*, p. 80.
2. Anthony Storr, *Sexual Deviation* (Harmondsworth and Baltimore: Penguin Books, 1964), p. 11.

confessional experience just described won my heart for ever to the Society of Jesus—though in later life I was not always to share their theological viewpoints. So great was the attraction that I actually made preliminary inquiries about how to become a Jesuit: a project with which I failed to follow through. A further consequence was that for many years I retained a lively devotion to the Sacred Heart. From this there slowly evolved in my mind an opinion which I still hold—that at the devotional level what moves us is not the Jesus as presented by New Testament scholars, or even in the creeds, but Jesus as we subjectively believe him to be.

Prior to this happy encounter with the Jesuits, my adolescent life was in disorder. I became taken up with music and the theater and made friends with people of similar interests, including actors and professional musicians. With the family at home I must have been very difficult for several years: temperamental, opinionated, with not a few aesthetic airs and graces. My father, who observed sympathetically all my whims and moods, once remarked that it would be very nice if boys could fall asleep at the age of seventeen and not wake up again until they were twenty-one. For a time I harbored the absurd thought that I was "misunderstood." I even wrote a three-act autobiographical "tragedy," which I called *The Misfit*. When I showed it to a local amateur producer, with whom I had become very friendly, he said he would get a company together and put it on the stage. Despite our warm friendship he never did, which I think was a tribute to his good judgment rather than a mark of inefficiency. He later gained a national reputation as a theatrical director in London and finally received a knighthood. Fortunately, this phase in my life was not destined to last—perhaps because I was fairly conscious of how miserable my conduct was and how uneasy it made my loving and, as I now see, fully comprehending parents. Many of these misdemeanors—involving much selfishness and lack of consideration—though often not technically "mortal sins," troubled me in mind more than explicit lapses into sensuality. They formed part of my at that time infrequent confessions to a priest.

Here may be the suitable place to redeem my promise to say something more about the sacrament of penance. The thoughts that follow are merely personal; they offer no general plea, still less any direct challenge to existing practice. My occasional embarrassing experiences with confessors left, I believe, no lasting scars. They may even have done good, since the sanction of a moderate fear has its place in early religious training. However, my emerging unscathed could well have been due to natural resilience and basic self-confidence on the part of the penitent rather than to any shrewdness or insight on the part of the confessor. There is plenty of evidence to show that many Catholics who in later life abandon the sacraments trace the cause to the block provided by the confessional. Again, the thought recurs: the Church knows how to deal with her children but not so easily with her grown-ups. Many of the problems facing ecclesiastical authority today, it seems to me, are not so much moral or doctrinal as psychological—how to cope with the adult mind.

For this and other reasons I am in sympathy with those who wish to recast individual auricular confession into a congregational penitential service: a short homily stressing the need to be converted from sin followed by self-examination and a confession in general terms of personal guilt, concluding with priestly absolution. As root-and-branch reforms are usually a mistake, opportunities for particularized private confession should be retained; but its difficulty must be recognized. This does not merely arise, as is often thought, from the refusal to accept a salutary rebuff to human pride; the difficulty is the one inherent in all verbal communication. The penitent uses words as they flow from his own mental and emotional background, whereas the confessor must judge the same words from his. No degree of articulateness, no amount of sympathetic imagination, can really bridge this gap. Judgment, therefore, could more safely and wisely be left to God.

The confessor's role might helpfully be transformed into that of a spiritual director, or guru, who could be consulted when need arose. This would probably require, however, some modification of the existing limits in the average priest's early training so that he should become, not simply in theory and corresponding ethical practice but by deep personal experience, a master of the spiritual life. Finally, as is now being more and more recognized, the questions that have to be asked—not so much by others as by ourselves—concern less our individual "sins" than what sort of people we are and in what direction lies the drive and tenor of our lives as a whole. A characteristically constructive, generous, self-giving person doubtless fails at times, even through self-indulgence, whereas someone who is ungenerous and egoistic—faults that diminish self-knowledge—might in all sincerity have few "sins" to confess. From the ultimate point of view it matters little how much the priest in confession knows about us; what counts is the extent to which we know ourselves and how that self-knowledge takes effect in the world around us.

When we are young, we feel our emotional experiences to be unique. As we grow older we learn inevitably that we were not rare exceptions; we were almost commonplace. So it was, to judge by what the psychologists have to say, in my own case. First, I recollect the fascination with a school friend, a boy, an emotion that brought with it the very opposite of intimacy, a shyness so inhibiting that I could scarcely bring myself to speak—with the result that our paths seldom crossed, and we never really came to know each other. Then, at Christmas parties, the kissing games with girls and the wakening interest, dreamy and childishly idealized, they aroused. I fell in love—for children's affections are often deeper, or at least more concentrated, than their elders'—with one in particular. The look on her face, the way she walked and moved, her exceedingly pretty dress of silk or satin (I was not then sure of the difference) filled me with a delicious fascination—for one who did not, and never could, belong to the humdrum, everyday world. I still sometimes wonder (though not too seriously) if that is not in some way the truest view of women: as beings to be looked at and pictorially enjoyed. It would doubtless be less than satisfactory to them, though it accords with my own happily celibate vocation. Thus I can still enjoy the vision depicted, and the almost miraculous verbal felicity, in Herrick's lines:

> Whenas in silks my Julia goes,
> Then, then (methinks) how sweetly flows
> That liquefaction of her clothes.

In my late teens, as was doubtless to be expected, the picture changed. Much of the idealism and tenderness fell away. I grew bolder and in one instance at least underwent almost every experience except the ultimate one. But even at eighteen my interest in the opposite sex, though lively for a time, did not involve any depth of passion. Nor did a lasting union—marriage—with its ties and responsibilities, attract. About that time, it must have been, I read and caught the mood of Rupert Brooke's lines, romantic and mildly cynical:

I dreamt I was in love again
  With the One Before the Last,
And smiled to greet the pleasant pain
  Of that innocent young past.

. . . .

The boy's woe was as keen and clear,
  The boy's love just as true,
And the One Before the Last, my dear,
  Hurt quite as much as you.[3]

Did these sentiments indicate a developing maturity—or mere heart-lessness? Perhaps we need not decide.

My mental inclinations, released from the forced labor of school, now claimed their full scope—or at least the scope that suited my tastes. I had read—somewhat, I confess, as a tour de force—the whole of Shakespeare, including the poems and sonnets, by my eighteenth birthday. Combined with this, I learned to appreciate the point of Milton's lines:

How charming is divine philosophy!
Not harsh, and crabbed as dull fools suppose . . .

The German philosophers (in translation) rather than the English held my attention, not in exhaustive studies, but sufficiently for me to feel their force. Kant and Hegel—both frowned on at that time in official Catholic circles—were easily at the top of the list. Kant's a priori categories and Hegel's dialectic of thesis-antithesis-synthesis impressed me as astonishing intellectual discoveries. The processes of formal logic, studied from other sources, I thought worthwhile mastering, at least at their elementary stage. This last investigation tempted me to an experiment.

At the time I was engaged in this reading I met a girl at a private dance and was attracted to the point of wanting to see her again. Opportunity, or courage, was lacking for me to ask her—as would be said nowadays—for a date. So I wrote a long letter, set out in careful syllogisms, leading to the conclusion that she had no logical choice but to consent to our going out together. She replied that she found the letter rather boring, that she had no time for logic, and that my conclusion did not appear to her to follow at all. However, she agreed to go out with me.

3. Rupert Brooke, *Collected Poems* (London: Sidgwick & Jackson, 1919), p. 80.

Looking back now on these and several parallel episodes, I feel that they were part of the pattern of things. They taught me at an early age to appreciate women, and unlike the great St. Augustine, I have little sense of regret, though I think I can honestly say that at the time I was truly sorry for any offense I had given to God. Soon my life was to take a very different course; but the conviction would remain that the sensuous and the spiritual are not meant to be entirely separated. Sensuality alone leads to incontinent promiscuity, extinguishing all awareness of the spiritual; but the aim of being purely spiritual can terminate in an arid inhumanity, helpful to no one, least of all oneself. Before leaving the topic, it may be to the point if I touch on another aspect of the phenomenon of sex. The Church seems now to be in a transition period with respect to the formulation of its moral as well as its doctrinal teaching, so that there should be no harm in an open, though quite tentative, expression of one's mind. This may be the less unacceptable to squeamish traditionalists, coming from one who is, in his own way, in love with Catholicism, attaches high value to self-restraint, accepts happily the ideal of monastic chastity, and who would not find life worth living outside the visible fold of the Church.

What the Victorians referred to as "the love that dare not speak its name" is today rather more talked about than in the past. "Homosexuality is a part of life that intelligent people should know about and understand," writes a recent authority. "Unhealthy ignorance causes an almost unbelievable amount of misery and frustration." [4] Most careful observers will corroborate this view; those who are ready to detect and condemn what they regard as effeminacy or homosexuality in others, and by implication to repudiate in themselves, are often sadly out of touch with the human condition. The first chapter of St. Paul's Epistle to the Romans may be inspired scripture, but it hardly presents a balanced picture of life as a whole, even life in the ancient world. It may be contrasted, for example, with the opinions expressed by Plato in his *Symposium,* where the situation is viewed rather more calmly. It would be hard to quarrel with the following judgment, based on extensive research:

A sexual practice which is considered acceptable in one time and place may be abhorred as a perversion in another; and even within the same culture, each individual may adhere to a different standard of sexual

4. D. J. West, *Homosexuality* (Harmondsworth and Baltimore: Penguin Books, 1960), p. 12.

behaviour, depending on the interaction between his upbringing and the strength of his sexual needs. It is safe to assert that there is no sexual practice which has not somewhere been condemned, and none which has not elsewhere been accepted.[5]

More pertinent to what is at present being touched on, and if true, of dominating importance, is an opinion expressed by an authority already cited: ". . . children are not born with the sex instinct specifically directed to one sex or the other. Exclusive preference for the opposite sex is an acquired trait, and involves the repression of a certain amount of homosexual feeling which is natural to the human being." [6]

This observation corresponds to my own experience and, I have little reason to doubt, to that of others. When in later years I came to lead a celibate life with its absence of feminine company, I found that natural affection—the groundwork, be it noted, for supernatural grace and charity—tended to be directed toward the members of one's own sex. In other words, the repression of homosexual feelings was to some extent relaxed. Here, however, a number of careful qualifications need to be made. One often reads in books touching on this topic that among male celibate communities, notably those concerned with educating boys, homosexuality is common practice. The verdict is usually guesswork, based not on direct investigation, but on certain physiological and psychological assumptions. Those with inside knowledge will testify that although lapses into overt homosexual acts do occasionally occur, they are extremely rare and if discovered encounter the full weight of community opinion against them. In any well-regulated monastery, for example, the sense of dedication to the highest religious ideals, responsibility for the welfare of each for each, especially the young, to say nothing of the taboos inherited from the prevailing culture, preclude indulgence in such anomalies within the bounds of the social group.

The casual observer could be misled by the fact that he may notice among religious groups composed of only one sex what might be called a homosexual tone. This means nothing more than an open friendliness among the brethren, an ease and naturalness with one another, amounting to a genuine affection, whose outward expression is normally much less demonstrative than we find sanction for in the Gospel (e.g., Luke 7:45, 22:48). Indeed, where such a state of

5. Storr, *Sexual Deviation*, p. 11.   6. West, *Homosexuality*, p. 12.

affairs is absent, where, in other words, because of ignorance or fear the natural homosexual tendency has been too violently repressed, the result will be an inhibiting of the love—experienced as such and distinct from well-intentioned "charity"—that is due to one's companions. Of this the penalty is frustration and consequent unhappiness. On the other hand, though overt acts be avoided, if the homosexual tendency has not been sufficiently repressed—so as to achieve a harmonious balance with the heterosexual tendency, which is no less natural—the result will be, at best, a thinly disguised misogyny —a distaste for the company of women. This is not uncommon in monastic and clerical circles generally, and it should give grounds for reflection. When a priest cannot on suitable occasions happily meet and associate with women and feel at his ease with them, he is obviously failing to make contact with half the human race, to his own great impoverishment. The difficulty, it seems to me, will not be overcome merely by relaxing the law of clerical celibacy, desirable as many think this to be—at least for the diocesan clergy who wish to marry. It should be as possible for a person dedicated to religion, who has learned to love without passionate involvement, to have at least as close a friendship with a woman as with a man.

The problem, as is so often the case, is one of achieving balance. In the celibate life it sometimes happens that because of his faulty spiritual training a priest or religious attempts to dampen down, or even extinguish, his natural emotional outflow to the members of both sexes alike. He may sincerely believe that God will take the place of what he is renouncing, and so he strives to sublimate his affections, only to be met with disappointment, for God accepts a full, but not an empty, heart. Disillusionment follows, and the spiritual life is apt to become a dreary routine instead of a fresh adventure every day. Such a priest or religious may face the world bravely, with a kind of tough geniality; but there could develop an uninviting hardness, a lack of sensitivity. Cut off from warm human contacts, he may seek compensations to distract him from his inner loneliness. Among these could be a reversion to the habits of earlier years, or overindulgence in those well-known opiates, intoxicants and tobacco. The latter, we may note in passing, is not unrelated to infantile human need. Part of the gratification provided by the pipe, the cigar, the cigarette, says Aldous Huxley, stems from something more primitive than the urge for nicotine. What we seek also is the pleasure of suction: we have returned to one of the earliest of earthly satisfactions, that of the infant drawing from its mother's breast.

Having felt called to embark on this series of self-disclosures, there is something more for me to relate before returning to the roughly chronological outline of my approach to the Benedictine life. I shall attempt to say something about the quality of my mind, or rather sensibility, as it appears to me. This has obvious relevance to the thoughts and suggestions being set down in these pages. But it also puzzles me, since I often find myself out of step with contemporaries who are at least as deeply concerned with the things of the spirit as I happen to be. For example, as I write I am surrounded by a monastic community, with whose members I feel myself to be in warm personal communion—a sentiment that, I have every reason to believe, is reciprocated. A number of these brethren are academically more accomplished than I, with talents and abilities beyond my range, combined with an evident Christian dedication to which I can make no claim. And yet none of them, I'm convinced, could, or perhaps would wish to, write a single paragraph in this book. The reader will, I'm sure, indulge me if I try to sort this out along with some larger matters in a series of more or less relevant digressions.

How important it is for the Catholic writer nowadays to achieve authenticity of spirit, to exhibit the kind of mental freedom from which it is evident that the conclusions of his inquiry were not laid down before the investigation began. When he feels that he has something original to say, he should be able to prescind from, without challenging, Church authority, so that any freshness of approach be not stifled by an encumbering ecclesiology. The Second Vatican Council has prompted a spate of able and conscientious work, often highly optimistic in tone; but as that spectacular juridical exercise could of its nature produce only a meager diet of spiritual refreshment, no piquant dishes were to be expected from its aftermath. What is most of all called for is the exercise of powerful and intuitive minds without party allegiance that can reach behind the concepts of current theological controversy, beyond the categories of conservative or liberal, Catholic or Protestant, Christian or non-Christian, and illuminate—for those whose interest is not in an ideology, however sacrosanct, but in that which can be disclosed as self-evident and a matter of experience—what the religious quest is really about.

To many it might appear that this deficiency has been met in our time by one religious writer of genius, Teilhard de Chardin. It may be so. In a way I wish I could think so; then I should not get into so much trouble with some of my friends! But Teilhard was too much the Westerner, perhaps too distinctively the French Catholic, to be able to take seriously any religious tradition but his own. He absorbed little from his contacts with the East. Teilhard was "relatively untouched in a cultural sense by his Chinese interlude," a writer in *The Times Literary Supplement* (December 25, 1970, p. 1517) points out, raising again the appropriate question mark. "For though one can detect a pattern of evolution in human history if one accepts the Omega *et tout cela*, it is very doubtful whether one should. . . . Part of the substructure of Teilhard's *Weltanschauung* was his Christian mysticism, but the other pillar, biology, is not connected properly to that superstructure. However moving Teilhard's vision is, it *is* only a vision, a non-scientific apocalyptic." To Teilhard, in a measure at least, may not the observation of another man of vision, W. B. Yeats, fittingly apply? "There have been men who loved the future like a mistress, and the future mixed her breath into their breath and shook her hair about them, and hid them from the understanding of their times."

Let me hasten to state that these remarks are not intended to indicate that the author sees himself as stepping into the theological breach. Suggestions, lines of thought, one serious question at least are what I have in mind; but their location there is so precarious, so embryonic, that I am as anxious to tell about their setting, how they came to exist, as to argue for their validity. In other words, I am not sure how much truth they have, or to what extent such truth as they can claim might mislead. That is why I want to provide, along with them, hints of their origin, of the sensibility that receives and harbors them, so that the reader may, if he thinks fit, dismiss them as idiosyncratic, far from the mainstream of Western religious thinking. Like Kierkegaard, in this one respect at least, I am the very opposite of a prophet. I speak with no authority and without too much confidence.

One difficulty is that of expression. As I write these pages, the recurring problem is not to think up what has next to be said but to cope with the inrush of multitudinous thoughts, which might just possibly bear upon my theme. When an idea presents itself, its clarity lasts only for a moment before it is marred (or could it be, enriched?) by an upflow of associations, so many and often so emotionally powerful that the cerebral process becomes overcharged, and I cannot continue. Sometimes, I have to get up and walk around the room, then sit, or even lie down, before I can begin to select from all the possibilities of statement what the final sentence is to be. It goes without saying that this manner of working—which, for all I know, may be a commonplace among authors—is both exciting and exhausting. But it may indicate a limited mental capacity, which should also be taken into account.

A moment ago I mentioned the "cerebral process" involved in a creative literary effort. The phrase may be roughly accurate; but it leads me to say that I find less and less empirical evidence for drawing a real distinction between one's mental state and that of the body. So far as I know, I am not much subject to moods, with their varying physical effects. Most of the time I am unfashionably free from *angst* and a sense of depression. Once as a youngster at home, when I thought my life was full of overwhelming problems, I overheard my father telling a friend that this particular son of his always seemed to be happy. Basically, I think he was right. Nowadays, when thoughts come from my own or another's mind, bringing a flash of insight, they set the pulse beat racing, so that I am, as it were, teetering on the brink of a minor ecstasy. This state of excitement seems to me as much physical as mental, though I have no notion how it is to be accounted for. Possibly the explanation lies in nothing more mysterious than body chemistry—a conclusion which would confirm my own impression that body and spirit are but complementary aspects of a single reality.

Related to these remarks were two personal experiments with mind-expanding drugs carried out during my recent journey to the Far East. The motive for these was only in part curiosity: when young people told me that they were on, or had been taking, a "trip," I wanted to know from experience what they were talking about. One of the experiments was with marijuana, or cannabis, in California, the other with LSD in Japan. Both experiences, in my case, were surprisingly agreeable, though I have no temptation to repeat either. Marijuana produced a heightened degree of sense awareness; outlines were sharpened, colors intensified, so that whatever one looked at took on a greatly added interest. A nightlong LSD session had the temporary effect of filling my mind (or was it just the brain?) with wave after wave of light. One of the participants assured me that it was the light of the Holy Spirit; but I remained skeptical. What the light did effect, however, was to bring out the facial appearance of my three male companions at its best; they seemed almost transfigured. Accompanying the visual sensations was an increased amiability, a compassionate affection, which lends support to the view that LSD could, under certain conditions that did not obtain on this occasion, act as an aphrodisiac.

Since these experiments of mine a good deal more has been discovered or at least written about hallucinogenic drugs. The prospect they open up is not reassuring; the risks of "mind blowing" in the sense of brain damage appear to be serious, and they should not be lightly incurred. Nor am I persuaded, at least in the present state of our knowledge, that they offer an entrance into the deeper realms of the spirit, which could not be more satisfactorily obtained without them. Whether marijuana, for example, is potentially more injurious than alcohol is an open question, and obviously it is not the mark of a civilized society to attempt to eliminate drugs by savage legal penalties. It seems possible that careful control of the supply and further research into their nature—which, of course, cannot be achieved without experiment—may show that the hallucinogens can be used to bring about truly beneficial results.

These experiments, brief and unrepeated, are mentioned because they may have some bearing on the quality of the mind composing the present essay. When someone tells me he is on or has taken a "trip," been "switched on" artificially, I know what he means, for I have shared the indescribable state of his sensibilities. What makes the situation pertinent to these explorations is that my habitual mental condition for as long as I can remember—though of less intensity and minus any abnormal hallucinations—is (I believe) that of being "turned on." Admittedly, this could be more a disadvantage than otherwise; it may account for the limited capacity to discipline the mental turmoil, a kind of ideational and imaginative total recall that I find so difficult to conceptualize and put neatly into words. It may also account for the doubtless excessive pleasure derived from being alone with my own thoughts and when in the company of others the frequent manifesting of a genuinely felt interest and affection by a verbal effervescence that people more gifted than I find hard to cope with and which is by no means to everyone's taste.

On the other hand, such a mental condition may have its advantages. It could enable the mind to reach intuitively to the heart of the matter with a speed and in a manner unattainable simply by academic scholarship. It could deepen and enlarge the understanding and, given an inclination to remain within the bounds of what is humanly intelligible and rational, enhance the mind's power to produce eventually clear and incisive utterance. It could, I believe, bring the mind quickly to the ultimate religious viewpoint, and enable it to stay there, steadily and without much danger of becoming dizzy or confused. Finally, it could predispose the whole personality to an *experience* of that by which the intellect has been enlightened and the imagination set on fire. So much for that brief, though eloquent phrase—"turned on."

To come to another aspect of the body/spirit unity. While living in the United States, thanks to the generosity of American friends, I was given the opportunity to take brief but extremely welcome holidays at some of the world's sunspots: California, Bermuda, Antigua, Barbados, Ischia, and the Grecian islands. My companions on these occasions, it must be confessed, were not as a rule monks and clerics, from whose company I had temporarily withdrawn, though to which I was glad enough to return. But such, if you will, is the waywardness of this particular spirit that it experienced not a sense of singularity or guilt but of exultation at the consoling warmth of God's beautiful world and with it, heartfelt gratitude to those who had made such adventures possible.

As life goes on, I find it more and more difficult to attach real meaning to the familiar distinctions between the profane and the sacred, between natural and supernatural. A comment, more luminous than many a theological treatise, has long lodged in my memory. It comes from a former professor of poetry at Oxford, A. C. Bradley: "The only secular thing on earth is the secular heart of man." Bradley!—of whom it was said that he had entered so deeply into Shakespeare's creative imagination, that he could tell you what Hamlet had for breakfast each morning. The source and exact wording of the witticism escape me but the verses are worth recalling:

> I dreamt last night that Shakespeare's ghost
> Sat for a Civil Service post.
> The English paper for that year

Contained a question on King Lear—
Which Shakespeare answered very badly
Because he hadn't studied Bradley.

To return to the sunlit beaches on which I spent a good deal of
time. "After two thousand years of Christianity," wrote Albert
Camus, winner of the Nobel Prize for Literature in 1957, "the revolt
of the body."

It has taken two thousand years for us once again to be able to show
it naked on the beaches. Hence the excess. And it has recovered its place
in our customs. What we now have to do is to restore its place in philosophy and metaphysics. This is one of the meanings of the modern
convulsion.[7]

Quoting Delacroix with approval, it was Camus again who would
point out that "it needs great boldness to dare to *be oneself*"[8] (Camus's italics). To spend periods lying relaxed in the sun was for me a
sensuous rather than a sensual experience—as it is, it seems certain,
for the majority. Apart from the well-known effects that sun-bathing
has on everybody, with me it was often an occasion for reviving my
awareness of the sun as the symbol—in many religions the supreme
symbol—for God. This symbolism is as compelling for much of Hinduism today as it was for the Egypt of 1400 B.C. When I was thirteen
I wrote a poem, a set of childish verses, and called it *Ode to the Sun;*
it was published in the school magazine, one of the few achievements of my early student days. Even at that age, indoctrinated as I
was with Catholic belief, it seemed to me entirely fitting that the sun,
source of all earth's light and warmth, should be a focus of worship.
It fascinated me that Socrates, having spent the whole night standing in contemplative thought, when dawn came, "made a prayer to
the sun and went his way."

Not until years later did I learn that the Egyptian king, Amenhotep IV, who changed his name to Ikhnaton (spirit of the sun disc),
made perhaps the first attempt in history to establish a monotheistic
religion; it took the form of sun worship. Compared with the polytheism that had gone before, it was a purified religion, and its liturgical worship found expression in such a hymn as the following, addressed to the sun disc, Aton, as the one true god:

7. Albert Camus, *Carnets 1942–1951,* trans. Philip Thody (London: Ham-
ish Hamilton, 1966), p. 84.   8. *Ibid.,* p. 158.

The dawning is beautiful in the horizon of the sky,
O living Aton, Beginning of Life!
When thou risest in the eastern horizon,
Thou fillest every land with thy beauty.

. . . .

Bright is the earth when thou risest in the horizon.
When thou shinest as Aton by day
Thou drivest away the darkness.
When thou sendest forth thy rays,
The two lands (Egypt) are in daily festivity . . .
All cattle rest upon their pasturage,
The trees and the plants flourish,
The birds flutter in their marshes,
Their wings uplifted in adoration to thee.
All the sheep dance upon their feet,
All winged things fly,
They live when thou hast shone upon them.[9]

A parallel approach to the Supreme Being (Brahman), much earlier in origin, as taught in the Chandogya Upanishad, still informs Hindu worship today. "The sun is *Brahman*—this is the teaching . . . When it was born, shouts and hurrahs, all beings and all desires rose up toward it. Therefore at its rising and at its every return shouts and hurrahs, all beings and all desires rise up toward it." [10]

Sometime in the early months of 1968 I visited Banaras (Varanasi), India's holiest city, on the outskirts of which the Buddha first preached his message. More than once I went down to the river Ganges, where the water was running swiftly—filthy and polluted to a Western eye but for the thousands lining its banks, sanctified by the mystique of their religion many centuries before the birth of Christianity. The sun was rising slowly over the further shore. Near where I stood scores of people—men, women, and children—were bathing in the river, some immersing themselves totally. Before or afterward, they would turn and face the great red globe of the rising sun; there they would sit in quiet meditation, or worship outwardly in a series of prostrations. Prompted by some impulse, I stooped and

9. Translation by James H. Breasted; quoted in Fred Gladstone Bratton, *A History of the Bible* (Boston: Beacon Press, 1968), pp. 57–58.
10. Chandogya Upanishad, III, xix, 1, 3, quoted from *A Source Book in Indian Philosophy*, ed. Sarvepalli Radhakrishnan and Charles A. Moore (Princeton: Princeton University Press, 1957), pp. 65–66.

dipped my hand in the flowing water and blessed myself with it. Perhaps it was a Christian's way of paying his respects to that which Hindus call "the river Ganga, the all-purifier."

It would be ridiculous to pretend that these associations play much part in the minds of the millions in America and Europe who flock to the beaches to perform their own acts of sun worship. One aspect of the matter, however, is worth reflecting on by those who acknowledge Camus's point about the unclothed human body: "What we now have to do is to restore its place in philosophy and metaphysics," and, he might have added, in theology. (Any nervous reader may rest assured that no plea is about to be made for theological sanctions encouraging exhibitionism or flouting accepted conventions.) What deserves to be carefully noted is that the total removal of clothing, or its reduction to a minimum, is an act of liberation not essentially related to the sex drive. Perhaps the chief reason why people go swimming and sunning is because it gives them a rare sense of freedom; they are no longer bound by the habits and customs enforced by everyday attire. Opportunity to be genuinely—that is, unselfishly—free is what, at our best, we most of all seek. (I say at our best, because unless we are clear-headed and courageous, we may prefer some form of servitude.) Transferred to the religious dimension this search finds its goal not in bodily nakedness but in being freed from the integuments of ignorance and sin, so that one becomes one's true self, naked before God. Thus the terms in which religion should be presented today, if it is to prove equal to the "modern convulsion," is essentially as a process of liberation at its deepest level. "So if the Son makes you free, you will be free indeed" (John 8:36). It has often been pointed out by those whose religious imagination can respond to symbolism, however excruciating, that when the Son performed the act by which, according to Christian belief, true freedom became possible for us, he did it without clothing.

It is time to end this psychosomatic interlude and return to the chronological point when I began seriously to feel the need to introduce a sense of purpose into my life. During my late teens and early twenties a devout Irish lady, intelligent and learned, used to visit our home fairly regularly. She regarded me amiably enough, even at the age of twenty-one, as a "precocious adolescent" and warned me against the dangers of acquiring a "fatal fluency." One day she suggested that I should join a Catholic lay organization called the Evidence Guild. It provided a training in apologetics and elementary theology with a view to proclaiming the Church's message, literally on the streets. I followed her advice and quickly found myself in congenial company and engaged in worthwhile work.

The study and the opportunities provided for leading a meaningful religious life appealed to me much more than the outside activities of the guild. The apologetic arguments carried conviction in those days. Christ claimed to be God; in making that claim he either spoke the truth or told a lie; he did not tell a lie; therefore . . . What statements could be more lucid? What argument more conclusive? To justify them one needed only to find and learn by heart the proof texts in the New Testament. It took some time for me to discover that matters were not quite so simple. I was happy, too, with the general intellectual structure of Catholicism as I then understood it and with the authoritative manner in which the Church proclaimed her message. Only after many years did I awaken slowly and almost imperceptibly from my dogmatic slumber —not then to any radical skepticism or desire to repudiate but with an awareness that when it came to speaking about God's revelation, even the Church, as Aquinas had pointed out, could only stammer. Basically, I feel that this is still my position.

During those years I learned, or so I thought, to combine extensive reading about religion with a personal effort to acquire more of its spirit. Hilaire Belloc and G. K. Chesterton, leaders of what their detractors called the "beer-and-religion" school, were then much in vogue among Catholics. I enjoyed Belloc's poems and essays for their craftsmanship, but it soon appeared that he was unreliable as a historian. Chesterton, behind the verbal fireworks, appealed to me by reason of his poetical, even metaphysical, approach to life and as a brilliant defender of orthodoxy. At times, though, I found his stream of paradoxes rather tiresome and it was with amusement that I came across William Ralph Inge's comment that Chesterton "crucified the truth upside down." Inge, then dean of St. Paul's, had a flair for the acidulous bon mot, particularly at the expense of the Roman Church. He once described Lourdes as a "lucrative imposture," though I don't think the remark affected one way or the other my own disinclination to visit that deservedly famous shrine.

As for my personal life, I went on most weekdays to Mass and

Communion, attended days of recollection and one or two weekend
retreats given by the Jesuit fathers. Asceticism, I became convinced,
must be given its due place. During Lent I kept the Church fast—
then quite rigorous—to the letter, inconveniencing the family not a
little. I read a book by Robert Hugh Benson about a young convert
from Anglicanism who scourged himself regularly, until he finally
became a Carthusian, the austerest monastic order in the Church,
and a life of Aloysius Gonzaga, a Jesuit saint so dedicated to the
ideal of chastity that he refused to look his own mother in the face.
(One of the Popes, in what was surely a less inspired moment, had
declared him to be the patron saint of youth.) The result, predict-
ably enough, was that I obtained for myself a hair shirt and cord
discipline from a convent near London's Marble Arch and put them
to good use.

Cheerfulness, however, kept breaking in. I was able to keep these
eccentricities completely to myself as I circulated normally and happily among my friends. Looking back on them now, I think the effect
of these self-inflicted penances may have been neutral, neither good
nor bad. Psychologically, they still retain some interest for me. Do
they substantiate the charge that there is not very far beneath the
surface of Christianity a sado-masochistic strain that needs to be
more clearly recognized? Do they perhaps indicate in the individual
a hidden sexual interest that, if it is too facile to call "unhealthy,"
should certainly be raised to the conscious level and honestly faced?
Whatever the answer to these questions, I am confident that such
practices are not to be encouraged. They were wisely ruled out completely in favor of the discipline of everyday monastic life when I
entered the Benedictine order.

Meanwhile, several of the monks from Ampleforth who were sta-
tioned in nearby parishes would occasionally come to our home to
dine with us and play bridge. Both my parents greatly admired the
Benedictines; we young people were encouraged to attend their
church services and to go to them for confession. All this, as I would
later understand, was part of a most kind and providential parental
"plot." My mother, though leaving me quite free, had never concealed her lack of enthusiasm for my Jesuit learnings, and she evidently feared that they might revive. She felt, justly or not, that the
Society of Jesus would deal too harshly with this freedom-loving son
of hers; he was more suited to a monastery where the English tradition of liberty under law entered as much into the life of the commu-

nity as the Rule of St. Benedict. How right, I'm sure, she was! In
September, 1930, at the age of twenty-three, I was received into the
novitiate at Ampleforth Abbey and entered on a way of life in
which, despite periods of difficulty, I was never to experience a seriously unhappy moment.

At the end of a year's probation, in which one learns the Benedictine ways and customs, comes the critical moment: the novice has to
decide if he wishes to make his vows and to be professed as a monk.
At the same time, the community, after elaborate investigation, must
pass its verdict on his suitability for the life. I was, of course, in no
doubt about what I wanted to do. In a preliminary interview with
the Abbot, held chiefly for the purpose of making sure that whatever
decision I made would be a free one, he said that he considered that
my real novitiate had been spent with my family at home. I took
this to be a graceful compliment to my parents and the way I had
been brought up. It was an unpleasant surprise, then, when later, in
the presence of the monastery council—a group of monks who act as
the Abbot's official advisers (to which, many years later, I was to be
elected myself) and constitute the governing body of the Abbey—he
asked me a direct question. Did I think that perhaps my ideas were
too democratic for me to be able to lead the Benedictine life? I believe I replied with a mumbled and doubtless not very convincing
negative. Evidently, the deviation, if such it was, did not weigh
heavily on the Abbot's mind, for in due time I happily made my
profession along with my companions in the novitiate.

The next two years, as I have already related, were spent in making up the deficiencies of my early schooling. Study was now no
problem; to be occupied with books seemed to me, apart from worship and meditation, the most sensible way to spend one's time. These
were also the years when like every church student I had to do
courses in scholastic philosophy. Though such pursuits are out of
fashion today, I found them fascinating. In the early thirties Jacques
Maritain was at the height of his powers, largely dominating the
Catholic intellectual scene in France and to some extent in England.
His work, though I later learned to make some minor modifications
of my own, has left a permanent impact on my mind. I think particularly of his elucidating the relations between art and prudence, truth
and beauty—which were then pressing "existential" problems for me
—and in general his discussions on the nature of knowledge.

So affected was I that I wrote some verses in iambic pentameters illustrating the Aristotelean theory of act and potency, dedicated them to Maritain, and (most presumptuously, as I afterward realized) mailed them to him at his home in Meudon. Shortly afterward came a gracious letter, together with a copy of that brief but precious essay, *De La Vie D'Oraison*, inscribed: *"au Révérend Père Aelred Graham, bien sympathiquement, Jacques et Raïssa Maritain."* It rests on the shelf before me as I write. Twenty years later I had the privilege of meeting them both on several occasions, in New York and at Princeton University, so making personal contact with two of the choicest spirits of our time.

My years at Oxford were spent in the main studying theology with the Dominican Fathers at Blackfriars. But residing at Ampleforth's Saint Benet's Hall with my monastic brethren, I was able to balance these rather abstract studies with the humanistic interests of the university. The Dominicans duly reported to my superiors that I had "a very subtle mind for theology," and after four years, I became the first English Benedictine to receive their degree of lector. Not, however, without suffering a minor breakdown, due to overwork. The Abbot was solicitous; he offered to send me on a holiday, protesting kindly that I was in danger of "burning myself out." But I preferred the diagnosis of one of my contemporaries, a wise and witty monk, who like me was later to become a prelate; he was acting as infirmarian at that time. He said that all I needed was a little rest, as I was merely suffering from an attack of "Aquinas pectoris."

As no study can hold my interest long unless it is related to human life, particularly my own, I tried to discover what it was in so improbable a personality as Thomas Aquinas that so absorbed my attention. His admitted saintliness was not enough. I decided that it was his concern for truth—finding it, living by it, and, as far as possible, stating it in words. "When anyone speaks the truth, he is invincible, whoever it be with whom he is disputing," he had written in his *Commentary on the Book of Job*. I conceived a desire to try always to speak the truth—but discovered it was impossible. Truth is a matter of nuances; it has so many facets. With care, when writing, one can get near to it; but in speech, when words so inadequately mirror thought, truth suffers badly. It suffers, too, when one has an itch to be funny, though I think that genuine wit can make truth memorable, polishing it like a diamond.

Looseness in the use of words may not matter so much. It is when one's word is no longer one's bond that we are in trouble. Dishonesty, unreliability, lack of integrity, these are what bring misery into people's lives—much more than occasional indulgence in sensuality. I wondered why the Church did not seem to take this view; I thought that priests should talk less about the Mass and the sacraments and more about natural virtue with which St. Thomas appeared so concerned—particularly the virtue of justice. I began to study the Platonic Socrates and found his death much more inspiring to contemplate than the life of many a Christian saint. "The death of Socrates," I was later to read in Karl Jaspers, "gives a picture of serene composure in nonknowledge filled with ineffable certainty." I wondered if there was any better way to die.

Under these influences I resolved to try to be honest and straightforward and open in all my dealings—a resolution that at best has only been moderately well carried out. Perhaps it was the recollection of past failures that made me so sensitive on the point. When I was nineteen I did a week's well-paid work at the expense of the strikers in a general strike, fearing all the time that their cause might be just. Soon afterward, I was convinced it was, even though Cardinal Bourne, Archbishop of Westminster, came out in support of the employers. Belloc and Chesterton both strenuously defended the strikers, and I was ashamed not to have been on their side.

A small incident five or six years earlier, which might have ended miserably, still gives me twinges of remorse. In those days the evening newspaper was sold by boys running through the streets calling out their wares—so that their voices became hard and cracked from overstrain. These boys were very poor, virtually in rags, often in bare feet. One night, when we heard the paper being called, my father sent me out for it with a penny—all that it cost. Unhappily I was hard up for pocket money at the time and chanced to have a foreign silver coin in my pocket, the size of a half crown. As the night was dark and rainy, I risked giving the newsboy this and took the change. Fortunately, within two minutes he had found out the deception; he followed me and banged on the front door until my father went to open it. I was tempted to run upstairs away from the scene but just managed to stay. The boy sobbed out angrily that he had been cheated and pointed at me. He must have been about my own age, thirteen. I also was in tears, but mine were of shame and fear. My father sized up the situation at once, and I saw him give the boy enough money to pay for all his papers for a week. To me my father said nothing, either then or afterward; he must have judged the punishment was already enough. The newsboy looked at the money, and his sobbing ceased. He did not speak but without raising his eyes put down his papers and held out his right hand, badly chapped and blackened from printer's ink, to me. I took it so warmly that we practically embraced. Then I watched him go silently out of the front door into the rain, his papers under his arm, his ragged trousers clinging around his bare, mud-stained legs.

Over forty years later this scene came back to me in all its poignancy. I was in Calcutta. As anyone who has visited that city knows, thousands of its inhabitants have nowhere to live but on the streets. They are often half-naked, diseased, and unbelievably poor and underfed. The sight of many of their deformities both repels and moves to pity. Yet somehow these people—many of them, at any rate—are sustained by their religion, kept patient by the seeming inevitability of suffering. It was at this time that I first heard the Indian proverb: "I felt sad because I had no shoes—until I met someone who had no feet."

Returning to Ampleforth from Oxford, I was soon engaged in passing on to others what I had learned. Within the year, at the age of thirty-one, came ordination to the priesthood. For fourteen years I was professor of theology in the Abbey and also at work on the teaching staff of Ampleforth College. The latter position brought me overall responsibility for religious instruction in the school, to which were added a sixth-form course on elementary "politics and economics" (roughly the equivalent of "civics" in the United States) and a class of English teaching with a group of the brighter fifteen-year-olds. As a pedagogical exercise the last was easily the most pleasurable of these three tasks, which is perhaps a slight index of my particular cast of mind.

With these youngsters I would try to bring life to the truism that it was not enough to have something to say; careful thought must be given to how to say it. Grammar and syntax were essential parts of the technique of prose writing, but it would never come alive unless you had at your disposal a large vocabulary and, even more important, cultivated an ear for the music of language. Without a multiplicity of words to choose from and a sense of how to arrange them aptly, I would repeat year after year, their writing could not fail to be dull. The most trivial incident became interesting if you knew how to describe it; a hair-raising adventure would fall flat unless properly told. An occasional generalization was permissible, but only if illustrated in concrete detail. Yet it was guiding students through texts of Chaucer and Shakespeare—Shakespeare above all—that gave me most pleasure.

On the nature of poetry, Aristotle had not said the first or the last word, but a word, it seemed to me, that was timeless. Poetry is to be considered "of graver and more universal import than history." The implications of this well-known maxim are worth reviewing today, not least by theologians, many of whom appear incapable of reaching beyond historical categories—themselves as much dependent on some antecedent philosophy as derived from factual records. History can undoubtedly be shown to involve more than what, in principle, Aristotle rather contemptuously thought—that it is merely "what Alcibiades did and had done to him." But that "more," particularly in the religious context, needs to be sorted out and critically analyzed. All of which is perhaps another way of suggesting that the poetry of religion may eventually turn out to be its most important aspect.

Such thoughts as these were not, so far as I can recollect, forced unduly upon the sensibilities of fifth-form schoolboys. Rather, their attention was drawn to the distinctive quality of Shakespeare's dramatic gifts, illustrated in such plays as *Julius Caesar, Macbeth,* and *The Tempest.* Brief passages from elsewhere—familiar to all Shakespearean students as touching the high point of creative genius—were presented for inspection in the hope that they would prove as evocative in their case as they were in mine. For example, Othello's "Keep up your bright swords, for the dew will rust them." Or Cleopatra's ". . . there is nothing left remarkable/Beneath the visiting moon." Or the manner in which, more than compensating for absent scenery, the approaching dawn is depicted by Horatio's words in the first act of Hamlet:

> But, look, the morn, in russet mantle clad
> Walks o'er the dew of yon high eastward hill.

And what Matthew Arnold regarded as the poetic phrase never surpassed by Shakespeare himself:

                            . . . daffodils,
            That come before the swallow dares, and take
            The winds of March with beauty.

The routine work of school teaching, given the conditions I lived
under, was an expression of the Benedictine monastic life. While engaged in these activities, I was also placed in charge of the parish
cared for by the monastery. For a period of five years during World
War II, I was in almost daily contact with the neighboring Yorkshire
country folk. Though temperamentally I felt myself far from the
ideal parish priest, for me it was a rewarding and agreeable experience. So much so that I was saddened to be relieved of it, to be appointed monastery guestmaster. This office, time-consuming and dis-
tracting, concerned with giving hospitality to visitors, I found such a
burden that after two years I asked to be released from it. The request, though eventually granted, did not sit well with my superiors,
so that for some time I was troubled in mind. My initiative, however,
did give me opportunities outside the teaching assignments just mentioned to do the writing to which I felt called, and for which otherwise I should have had neither the leisure nor the nervous energy.
During these fourteen years at Ampleforth, 1937 to 1951, I published
three books. Inevitably, they brought me some public notice and
what was more important, a number of valued friends outside the
monastery.

Over the years Benedictine community life, consisting of regular
public worship and personal prayer, punctuated by times for recreation and even holidays with one's relatives and friends, proved very
much to my taste. It has been the chief formative influence, leading
to whatever degree of spiritual maturity I may have attained. To
live in close daily contact with fifty or sixty other people teaches one
much about human nature in general and oneself in particular—
though to learn those lessons successfully is difficult and rare. For St.
Benedict, a monastery is a "school of the Lord's service," and no
description could be more apt. One strives to *love* each of one's
brethren, while allowing that one does not *like* them all, though I
now incline to the view that the familiar distinction between loving
and liking is a piece of sophistry, a way out from what is implied in
the obligation to love one's neighbor as oneself. There appears to be
no sanction for it in the New Testament.

Of one personal relationship during my early monastic life, which affected me deeply, I cannot forbear to say something. Entering the novitiate with me was a young Irishman from Dublin; unlike myself, he had been educated in the school at Ampleforth. He was four or five years my junior, and our mental outlooks were quite dissimilar; yet within a few weeks we became close friends. He had a most interesting mind, which gathered to itself stores of information—not, so he found, too easy to organize but readily made available to the many who listened to his fluent and entertaining talk. His spiritual ideals, tinged in those early days with a deep streak of asceticism, were of the highest, and they formed the real basis of our relationship. So often did we meet and talk together, and so obviously acceptable did we find each other's company, that in a less enlightened monastic community the affair might have been characterized, with pejorative overtones, as a "special friendship." Though it must have been manifest to all, neither he (so far as I know) nor I ever received a word of adverse comment from those in authority. No doubt they judged that our regard for each other—since, by our own resolve, it excluded no one else—benefited us both.

Being the older, I think I was the dominant partner. Though we were both beginners in the Benedictine life, he liked to talk over his problems with me; they often burdened and perplexed him, and he seemed to find some of my comments helpful. With the passing years he gradually became, through struggles and suffering, his own man, genuinely but quite unpretentiously a master of the spiritual life. He was placed in charge of the novices and attained a high reputation outside the monastery as a retreat giver. Toward the end of his life, though in failing health, he was in much demand by the younger generation as one who could enter into their lives and understand their problems. When he died, relatively young, in 1967, his loss was keenly felt—most of all, I was presumptuous enough to think, by me.

His insight had always been there, and privately, until I left for the States, I was able to profit by it. We never fell out or had a quarrel, but from time to time we were quite free in assessing each other's characters. I was convinced that he knew both my strong and weak points better than anyone else in the monastery. On that topic, partly because his manner of speech was memorable, but mostly because I knew that his shrewd observation stemmed from deep

affection, I don't think I have forgotten anything he had to say. The
burden of it was that I could be "quietly but frighteningly self-
reliant." He said that when I was concentrating on anything that interested me, writing most of all, I was apt to be withdrawn and aloof;
perhaps there was a strain of hardness that made me insensitive to
people's sufferings. "A lot of things are going to have to happen to
you," he told me once, laughing and genuinely in jest, "before you
become that true self you're so interested in." His words, cheeringly
different when I left for America, are as clear in my memory now as
when they were spoken: "You'll do all right there, because beneath
it all you're really kind." And he added, "But don't neglect to ask
people to do things for you."

When we reach a certain level of religious understanding, the
light we seek is not what confirms us in our present position but
something that leads us beyond it. Thus a man's most deeply felt
interests are usually an indication of his potential, rather than his
actual, spiritual state. We pursue a philosophy of life not for its intellectual delights or on account of its rational coherence but because it
answers a personal need. For this reason a preacher is at his most
convincing when, often unconsciously, he is condemning attitudes
clearly detectable in himself, when he is pointing to a path that he
most of all should be following.

So it was with my own interest in Buddhism. I have no recollection of the precise time when this began, though I recall at a very
early age hearing my father speak with great reverence of the Buddha. In my late teens, I read something of his legend—though from
what source I cannot remember. I was filled with enthusiasm for the
ideals I found there, which I myself most seemed to lack—clarity of
purpose, serenity, control of the flesh, and most of all, gentleness,
compassion, selflessness. It did not occur to me to doubt that these
inviting spiritual prospects were also to be found in my own Catholic
religion. My simple conviction was that the Church believed in truth
and therefore I was free to be interested in truth, wherever I found it
most appealing. The Buddha and his way of life struck me as very
appealing indeed.

When I was at Oxford, I bought and studied Canon B. H. Streeter's *The Buddha and the Christ*—the Bampton Lectures for 1932.
They aimed at presenting a "bird's eye view of the origin, develop-

ment and dominant conceptions of the two greatest of the historic religions, Buddhism and Christianity." This book impressed me greatly at that time, though I was later to learn that it was but little regarded by those who knew Buddhism from the inside. One of them, an expert in the Hindu-Buddhist tradition, suggested that the most pertinent sentence in it was an Eastern proverb: "Only a Buddha can fully comprehend a Buddha." Still, I was grateful for this book, and I think that from Streeter's rather limited standpoint he made good use of the knowledge available forty years ago. Perhaps it was all a little ambitious, as he admits in the preface, alluding to the book's subtitle—"An Exploration of the Meaning of the Universe and of the Purpose of Human Life"—in not much more than three hundred pages.

In the early summer of 1951 a major upheaval occurred in my life. I was asked by the Abbot of Ampleforth—by virtue of the office that he then held as president of the English Benedictine Congregation—to accept the priorship of one of its monasteries in the United States: the Priory (since become an Abbey) of St. Gregory the Great, Portsmouth, Rhode Island—Portsmouth Priory, as it was then more generally known. The assignment came by way of a "request," because such an office cannot be imposed as a precept of obedience. The acceptance or rejection of prelacy—a status involved in becoming a conventual prior—is a matter for the free exercise of the individual conscience. However, loyalty and a sense of what is fitting extend far beyond what some might consider canonical technicalities, so that I was glad to say yes, as well as honored to have been asked. The result was that in August, 1951, I landed for the first time in the United States to find myself superior of a Benedictine community composed of nearly thirty members, all of them American citizens and none of whom I had met. It was something of a challenge.

The term of office, begun when I was forty-three, was for eight years. It speaks eloquently for the spirit of the Portsmouth community that I was warmly received and given full co-operation. Together we had our problems and difficulties, and together we managed to face, if not always to solve, them. At the end of eight years I was honored by a unanimous request from the priory's governing body that I should be available for and accept election by the Portsmouth community for a second term. The details of those sixteen years' continuous administration can doubtless be found in the monastic chronicle at Portsmouth. Here I shall only touch lightly on their more public aspects, dwelling briefly on personal topics that might be of some general interest.

In almost all American religious and educational institutions one of the functions of their chief executive is to enlist the financial support of friends for a development program. Portsmouth was no exception, so that I soon found myself a practitioner in the art of fund raising and a client of a distinguished group of architects. Traveling, as might be expected, was necessary, not only on the Eastern Seaboard but to the Midwest, California, Texas, and the Deep South. Resistance to these efforts was, fortunately, slight, and I soon experienced the warmth of American friendship. These journeys were often linked with engagements to lecture and give retreats. As a result, I visited a large number of colleges and religious houses over the years. Both the sightseeing and the friendly encounters helped, I think, to broaden my outlook on life, remove some of the British insularity, and deepen my sympathies; but being by then solidly established in phlegmatic middle age, there were few experiences that affected me like those of earlier years.

The visiting was sometimes reciprocated. Once, a professor from M.I.T. (Massachusetts Institute of Technology), an expert in the phenomena of religion, came to see me. His first question was to ask if I had ever undergone a "religious experience." I said no, and he seemed disappointed. What I now think I should have said is that if he would eliminate all notions of trances, visions, extrasensory perceptions, and particularly, exceptional virtue of any kind, then all my life was a religious experience. But this would have been too complicated at short notice, besides being portentous and a little ungracious. All it would have signified, in any event, was my agreement with Paul Tillich's point, that "religion is not a special function of man's spiritual life, but it is the dimension of depth in all of its functions."

Later my kindly professor friend invited me to dine at his home in Massachusetts, along with one or two other guests, his wife and family. He had two charming teen-age daughters, who found—or so I thought, perhaps wrongly—our grown-up, somewhat academic talk rather overpowering. During a lull in the conversation the hostess asked me where in England I had been born. I said that I came from the same town as the Beatles and added that I admired their talents. For the two girls the situation seemed to be most agreeably transformed. That same morning their mother had been standing in a queue for several hours to buy tickets for a forthcoming Beatles concert. This little incident gave me as much pleasure as anything else that evening.

Among my nonroutine activities at Portsmouth was that of defending our monastery and school against the promoters of an oil refinery, who wished to locate on adjacent land. A good deal of publicity, litigation, and general anxiety were consequently involved. Finally, the refinery entrepreneurs abandoned their project. A happier affair was my part in the founding of a Benedictine priory and school at Saint Louis, Missouri. A group of dedicated laymen, interested in such a foundation, appealed first to Portsmouth. It was at once apparent that we lacked the required manpower, and the question was raised of my trying to interest my own monastery in England. Throughout the initial inquiries and subsequent negotiations, involving a number of people's going and coming across the Atlantic, I acted as intermediary. It brought great satisfaction to my friends in Saint Louis when after careful consideration Ampleforth decided to undertake the venture. Saint Louis Priory and School, having undergone some inevitable teething troubles, is now solidly established.

Over the years, while living in America, I met—sometimes casually, sometimes by design—a number of prominent persons in both church and state. As I write, I retain vivid recollections of only two. One is John Chafee, then Governor of Rhode Island—later Secretary of the Navy in the Nixon Administration—with whom agreeable business relations developed into personal friendship. The other was a pleasant encounter on the monastery steps. One cloudless morning, a Sunday, I found sitting there, with a shield protecting her eyes from the sun and a prayer book in her lap, a lady whom I quickly recognized—Mrs. Joseph Kennedy. Rose, as she is known to all the world, would drive over fairly regularly from nearby Hyannisport for the priory's annual June retreat. We chatted for a while about Jack, who was then campaigning for the nomination that brought him his ill-fated presidency, and Bobby, who had done some of his schooling at Portsmouth. I remarked on how sensible I thought her sun shield, now removed from her forehead and carried in her hand.

She asked me if I would be kind enough to accept it. As we parted, she handed it to me, smiling, and said: "The last person I gave one of those to was the Duke of Windsor."

During my priorship in the States I made several visits to Rome. On each occasion I had the honor of being received by the reigning Pope. The audience with Pius XII took place in the company of a small group, seated until the Pope's arrival in designated places before the high altar in St. Peter's. It was a splendid, if somewhat daunting, affair. I watched the Pope being carried in his *sedia gestatoria* up the main aisle of the basilica, cheered by the thousands present and distributing blessings on every side. Then he dismounted, walked round the small circle of the privileged, speaking a kind word to each of us and asking that we convey his blessing to our friends at home.

The meeting with "good Pope John" occurred at a congress of Benedictine superiors at the Collegio S. Anselmi de Urbe. Here I had the good fortune to observe a characteristic incident. After the Pope had greeted us warmly, exchanging a word or a joke with those who spoke Italian, his small entourage gathered about him to assist his departure from the college. Most of those present had already moved to the exit gates—a fact of which I was unaware—to cheer him on his way. Thus I happened to be among the group of no more than half a dozen who followed the Pope as he walked slowly along the ground-floor corridors. We reached the kitchen doors, where a band of Sisters, who took care of the cooking and serving, were gathered on their knees awaiting the Papal blessing. The Pope stopped, began animatedly talking with them, and then walked into the kitchen for a minute or two's inspection. The joy this gesture gave the Sisters should need no telling.

I was received on two occasions by Pope Paul VI. On one of these, before departing on my journey to the Far East, I was also conducted into the presence of the Cardinal Secretary of State, Amleto Cicognani—whom I had met when he was Apostolic Delegate in Washington, D.C.—and Cardinal Paolo Marella, head of the Secretariate for non-Christian Religions. Walking through the lofty Vatican corridors, seated on gilded chairs in damask-hung antechambers, I thought for a passing moment: what a leap of the imagination it must require on the part of those habituated to these baroque splendors to enter into the problems of the late-twentieth-century world. During my first meeting with Pope Paul he was so gracious as to hold one of my hands in both his and ask, before passing on, that I pray for him. By chance—if it was entirely by chance —a Vatican photographer caught the encounter with his camera. The result now holds pride of place in the room where I write—an assurance to all visitors of the occupant's unimpeachable orthodoxy.

While at Portsmouth I found it possible to delegate to others a major part of the work of routine administration. The credit for this is due entirely to the willing co-operation and high abilities of the resident community. The result was that I had some time to practice my favorite hobby—saying what I think in print. Three books and a number of essays saw the light during those years. In the early fifties I published in the *Atlantic Monthly* a critique of the message embodied in Thomas Merton's writings. It created something of a stir, as *Time* Magazine noticed it and brought out a lengthy summary in its religion section. In substance, I wrote that Merton in his penitential period had been overreacting against the world and its ways and that his message was marred by a somewhat strident ascetic tone. But my own tone left much to be desired, as several correspondents pointed out, and I soon regretted the manner, if not entirely the matter, of my essay. I felt an *amende honorable* was called for, so I invited myself to Gethsemani Abbey, where I was most hospitably received by the Abbot and Father Louis—Thomas Merton's name in religion—himself. He and I had long talks together and became firm friends. We were in close touch during the months preceding his ill-fated journey to the East, which was to be so abruptly cut short, because, as he said, I had been that way before him. It was pleasant to be able to introduce him to those who had been kind to me, both in India and Thailand. The journey promised much fruit, as he had mellowed and attained an insight far deeper than anything revealed in *The Seven Storey Mountain* (published in England under the title *Elected Silence*). His tragic death in Bangkok, startling and saddening his many friends, can only be accounted for as one of "the many ways of mystery and many things God brings to be."

At an earlier date and unconnected with Tom Merton's death (he seemed to prefer being called Tom, at least by those close to him

outside the monastery), one of his friends, who was on the editorial
board of a Catholic periodical, sought me out when I was on a visit
to New York. He wanted to talk with me about the journey I
planned to make to study Eastern religions in their native setting. He
had considerable knowledge of Hinduism and Buddhism, and we
discussed them together. He alluded to the parallel between Gautama the Buddha and Jesus Christ. Gautama emerged from Hinduism as Jesus had come from a Judaic background. Each was critical
of, and to some extent in revolt against, his own religious tradition.
To a neutral observer the stories surrounding the Buddha were no
less impressive than those that portrayed Christ. Then came the
question: Did I think, as a Catholic, he could hold that the Buddha
embodied a revelation from God equal to Our Lord's? I said that
they were in different situations and dealing with different questions.
But he continued to press the point. I said that no orthodox Catholic
theologian, at least in the present state of doctrinal development,
would admit the equality. He said that he personally believed that
the Buddha was just as wonderful and inspiring as Our Lord was.
He added that very few Catholic theologians knew anything about
Buddhism, and that what little they did know was viewed in the
light of their own theological prejudices. I said that I would think
about it. With that, and a friendly handshake, we parted company. I
am still thinking about it.

Shortly after Tom Merton's death, I received a letter from a Buddhist monk, with whom I had effected their meeting in Bangkok. It
contained the suggestion that Merton's spirit was so sympathetic to
Buddhism that it might well be he would have his next birth as an
adherent of the Buddhist faith in Thailand. Here, of course, we have
an allusion to one of the central doctrines of the Hindu-Buddhist
tradition—metempsychosis, or rebirth. This belief was held by some
of the early Church Fathers, notably Origen, St. Gregory of Nyssa,
and possibly others[11]—but it does not call for discussion in our present context. Linked with it, however, and less alien to popular Christian thinking, is the Oriental doctrine of karma. The meaning of this,
in effect, is that our past actions by their direct causal influence have

11. See *Reincarnation—An East-West Anthology,* ed. and comp. Joseph
Head and S. L. Cranston (Wheaton, Ill.: Theosophical Publishing House, 1961),
p. 35ff.

made us the kind of people we are at the moment, and our present actions are shaping our future destiny. Actions in this case include not only external acts but our inner thoughts and wishes, which often operate at the unconscious level. Accordingly, a Buddhist would say that it is just a person's karma that he should behave thus and so, or that this or that should happen to him. It follows that there is "good karma" and "bad karma," showing that karma has strongly ethical overtones. If a man's general line of conduct is beneficent and effective, if he succeeds in worthwhile undertakings, he has good karma; if his acts are selfish (it being a matter of indifference whether or not he be aware of the fact), or if it always seems to happen with him that things go wrong, so that we call him unlucky or accident-prone, a Buddhist would say simply that his karma is bad. There is a familiar parallel to this in the Christian tradition: "Do not be deceived; God is not mocked, for whatever a man sows, that he will also reap" (Galatians 6:7).

In view of several past events the thought occurs to me whether it might not be an aspect of my own karma to assist a little toward the mutual understanding between Christians and Buddhists. Near the end of my first term of office at Portsmouth in 1959 a young student from Harvard wrote to me. He had become a convert to Catholicism in his teens but retained a still earlier interest in Buddhism, particularly the Tibetan tradition. He thought the Catholic teaching on the Incarnation of vital importance, but at the same time, at this extraordinarily early age, he had been much helped by Eastern spirituality. He wanted to hold together his Catholicism with his Buddhism, and he was actually studying Sanskrit with a view to reading original Buddhist texts. As might have been expected, this seemingly premature attempt at a religious synthesis gave rise to problems, both theoretical and personal. He was troubled in mind, and someone had advised him to come and talk with me.

Immediately, we established a warm personal rapport, which was to remain the basis of what developed into a permanent friendship. As with so many troubled youngsters, coping with his difficulties depended on his finding a friend and confidant whom he could wholly trust. Such light as came to him through me, he would sometimes say, was indispensable. From the arcane processes of the psychiatrist's clinic he profited little. But the relationship was mutual.

His gifted and intuitive mind scintillated into apt and articulate speech, and he responded to my counsel with affectionate loyalty. Thus the time and thought I was able to give to his recurrent problems were more than rewarded. His company was a delight, and we would take holidays together. Now in his early thirties he is able to consider with a mature mind what Catholicism and Buddhism might have to give to each other. He shared my journey to the East, handling all its incidental chores; a chela traveling with his guru—as he lightheartedly described it—through Buddhist lands.

Another no less happy friendship came to me through my interest in Buddhism and lengthy sojourn in America, leaving me with lifelong gratitude to both. Invited to Harvard to lecture on the substance of one of my books, I made contact with the Cambridge (Massachusetts) Buddhist Association. Its guiding spirit was a lady, neither too old nor too young, who appeared interested in what I had to say. Subsequently, she paid periodic visits to the priory so that we might talk together. Reciprocally, I would occasionally visit the association's headquarters to take part in their zazen (sitting meditation) sessions. As she was a devout Buddhist, loving her faithful husband, with whom also I became on friendly terms, there appeared to be no impediment to "the marriage of true minds." Her creative and generous spirit brought me much joy, not to speak of the help I received from her expert knowledge and practical good sense. It was a delight to visit with her and her husband at their home in Cambridge, or to spend a few weeks—partly in study and reflection, partly in the "sun worship" already described—at their secluded summer home on Cape Cod. From these experiences, among other things, I learned how Buddhism extends its concern not only to mankind but to the animal world, "all sentient beings," particularized in this case by two large and splendidly evolved dogs with whom I used to play ball and take for adventurous daily walks.

But it is time to bring these self-disclosures to an end. My sixtieth year coincided with the end of my second term of office at Portsmouth. A younger man was needed (it was he who was to become Portsmouth's first Abbot, the priory being raised to the status of an abbey in 1969), and more and more I felt the call to be related to people, not within an official or juridical framework, but just as fellow human beings. It would be good to return to my own brethren at Ampleforth, where in October, 1968, I was to find myself as much at home as if I had never been away. The journey back to England was, as it were, westward to the East—Japan and Thailand, thence to India, Iran, Israel, and Greece. Such a route, with so many opportunities for enrichment, taken in slow stages over many months, was made possible by the generosity of American well-wishers. My deep sense of gratitude to them remains undimmed. Not least does this extend to a most generous and kindly doctor from the beautiful island of Ischia, settled in the United States, who carefully provided me with all the elaborate medication needed for my journey. The relationship was very much more than professional: a developing friendship with him, his wife, so solicitous for my welfare, and the numerous members of their family, remain among the happiest memories of my life in America.

Early in June, 1967, having resigned the priorship, I left Portsmouth for California. Here again I was in the hands of the kindest and most considerate of friends, to whom I had been introduced by an outstandingly helpful and gifted colleague at the priory. I felt some weeks were needed to plan and reflect on my forthcoming pilgrimage to the East; they were spent at a beautiful ranch sixty-odd miles to the north of San Francisco. It was owned by a lady, a widow, an ardent member of the Episcopal Church, whose kindliness and sensitivity left her with no problems in giving hospitality to a Roman priest. Such was her largeheartedness that she could also welcome under her roof certain San Francisco hippies, several of whom I was glad to become acquainted with, so learning—not without sympathy—something of their outlook on life. She provided me with the best of both worlds: sunshine and hours of solitude through the midweek, hosts of visiting friends at weekends. A strong personality, yet marked by a truly Christian humility and diffidence, it was with humorous affection that a local social columnist once alluded to her as "St. Helena's grandest grande dame." May God's blessings always be with her!

A few days after I left the priory a colleague, who more than any other had helped me with complete selflessness over the previous sixteen years, was kind enough to send me a press clipping, an editorial from one of New England's leading daily newspapers, the *Providence Journal* of June 9, 1967.

The Very Rev. Aelred Graham, head of the Benedictine priory and school in Portsmouth and a quiet influence for good in the state for 16 years, has slipped from Rhode Island as unobtrusively as he lived among us. His civilizing demeanor will be missed.

A priest, a scholar and highly intelligent observer of life whose special interests lay in relations between the Catholic Church and modern democracy, Prior Graham breathed ecumenicism before it was a household word.

With kindly humor, he pierced pretensions among people of his church, saying: "Could it not be, with many of us, that the time we employ in denouncing, let us say, the evils of Russian atheism, would be more profitably devoted to asking what sort of God it is that we ourselves believe in?" Or, "What we tend to forget is that there can be such a thing as bad religion. And when religion goes bad—then, almost literally, there is the devil to pay."

He believed that a Catholicism which has nothing more positive to say to contemporaries than that they should close their ears to evangelist Billy Graham and their eyes to *Baby Doll* [a movie briefly censored in Providence] is bad Catholicism. He criticized the Catholic press for being overly hostile toward non-Catholics. Prior Graham is a doer as well as phrase-maker. He launched a development program at Priory School, among the finest schools of its kind in the country. He hired Pietro Belluschi, then dean of architecture at M.I.T., to design a church and monastery on priory grounds. The Church of St. Gregory the Great, opened in 1960, is an architectural landmark which still draws students and practicing architects to Portsmouth.

He fought location of an oil refinery near the priory grounds, cooperated in the expansion of the Kaiser Aluminum & Chemical Corp. at Arnold's Point, and sought what he thought was best for the people of Portsmouth.

Prior Graham has resigned as prior and has left Rhode Island on a visit to the Far and Middle East where he will study non-Christian religions, particularly Buddhism. Quiet though he was, he has left his mark on Rhode Island.

It was a gracious send-off, although I must admit that the architectural developments here alluded to owe more to the talents and energies of several members of the Portsmouth community—especially a monastic friend who was a graduate in city planning from Massachusetts Institute of Technology—than to any unwonted efforts of mine. Before unfolding the fruits of my experience in the East, however, we must give some attention to the faith of the Christian West. Jesus Christ, for me as for Thomas, will always remain "My Lord and my God" (John 20:28). Catholicism still presents itself basically in the way I have known it since childhood, as Holy Mother Church. Though here, as elsewhere, we must learn with St. Paul, sometimes reluctantly and often at the risk of being misunderstood, to give up, in religion as in other areas of life, "childish ways" (1 Corinthians 13:11). So perhaps, without too much presumption, it can be said that she now has from me the loyalty of a son "come of age."

4. Christianity's Response to Jesus

i. The Historical Jesus and the Ideal Christ

In 1947 I published a meditative study entitled *The Christ of Catholicism*. Well received in the circles for which it was intended, it was adopted as a textbook in several Catholic colleges. But its over-simplified thesis—"the Christ of Catholicism is the Christ of reality" —has since worried me a little. A professor from the Harvard Divinity School, in a friendly encounter, commended the book's devotional tone but complained that I was reading the orthodox theology of the Incarnation into the four Gospels instead of using the Gospels, carefully differentiated, to evaluate that theology. This struck me as a valid comment, and it has remained in my mind ever since, even though I stand by the substance of what I then wrote.

On the other hand, a familiar distinction employed until recently by New Testament scholars, between the Jesus of history and the Christ of faith, has difficulties of its own. History in this context is usually accepted as meaning what actually happened—the event, without any subsequent interpretation. Thus the statement "Jesus of Nazareth met death by crucifixion" would doubtless be generally accepted as historical. But when St. Paul accuses the "rulers of this age" of having "crucified the Lord of glory" (1 Corinthians 2:8), with what kind of statement are we dealing? For orthodox Christians this statement is true. But in what sense is it true? Clearly not in the sense of an observed fact: Paul was not present at the Crucifixion. And in any case it emerges from the context that he is speaking in terms of his personal faith, a faith that does not "rest in the wisdom of men but in the power of God" (verse 5). So convinced was Paul that his understanding of the death of Jesus corresponded to reality that he was able to impress his conviction of the truth on others, with the result that it has entered into the Church's accepted tradition. Nevertheless, his words represent inspired interpretation rather than factual observation.

When biblical scholars and theologians speak of the "Christ event," I understand them to mean the personality and life work of Jesus understood in the light of all that is set down in the New Testament, possibly also in the light of the Old Testament, interpreted as a prelude to and consistent with the full Christian revelation. Here we have the approach of biblical theology: a method of elucidating the significance of Jesus hallowed by a long tradition, from the early Church Fathers down to the latest interpretations of committed Christians in our own day. Illuminating as this method of approach may be, it contains implications that are not always brought to light. Any historical personality or event, I suggest, can be viewed at three different levels: (1) observation; (2) interpretation; (3) reflection. This triple classification does not represent degrees of truth content; thus (2) and (3) could be "truer" than (1). But in studying the origins of Christianity it is important not to get the viewpoints confused.

Consider for a moment level (1), that of observation: if we interpret this phenomenologically as pure description based on the direct evidence of sight and hearing, how much of what the New Testament tells us about Jesus was immediately observed? Very little, it seems to me. The Gospels do not pretend to be detached chronicles of what actually happened; they aim at bringing out the religious significance of what happened. This is as true of Mark, commonly regarded as the most "primitive" account, as it is of John, whose presentation of Jesus is usually looked on as the most theological. Thus Mark does not set out simply to narrate the life story, or even the public ministry, of Jesus of Nazareth; the evangelist's concern is with the "good news" of the Jesus, whom he believed and wished his readers to believe was the Messiah and Son of God (Mark 1:1). Though Mark (15:35) attributes to Jesus on the cross the apparently despairing but in its full context triumphant opening verse of Psalm 22, the Passion story does not terminate with Jesus' dereliction. For the evangelist the climax lies in the words of the centurion at the foot of the cross: "Truly this man was the Son of God" (15:39).

With regard to the Fourth Gospel we need not here enter into the question of its authorship. For at least one incident eyewitness authority is claimed: the emission of blood and water from Jesus' side after his death on the cross: "He who saw it has borne witness—his testimony is true, and he knows that he tells the truth—that you also may believe" (19:35). But there is some doubt as to the authenticity

of this verse, and it is just possible, though by no means certain, that
when the Gospel was first made public (perhaps in Gnostic circles),
it was without 19:35 and that this verse was subsequently added to
secure for the book authority (that of eyewitness = the beloved disciple = an apostle) among the orthodox.[1] In any case, the verse
echoes the purpose, that of evoking religious belief, for which the
Fourth Gospel was written: "that you may believe that Jesus is the
Christ, the Son of God, and that believing you may have life in his
name" (20:31). John's Gospel may tell us as much of what actually
happened as do Matthew, Mark, and Luke. Indeed it may tell us
more, but like them it is the product of committed Christian faith,
not of detached observation.

Luke's Gospel makes the most explicit claim to be derived from
the testimony of eyewitnesses (Luke 1:2); we are offered "an orderly account" (1:3) of what was handed down from the beginning.
Scholars are agreed, however, that none of Luke's written sources
could have been composed earlier than twenty years after the ministry of Jesus. Behind these sources lay the oral tradition concerning
what Jesus had said and done. Luke did not of course falsify his
materials, but he shaped them to his particular purpose. The Gospel
and Acts of Apostles belong together and, being addressed to Theophilus (possibly a high official in the Roman government), they are
intended for the world in general, not just for use within the Christian community, as was the case with all the other books of the New
Testament. Luke's two-volume "apology for the Christian faith" appears to have been published in order to meet the situation within
the Empire after Nero's persecution had ended. The infant Church
was in a precarious situation, its members fearful and in need of
reassurance, its enemies ready to extirpate this hated Jewish sect.
Luke is concerned to gain for the Christians at least the tolerance
shown by the Emperor to Judaism as a whole.

The author's purpose was to supply Theophilus and others like him with
the solid truth about the calumniated movement. Have Christians been
condemned as the felonious followers of an executed felon? He will show
that Christ and his disciples have justly been pronounced innocent by the
representatives of Roman law. Is Christianity despised as an eccentric,
foreign superstition? He will prove that it is the true fulfillment of the
religious aspirations of the Old Testament, deserving all the tolerance

1. See C. K. Barrett, *The Gospel According to St. John* (London: S.P.C.K.,
1967), p. 464.

Rome has shown to the Jews, and that, unlike the nationalistic creed of the Jews, it is a world religion, adequate to meet the spiritual needs of a world empire. Have Christians been denounced as revolutionaries who are turning the Roman world upside down? His story will tell how Christ turned his back on political revolution in order to accomplish a profounder revolution in the realm of ideas and values. Are Christians suspected of antisocial behaviour? He will portray the author of their faith as a figure of nobility, grace, and charm, able to reproduce the same qualities in the lives of his followers and to raise to decency and dignity even the outcasts from the society of men.[2]

In Luke we notice an advance on the interpretations supplied by Matthew and Mark, a development in Christian thinking from what happened to how what happened is to be understood. Thus to take one small example: Matthew and Mark never refer to Jesus as "the Lord" in narrative, whereas Luke does so fourteen times. We have already touched on the theological motive for Mark's Gospel. More specifically, it seems to have been written to establish Jesus as the long-awaited Messiah and to explain how it came about that, as such, he was rejected by his own people. Matthew's Gospel was written to show that Jesus' ministry, and particularly his death and resurrection, were the fulfillment of Old Testament prediction. Thus for Matthew the evidence for what Jesus did and endured is to be found in the writings of the prophets, who lived long before the events they are alleged to have foretold. So we have the frequently recurring formula: *"This took place to fulfil what the Lord had spoken by the prophet"* (see Matthew 1:22, 2:15, 17, 23, 4:14, 8:17, 12:17, 13:35, 21:4, 27:9). Finally, we may note in passing that despite the fact that Jesus was purely Jewish all four Gospels—Mark notably, and John most of all—are what nowadays would be called "anti-Semitic" in tone. The main reason for this is not hard to find: the Gospels have as their nucleus some early narrative of the Passion involving an act of judicial murder under the Roman procurator, Pontius Pilate. When the Gospels were issued, however, the Church was making its way within the Empire and at the mercy of its officials. From this situation would naturally arise the tendency to exculpate Rome from the crime as far as possible and to pin the blame on Jesus' Jewish enemies.

Here it will be in place to say a word about *Formgeschichte*

2. G. B. Caird, *The Gospel of St. Luke* (Baltimore: Penguin Books, 1963), pp. 14–15.

(form criticism). Nearly twenty-five years ago I described it rather naïvely as "but the latest example of the unbridled rationalism which has undermined the whole structure of traditional Christianity." There may still be a point in this crude description, but I now think that despite some arbitrariness in applying the method its initial principle must be acknowledged: the contents of our Gospels can only represent a small portion of what Jesus said and did, and that portion must have been selected and shaped in accordance with what most needed to be told to the communities in which the Gospels circulated. Thus they are as much evidence of the special interests of the primitive Church as of the events and sayings they relate. Therefore, it seems to me that the Gospels—to return to our three levels or viewpoints of observation, interpretation, and reflection— fall nearer to the category of interpretation than of direct observation.

Subjective interpretation, inspired and true within its terms of reference as it may be, permeates the message of St. Paul. Accordingly, the significance of the life work of Jesus is not to be found in any day-by-day account of his ministry, including its tragic yet triumphant end, but in what God had revealed to the mind of Paul. "Even though we once regarded Christ from a human point of view, we regard him thus no longer" (2 Corinthians 5:16). God was in Christ reconciling the world to himself through the Cross. There resulted a new creation; compared with this, with being "in Christ" as the resurrected and ascended Lord, it was of small importance to have kept company with him during his earthly life. Thus Paul lifts the historical mission of Jesus to a higher level than that of history; he eternalizes it, so to speak, transforming it into a Christ cult. To this cult, as a notable Pauline scholar has pointed out, those who concentrate on the historical aspects of Christianity are apt to become insensitive.

Many of us have become cult-blind through a modern cult, the cult of the historical. And accordingly they try with historical means either to give Christianity a sure foundation, or to explode it into the air as a troublesome ruin. But Christianity, if it is a reacting Christ-cult, cannot be exploded, and requires no historical justification. Its foundations are good. It stands today on the same basis upon which it stood originally, that is, it reveals the ever present God through the ever present Saviour.[3]

3. Adolf Deissmann, *Paul: A Study in Social and Religious History* (London: Hodder & Stoughton, 1926), p. 122.

Christian faith, as I understand it, is focused, not on the historical Jesus but on the risen Christ, whose significance is divinely revealed. Thus Bultmann is correct in his statements that "even the historical Jesus is a phenomenon among other phenomena, not an absolute entity . . . Faith in God leads to acknowledgment of the person of Jesus, not vice versa." [4] Nevertheless, if Christianity's true character is to be fully unfolded and its place in the religious history of mankind properly understood, then what Jesus of Nazareth actually said and did in first-century Palestine remains of capital importance. The New Testament, we have argued, is in the main an inspired interpretation of Jesus. We shall presently suggest that the more developed theology of the Incarnation is the work of human reflection, safeguarded as its findings may be from positive error. But interpretation is bounded by the limitations of the interpreter, and reflection is dependent on the acumen and integrity of the minds so engaged and the data with which they are provided. Thus each of the New Testament writers was as much a man of his time as any other author setting his pen to paper. The bishops who reached the conclusions they did about the significance of Jesus at Nicaea in 325 A.D. and Chalcedon in 451 could speak only in terms of the philosophical categories then available to them against the cultural background of the Graeco-Roman world. Those who formulated the early Christian creeds were in no better position to address themselves, for example, to the disciples of Confucius or the Buddha than were these to proclaim their own distinctive message to the inhabitants of the Mediterranean seaboard.

Prescinding for a moment from the total theology of the redemption, with its foreordained pattern of what God's only-begotten Son had come on earth to do, I am persuaded that Mark 1:14–15 (particularly verse 15) constitutes an accurate historical summary of Jesus' message: "Now after John was arrested, Jesus came into Galilee, preaching the gospel of God, and saying, 'The time is fulfilled, and the kingdom of God is at hand; repent, and believe in the gospel.'" The kingdom means God's direct intervention in the existing world order, the overwhelming of the powers of evil, and the establishment of the rule of righteousness forever. The kingdom was about to break in on the cruel and despotic Roman administration of Palestine; the kingdom could be expected at any moment. There-

4. Rudolf Bultmann, *Faith and Understanding* (London: S.C.M. Press, 1969), pp. 31, 32.

fore, God's people must be converted, transform their lives, so as to be ready for the kingdom when it came.

But in what sense, if any, has the kingdom come? "Lord, will you at this time restore the kingdom to Israel?" (Acts 1:6). The Jesus who at the beginning of his ministry, as we have just noted, proclaims authoritatively that the time is fulfilled, God's Sovereign rule is at hand, is represented after his resurrection as answering the most urgent question in the mind of his followers with a put-off: "Lord, will you at this time restore the kingdom to Israel?" "It is not for you to know times or seasons which the Father has fixed by his own authority" (Acts 1:6, 7). St. Paul employs the terminology of the "kingdom" quite frequently (e.g., Romans 14:17; 1 Corinthians 4:20; 6:9 and elsewhere) and clearly lives in expectation of its arrival; but for him the emphasis has shifted to his personal communion with Christ, linked, at least in his earliest letters (1 and 2 Thessalonians) with Jesus' second coming. In the Fourth Gospel the doctrine of the kingdom has almost, though not quite (e.g., John 3:3, 5), disappeared, to be replaced with even greater emphasis than in St. Paul by the proclaimer of the kingdom, Jesus himself. Thus, without erecting a sharp antithesis between the two proclamations, it seems correct and also illuminating to observe with Bultmann and many others that while Jesus proclaimed the kingdom, the Church proclaimed *Him*.

In the mind of the early Church the coming of the kingdom is linked with the return of Jesus as the Son of Man in glory (Mark 14:62). Meanwhile, in view of the firm belief of Jesus' disciples in the Resurrection and the visionary experience of Paul on the Damascus road, Jesus had been recognized as the Messiah and Son of God. Above all, "Jesus is Lord" (Romans 10:9; 1 Corinthians 12:3). "Let all the house of Israel therefore know assuredly that God has made him both Lord and Christ, this Jesus whom you crucified" (Acts 2:36). It is this process of recognition that transformed the historical Jesus into the ideal Christ. The risen Lord, as preached by Paul to the pagan Roman Empire, would be declared to be "consubstantial with the Father" at the Council of Nicaea, and to have "two natures," one divine and the other human, at the Council of Chalcedon. These formulations have not been modified in the official teaching of the Catholic Church for over 1,500 years.

It is not the purpose of this essay to question the verbal formu-

laries drawn up by these councils, merely to point out their limitations. When we look into the proceedings at Nicaea, we find that, as
was made clear on that occasion, the key word ὁμοούσιον ("the
same essence") is not in the New Testament. The debates concerning its meaning were predominantly in terms of Greek philosophy.
The word οὐσία in current terminology had various equivalents.
For the Platonists it meant one thing, for the Aristotelians another,
and for the Stoics yet a third. It is true that Athanasius, whose view
on the matter was to prevail, disclaimed these philosophical associations, declaring that "what the Greeks say is nothing to us." But he
was obliged to admit that he had to rely not on the wording of Scripture but on what he conceived to be its "sense." Even so, it was
readily acknowledged at Nicaea that all words have their limitations;
God is ineffable, and human language is necessarily inadequate to
things divine.

The abstruseness and subtlety of the orthodox doctrine of the
Incarnation were increased by the Council of Chalcedon. The unity
of the Lord's divine person is asserted, subsisting in two natures, one
divine, one human. These two natures are united without confusion
or intermingling, without alteration or change of their distinctive attributes, without any division of person, or any subsequent severance
of the two united natures. Here we have the Catholic ideology at its
most intricate, and it is not surprising to find even a highly conservative Christian scholar qualifying his agreement with the remark that
". . . the Council may be said to have failed to recognise the *ethical*
aspect of Christ's humanity as the unique archetype of manhood—a
point which held such a prominent place in the thought of earlier
writers like Irenaeus and Athanasius." [5]

In an earlier chapter I have indicated my own conception of religious faith;[6] it is based on a disclosure from God as primary truth.
The object of Christian faith, therefore, is not the historical Jesus as
he can be disentangled from what the New Testament says about
him, but the Jesus, or rather the Christ, as proposed to us in the
understanding of the Church. So we find it implied in the New Testament itself: "For flesh and blood has not revealed this to you, but
my Father who is in heaven" (Matthew 16:17); this is echoed in St.
Paul's position, when he says he is no longer interested in Christ

5. Robert L. Ottley, *The Doctrine of the Incarnation,* 7th ed. (London:
Methuen & Co., 1929), pp. 429–30.   6. See pp. 6–7.

"according to the flesh" (2 Corinthians 5:16), that is, from a human point of view. Nevertheless, the Church's understanding of Christ cannot be entirely detached from the historical Jesus in a series of free-floating concepts or Platonic ideas, since the roots of Christianity, if not its full flowering, are buried in what actually happened on this earth. Therefore, if it could be shown incontrovertibly by the processes of scholarship—and let orthodox theologians be allowed to say that it is a big "if"!—that the traditional interpretation of Jesus and his message and the Church's reflection upon it need to be reviewed in a hitherto unrecognized perspective, then this conclusion must be courageously faced and accepted, disturbing as it might prove to be to not a few prejudices and vested interests.

To return briefly to our first records: I think there are grounds for the distinction, now a commonplace among scholars, between the emphasis in the belief of the original Palestinian community, grouped around James and Peter at Jerusalem, and the character of the message proclaimed by Paul, and in the Fourth Gospel, to the Hellenized communities in various parts of the Empire, including Rome. The Palestinian community continued the cult of Judaism, worshiping steadfastly in the temple (Acts 2:46; 3:1). Their proclamation was that of Jesus himself, who preached the *coming* of the Kingdom of God. They believed that Jesus, the crucified prophet, would come again as the Messiah; they were a community waiting for the age that was still to arrive. But for Paul and John, author of the Fourth Gospel, the new age has already dawned, although the community, become the "church," is still and will remain "eschatological," looking forward to the Lord's coming in judgment (1 Corinthians 4:4, 5). He is to come from heaven: ". . . from it we await a Saviour, the Lord Jesus Christ, who will change our lowly body to be like his glorious body, by the power which enables him even to subject all things to himself" (Philippians 3:20, 21).

With the indefinite postponement of the expected event—the appearance of Christ as judge and the establishment of a new world order, the Messianic age—the attention of the Christian communities was focused more and more on the cultus. "Kyrios," the Lord, becomes the most popular designation for Jesus, as the resurrected and idealized Christ. He is now recognized as a cult, even a mystery, Deity, who works supernaturally in the Church as a cultic body. In his death and resurrection the faithful are able to participate through the sacraments. By the early second century we find essentially all the elements constituting Catholic piety down to our own time.

How, then, does the influence of Jesus, acting through his spirit, take effect on his followers today? In various ways, it seems to me. No one, obviously, can make contact with Jesus of Nazareth in the direct manner of the first disciples. Similarly, the experience of Paul on the Damascus road, with its world-shaking consequences, has occurred only once. The encounter with Jesus in the sacraments, even the Eucharist, is symbolic rather than evidential; it presupposes a faith whose object is unseen, and it is dependent in large measure on what might be called the psychological dispositions of those partaking in sacramental worship. For Lutheran piety Jesus becomes known in the announcing of the divine "word"—understood, not as eternal truth, but as God's proclamation (kerygma) in history, to which man must respond by an existential decision based on faith. For everyday Catholicism, Jesus is to be found chiefly in the mood induced by adoration and worship, either privately, or more effectively in the public worship of the Mass. He is a transcendent, externalized figure, theoretically at one with but for all practical purposes far above the human race as its Saviour and Redeemer, who is best approached through the liturgical services of the Church. The linking of Jesus to the empirical Church has taken place also at the juridical level—with the concept of the bishops as the successors of the apostles and the Pope as the "vicar of Christ." The result of all this is that typically Catholic spirituality tends to be more and more assimilated to the ecclesiastical system, as this finds its expression in public worship.

The adequacy of these conceptions, for those who are seriously interested in religion, appears in some doubt at the present time. Here the question of their truth does not arise, for "truth" in these matters is usually determined by certain antecedent assumptions, by how positions are to be understood. But at least it may be suggested that we need to find another perspective if we are to reach a level where a religious presentation evokes an immediate response. Anyone who has talked with missionaries in contact with the ancient, civilized religions of India and Japan will quickly learn, in comparison with these native traditions, how powerless to arouse interest institutional Christianity can be. The Christian Church is probably not yet under sufficient pressure to embark on the radical self-ques-

tioning it will eventually have to face if it is to disentangle what in its
heritage is authentically religious from what is the product of the
cultural synthesis stemming from Jerusalem, Athens, and Rome.
Meanwhile, we shall do well to observe the order of priorities set
forth in the Christian creeds, where belief in God is the prelude to
and not the consequence of faith in Jesus Christ. This is incontest-
ably the order upheld by Jesus himself. The Judaeo-Hellenistic-
Roman tradition has its own story of God. There are good grounds
for suspecting that it is not the whole story.

ii. Adjusting to the Great Non-Event

The aspiration of the Lord's Prayer, "Thy kingdom come," remains unfulfilled. The Messianic kingdom, as it was understood by
Jesus' contemporaries to have been announced by him, never came.
This is the great "non-event." "Truly I say to you, there are some
standing here who will not taste death before they see the kingdom
of God come with power" (Mark 9:1). Here we have Christian
eschatology—the doctrine of how the existing order is to end—re-
portedly in the words of Jesus himself. Some scholars have read into
this prediction its fulfillment in the presence and activity of Jesus
during his lifetime by what they call "realized eschatology"; but the
interpretation appears forced, and it has not won wide acceptance.
Through most of the New Testament records the expectation persists
—now in a more, now in a less, lively form—that the "last times" are
upon the world. What was expected did not happen. Today Christians take this in their stride. But that the Church survived such an
anticlimax is astonishing—a proof of its inner vitality and gift of
adaptation to circumstances. The original expectation, I am persuaded, was not of how the world would eventually come to an end
but of the establishment by divine intervention within the lifetime of
Jesus' disciples here on earth of the Messianic kingdom. "Thy kingdom come" was a plea precisely for this.

It is true that the picture has changed almost beyond recognition
between St. Paul's writing of 1 Thessalonians and the appearance of
the Letter to the Ephesians—"the crown of Paulinism." The irrup-
tion of God's kingdom into the world is here no longer considered;
what dominates the author's mind is the universal mission of the

Church; there is to take place a gradual growth toward a final consummation (Ephesians 2:21; 4:13) rather than a catastrophic imminent return of Christ. There are hints of this long-term development even in our first evangelist. Mark 13:10—"And the gospel must first be preached to all nations"—though possibly an interpolation, indicates how the minds of early Christians were moving away from predictions of the disasters heralding the Messianic age to the more positive business of conveying the good news of salvation to mankind in general. As the Christian Church came into contact with the pagan world, the doctrinal emphasis of the Palestinian community centered at Jerusalem shifted to the themes stressed in the Pauline epistles and the Fourth Gospel. The notion of a Messianic kingdom presently to be established had lost its vitality, even for the Greek-speaking Jews scattered over the Empire; to the pagans such a notion meant less than nothing. Moreover, any hint of a kingdom that might be conceived as a rival to the Roman rule would be fatal to the new religion. Accordingly, other aspects of Christian belief could more suitably be stressed.

Such conceptions as those of a divine Redeemer, a Saviour, one who would be a light to the world, one who had pre-existed and dwelt with God, who had come down to earth and now returned to the region whence he came, the knowledge of whom and of the God who sent him was in itself salvation or eternal life, were ideas in common currency among the religions of the pagan world at the time Christianity was adapting itself to an alien environment. We may note the transformation even within the New Testament: two sayings, both ascribed to Jesus himself. Compare "The time is fulfilled, and the kingdom of God is at hand; repent, and believe in the gospel" (Mark 1:15) with "And this is eternal life, that they know thee the only true God, and Jesus Christ whom thou hast sent" (John 17:3). A pagan audience could make little or nothing of the first of these sayings; the second would be pregnant with meaning. Yet the meaning attached to it would vary with different audiences, as they interpreted it against their particular religious background and according to their own spiritual needs. Hence the growth of various types of Christianity.

The manner in which the Christian Church adjusted to what I have called the "great non-event" can best be understood in terms of the long controversy with Gnosticism. It is worthwhile giving some attention to this since it is instructive in itself and could have bearing on the Church's situation in the intellectual climate of today. To take the latter point first: Is the faith of a Christian basically a matter of "trust" (*pistis*), as in Romans 3:28? Or does faith connote "knowledge" (*gnosis*, the word from which "Gnosticism" is derived), as in, for example, John 14:9? Probably it is compounded of both, as is indicated by the context of the verse just cited—which refers to Jesus questioning Philip about his knowledge of him; though much will depend on which is given the greater emphasis, whether "knowledge" or "trust." Protestantism, as represented by Luther, tends to take the Pauline view of faith, which is basically a matter of *trust* in God. Catholicism, if Aquinas is still a representative spokesman, favors the Johannine conception: faith implies *knowledge* of God, at least in the sense that the believer's intellect is focused on ultimate truth (*Summa Theologica* II–II, iv, 2). The implications of the Catholic position are deep and far reaching; they are still insufficiently explored.

It is a mistake to view Gnosticism, either as a single unitary system or merely as a heresy opposed to Christian orthodoxy. The term covers a great variety of opinions, more or less philosophical, which may or may not have been systematized, and it was only gradually that certain Gnostic views came to be seen as incompatible with Christian truth. Gnosticism is a pre-Christian phenomenon.

The Gnostic movement, then, was the result of that mingling of diverse beliefs which had long been in process in many different centres; and it had developed itself, in all its essential features, before the Christian era had fairly begun. Of this pre-Christian Gnosticism we still have an impressive monument in the so-called Hermetic literature of Egypt—a literature which was compiled from sources that were certainly in existence in the first or second century B.C.[7]

The word "gnosis" is often employed by religious and philosophical writers to denote an intuitive vision of truth, as contrasted with a wisdom that comes by reflective thought. These two kinds of knowledge have both to be taken into account, when evaluating the purpose and character of Gnosticism. On the one hand, the Gnostic is in

---

7. E. F. Scott, "Gnosticism," in *Hastings' Encyclopaedia of Religion and Ethics* (Edinburgh: T. & T. Clark, 1937). The outline of Gnosticism given here is much indebted to this article.

possession of an occult lore; he participates in rites that are called "mysteries"; he is instructed in magical watchwords and secret names. On the other hand, he undergoes a mystical experience whereby he allegedly apprehends the true nature of God and enters into communion with him. The idea of gnosis is closely linked with revelation: all Gnostic systems assume that man is unable of himself to attain to the higher knowledge; this is to be communicated to him by a being from the higher world.

According to Christian tradition, one of the chief Gnostics was Simon, the "sorcerer," whom Peter and John encountered at Samaria (Acts 8:9ff). Samaria, with its mixed population, was no doubt an early center of Gnosticism. But Gnosticism manifested itself in so many widely separated areas and in such a variety of forms that it can only be regarded as the outcome of ideas and tendencies that infiltrated the general life of the time. Insofar as Gnosticism affected the presentation of the Christian message and its influence both positively and negatively was great, more was involved than what has been called the "Hellenization" of Christianity. Hellenism itself had been subjected to religious influences from the Orient. As early as the Babylonian empire's yielding to Persia in the sixth century B.C. and the imposition of the Persian dualism on the Semitic provinces, a syncretistic process, which was to continue into the Christian era, had begun. The process was intensified by the conquests of Alexander and during the Hellenistic period proper, from roughly 320 to 50 B.C. The Hellenic culture, now diffused over the East as far as India, acted as a solvent on the native forms of belief. Since Plato's time the idea that a deeper wisdom was to be found in the Oriental mythologies had obtained currency, and the ideas surging in from the East evoked a ready response from eclectic thinkers. Eastern myths and observance were interpreted in the light of Greek thought, combined and recombined in new syntheses.

With the coming of the Roman Empire the syncretistic process in the religions of the ancient world was complete. All national boundaries were broken down; the Eastern races could hold free intercourse with one another and with the peoples of the West. Moreover, the Stoic philosophy—with its stress on the virtuous life and the law of nature—became everywhere prevalent. It was to enter deeply into the Christian tradition, as could easily be shown by a line of continuity, in this respect at least, from St. Paul to St. Thomas

Aquinas. All over the East and around the Mediterranean seaboard
religious fusion was proceeding apace; but it advanced most rapidly
in such cosmopolitan centers as Antioch, Alexandria, and the great
cities of Asia Minor. In each of these centers there arose a mixed
religion, to which the local type of belief—Syrian, Egyptian, or
Phrygian—naturally contributed the largest share. So rich was the
diversity of this religious ferment that it had plenty to offer, both to
the superstitious masses and the sophisticated intellectuals. Thus we
find a strange mixture of crude mythology and lofty speculation in
the typical Gnostic schools.

Even Judaism, the most sharply defined and most exclusive of all
Eastern faiths, had become involved in the general syncretistic
movement. Babylonian, Persian, and Hellenistic influences are all
easily traceable in the Old Testament literature. At the time of Christ
there were unorthodox sects in Palestine itself; for example, the Essenes, of whom we have learned much since the discovery of the
Dead Sea scrolls—if indeed they were Essenes who dwelt in the
monastery at Qumran. These sectaries, according to the not very reliable historian Josephus (born at Jerusalem about 37 A.D.), had a
good deal in common with the life of the Pythagoreans, who in their
turn are thought by some to have had affinities with Indian
Buddhism—so that the lines of demarcation between one religion
and another become increasingly blurred. Outside Palestine, notably
at Alexandria in the work of Philo, a studied attempt was made to
bring the Old Testament teaching into harmony not only with Stoic
and Platonic ideas but with the native traditions of Egypt. Here also
was the probable birthplace of the so-called Hermetic literature, ancient writings attributed to the "thrice-great Hermes," some of which
may date back as far as the first century B.C. Both in Philo and the
Hermetic writings can be found a cosmic Logos, which is at the
same time a "son" of God.

The Eastern religions had some kinship with Christianity in their
presuppositions and motives. They represented a striving after an
unworldly purity, a longing for redemption, and a belief that the
true path to blessedness, to the authentically happy life, could be
discovered only in the light of divine revelation. These aspects of
the Christian message, therefore, were highly acceptable to the
Gnostic teachers. At the period of entering the pagan world Christianity was still in the process of free development. Within the Church

itself its teachings were subject to constant revision, and the Hellenistic thinkers did not hesitate to modify them yet further in accordance with their own preconceptions. As might have been expected,
the first Christian missionaries, if they were to make sense to their
hearers, were all but compelled to present the Gospel in terms and
imagery derived from the pagan cults. Thus the salvation brought by
Christ had been expressed even by St. Paul in a manner that easily
suggested the current beliefs.

Primitive Christianity, springing from the soil of first-century
Judaism was, as we have seen, apocalyptic in character. But such
visions as those described, for example, in Revelation, chapter 20,
though possibly consoling to those for whom they were first intended, could make little appeal to the Hellenistic world in general.
The main task laid upon Christian thought at the end of the first
century was that of transforming its apocalyptic beliefs, with particular reference to the expectation within the historic process of the
establishment of the Messianic kingdom, into their spiritual equivalents. It was thus that membership of the kingdom that did not come
came to be thought of in terms of personal immortality, making
possible a blissful hereafter. In this way Christianity itself partook of
the prevailing religious syncretism; for a time the boundaries between the Church and the contemporary cults were ill-defined. The
door was open to the so-called Gnostic movement and the adoption
of Christianity into the various syncretistic systems. At the same
time, the Church was becoming aware of the danger that threatened
it from the encroachment of foreign beliefs and the need to make
clear its uniqueness at the cost of a life-and-death struggle.

Christian polemical writers were disposed to deal with Gnosticism as a philosophy, and to criticize its extravagant speculations.
But its real nature, the basis of both its wide appeal and its danger to
the Church, was religious. The central idea of Gnosticism, as of all
the mystery religions, was the goal known variously as redemption,
salvation, liberation, or final enlightenment by means of revelation.
Redemption is understood as deliverance from the material world,
which is regarded as intrinsically evil. Gnosticism based itself on the
Persian dualistic conception, for which light and darkness appear as
two natural principles in eternal conflict. Under the influence of
Greek speculation the contrast of light and darkness became that
between spirit and matter—the lower world of sense and the higher

world of pure being. These two are irreconcilable opposites, though they have come to be mingled together. All the evil and misery in the world arise from this forbidden mixing of antagonistic principles: light with darkness, spirit with matter. Here we have the grand calamity that has made necessary a work of redemption.

The idea of deliverance from the material world carried with it the prospect of an escape from bondage to freedom. In ancient Hellenic thought fate was the power above the gods, and at the beginning of the Christian era the sense that everything happened of unavoidable necessity had been greatly strengthened by Oriental fatalism. This was linked with astrological beliefs that had come down from the Babylonian religion. Humanity's ineluctable destiny was written in the stars. By their influences, controlling him from his birth, man is forced under the yoke of mechanical necessity despite his deep-down conviction all the time that he is called to freedom. Gnostic thought aimed at dealing with this situation, and its motive was a genuinely religious one—to secure for the human spirit the liberty that is implicit in its nature. But if the soul was held captive by planetary powers, it was by overcoming those powers that freedom was to be won. An ascent must be made above the world rulers and powers represented in astral mythology; the presiding demons can be subdued or deceived by means of charms and passwords. To the end of circumventing the hostile rulers the secret discipline of Gnosticism was mainly directed. The adept was prepared for his future journey by sacraments and lustrations and by instruction in the hidden names of angels—themselves scarcely distinguishable from the stars—and the words and signs by which they could be overcome. All the resources of magical gnosis were called into play to effect the deliverance of the soul from the cosmic powers that had brought it under the bondage of necessity. It is against a background like this that St. Paul's outburst of confidence is best understood— that through God's love manifested in Christ the chain of necessity has been broken:

> For I am sure that neither death, nor life, nor angels nor principalities, nor things present, nor things to come, nor powers, nor height, nor depth, nor anything else in all creation, will be able to separate us from the love of God in Christ Jesus our Lord (Romans 8:38–39).

Where Gnostic thought was eventually to come into collision with the Christian Church was in relation to two doctrines: the resurrection of the body and personal immortality. Since matter was regarded as essentially evil, salvation lay in the soul's separation from the body. The soul, thus freed from its limitations, is simply to be reunited with the "pleroma"—the fullness of the divine being.

Among the manifold variety of Gnostic schools there are certain basic doctrines common to all. At the head of the universe stands the Supreme God, who is not so much a personality as the impersonal ground of all existence. Often he is conceived as pure light; elsewhere he bears names that serve to emphasize his absolute transcendence—Father of All, Unbegotten, Ineffable, the Unapproachable, the Abyss, the Unknowable. Other sects refer to him as "the Man," or the "primal Man." From the Father or Supreme God there proceed a number of beings in a descending scale of dignity, who are arranged in pairs of male and female, the minor deity and his consort, and in their totality make up the pleroma—the fullness of all blessedness and perfection. The divine existences, while distinguished from one another, are the manifestations of one God, who is himself impersonal and unknowable.

The need for redemption arose because of the fall from the pleroma of the member standing lowest in rank, known as an Aeon. To the Aeon or Power is usually assigned the name of Sophia (i.e., Wisdom), a name suggested by the Old Testament conception of the Wisdom by which the world came into being. Sophia is the fallen divinity through whom the light becomes immersed in darkness, and she is also the intermediary between the higher world and the spiritual nature that has been exiled from it. Thus she is regarded not only as the object of redemption but as herself assisting in the redemptive process—watching over the light until deliverance comes. The work of deliverance is undertaken by a Power of supreme rank, a Saviour (*Soter*)—identified, according to Gnostic thought, with Christ.

The Saviour comes down through the sphere of the "world rulers" (archons), taking on himself the form of the spirits of each world as he descends. Arriving in the world of darkness, he gathers to himself the scattered seeds of divine light and finally reascends along with the rescued Sophia into the pleroma. The figure of the saviour is itself older than Christianity and has many counterparts in the Hellenistic cults. Its prototype may possibly be found in the Babylonian light god Marduk, who descends unrecognized to do battle with Tiamat, the monster of Chaos. Further elements are borrowed from the myths of Attis, Osiris, and Mithra, although all the definite features are blended together and resolved into one abstract conception. The dominating characteristic of Christian Gnosticism is the identification of the mythical Redeemer with Christ, with whose history the pagan traditions are interwoven.

The Gnostic Saviour, however, always remains distinct from the historical Jesus, who appears simply as a man of pre-eminent spiritual nature, united for a given time with the heavenly Redeemer. The union is variously interpreted as taking place at his birth, or when he is twelve years old, or according to the more usual view, on the occasion of his baptism. Before the crucifixion the divine being, who is incapable of suffering, separates himself from the crucified. The Gnostic Redeemer originally had no connection with Jesus. He was simply an abstraction of features common to the mythological saviors, and this abstract figure was combined artificially with the Jesus of history. For this reason Gnosticism was unable, in spite of all efforts, to establish any real identity between the Redeemer and Jesus. It could find no way of bridging the gap between spirit and matter. Much of the prologue to the Fourth Gospel—John 1:1–18—could be interpreted as echoing certain Gnostic theories. Where it emerges as uniquely Christian is in the incarnational statement of verse 14: "And the Word became flesh and dwelt among us."

St. John combines hostility to and a certain sympathy with Gnostic thought; though in his first Epistle he is clearly opposing some form of Gnostic docetism—that is, the doctrine that the humanity of Jesus is apparent rather than real. Elsewhere in the New Testament the lines are being drawn between what was to develop into orthodox Christianity and the prevailing syncretism. The false teachers who are condemned in Colossians seem to belong to a variety of Jewish Gnosticism. The heresies referred to in the Pastoral Epistles and in the message to the churches in Revelation are even more clearly of the Gnostic type. Nevertheless, in their efforts to commend their message to the pagan world the Christian communities wisely assimilated much from current religious thought. But the need eventually became clear for the Church to establish its own identity if it was not to be dragged into the vortex of contemporary syncretism and so disappear as a separate religion. Early in the second century Ignatius, bishop of Antioch, wrote a series of letters marked by the strongest antagonism to the new doctrines, and for the next hundred years the conflict with Gnosticism dominates the theological life of the Church. Chief among the objections to Gnostic thought were that it taught the existence of a higher God than the one who created the world, that it drew a distinction between the Creator and the Redeemer, that it repudiated the Old Testament, that its docetic view of Christ eliminated him from the historic process, that it denied the Resurrection, and that its ethical teaching fluctuated between extreme asceticism and self-indulgent libertinism.

The results of the conflict are worth reflecting on today, when the Christian forces that in fact were to prevail themselves appear to be in some danger of dissolution. The Church took its stand on its universality. By the strict enforcement of unity in creed and worship it sought to make its Catholic character more manifest. There was established a "rule of faith"—an authoritative standard of belief by which all innovations could be tested. From this arose the formal creeds of succeeding times, which still remain the test of orthodoxy. Slowly the official canons of both the Old and New Testament scriptures were formulated, largely, in both cases, for controversial purposes: to provide ammunition for the anti-Gnostic polemic rather than as a result of calm reflection on the nature of the Christian religion and what might be compatible with the future spiritual needs of the faithful. Not the Church but the Gnostic Marcion was the first to draw up a "canon" of early Christian literature, acceptable to him and his considerable following; he also rejected the Old Testament *in toto*. The Church replied by eventually declaring canonical all the documents that form our New Testament, and since it supported certain crucial Catholic doctrines, took over without more ado the whole canon of Jewish scriptures, which had been set up by the Rabbinical Council at Jamnia near Jerusalem about 90 A.D. These are the essential elements in forming the contents of the Bible as we have it today. It was a curious and undiscriminating arrangement, still deserving far more attention from scholars and theologians— particularly from Catholics, who are under no compulsion to become bibliolaters—than it has so far received. The divinely sanctioned violence and warfare, the zestful accounts of bloodshed and slaughter, the complacent ritual of animal sacrifice—horrifying to the millions for whom a central religious belief is that "all sentient beings" must be respected—are painfully familiar. It is this literary heritage that impugns the credentials, if the claim were not questionable on other grounds, of institutional Christianity to be a religion of gentleness and peace. Selected almost at random, here is a choice item to be found in the "good book" for the edification of Christian readers:

When the people of Israel were in the wilderness, they found a man gathering sticks on the sabbath day. And those who found him gathering sticks brought him to Moses and Aaron, and to all the congregation. They put him in custody, because it had not been made plain what should be done to him. And the Lord said to Moses, "The man shall be put to death; all the congregation shall stone him with stones outside the camp." And all the congregation brought him outside the camp, and stoned him to death with stones, as the Lord commanded Moses (Numbers 15:32–36).

Gnosticism not only provoked a reaction; it produced lasting positive effects on the Christian religion. Gnostic thought and practice could not have diffused themselves so widely over the world in the first two centuries unless they had answered some genuine human need. As a result, the Church's tendency to set a high value on asceticism was strengthened; Christian monks of the third and subsequent centuries no longer appealed to Gnostic doctrine. But the nature of their contempt for the world could scarcely be distinguished from the earlier dualism. Moreover, religious sacramentalism was reinforced. Gnosticism had captured the popular imagination by its use of symbolic rites, which were considered in themselves sufficient to ensure all spiritual blessings. In place of the heretical ritual the Church now elaborated its own. The efficacy of the Christian faith was more and more identified with the value of the sacraments.

Perhaps the most enduring of all the effects traceable to the Gnostic movement is that effort toward a direct intuition or experience of the divine, which has received the designation "mysticism." Linked as it is with the Greek mysteries, the use of the term is understandable; but nowadays the phrase "religious experience" seems preferable, since it has no necessary connection with the occult or irrational, which formed a feature of the Greek and Oriental religions. What men are seeking, perhaps more eagerly today than ever before, is to reach beyond the creeds, ethical codes, and cultic observances of institutional religion in order to obtain a personal conviction through direct experience that such terms as God, Ultimate Reality, the Ground of Being, or what I have called on an earlier page, pure Existence, make sense. That Catholicism is able to offer such a goal—obscurely and, it often seems, rather reluctantly—is because of Christianity's long and fruitful dialogue with Gnosticism.

The Gnostic teachers, unlike the first Christian missionaries, were men of philosophical culture, and their free attitude to the nascent Catholic tradition prompted them to investigations from which the more orthodox writers held back. Thus Gnosticism stimulated the development of the Church's theology. Gnostic literature abounded in hymns, many of them of great beauty, and these were often taken over and adapted to the services of the Church. In fact, the Christian hymn may be reckoned a contribution made by Gnosticism to orthodoxy. For all these reasons Catholicism's irreconcilable opposition to Gnosticism, though necessary if the distinctive character of the Christian religion was to be preserved, was in many ways a misfortune. Not only was the Church deprived of influences that might have proved helpful but the extravagances of Gnosticism were only the other side of that freedom that was the birthright of Christianity, according to the Pauline dictum—"where the Spirit of the Lord is, there is freedom" (2 Corinthians 3:17). To check the inroads of Gnosticism the Church had to curtail freedom. Dogma was made rigid; the idea of new revelation was forbidden; ecclesiastical government became official and oppressive. The contrast between the third and fourth centuries and the primitive period indicates a measure of the loss that the Church sustained by its triumph over heresy.

It was in some such manner as I have just outlined that organized Christianity adjusted to the postponement of its original hopes and set out on the long journey to an unknown future. What of the situation in our own time? The Gnostics in today's world are, I suppose, the men of science, whose influence through their technological discoveries is all pervasive. The challenge that they throw out is not, as with the early Gnostics, that we should compete with them in terms of myth and ritual but that we should meet the test of evidence and experience, a test that after all is not without its sanctions in the New Testament. Religion is to be judged empirically by its fruits (Matthew 7:20); kinship with God is made evident to us by experience—"the Spirit himself bearing witness with our spirit that we are children of God" (Romans 8:16).

"Can religious beliefs also be viewed as working hypotheses, tested and validated by experience?" asks a recent winner of the Nobel Prize for physics in an article titled "The Convergence of Science and Religion." [8] "To some this may seem a secular and even an abhorrent view. In any case, it discards absolutism in religion. But I see no reason why acceptance of religion on this basis should be objectionable. The validity of religious ideas must be and has been tested and judged through the ages by societies and by individual experience. Is there any great need for them to be more absolute than the law of gravity? The latter is a working hypothesis whose basis and permanency we do not know. But on our belief in it, as well as on many other complex scientific hypotheses, we risk our lives daily."

Seeking partnership rather than enmity between religion and science, Dr. Townes considers the case of Galileo and draws some interesting conclusions. With the two final paragraphs of his article the present chapter may also fittingly conclude.

Galileo espoused the cause of Copernicus' theory of the solar system, and at great personal cost because of the Church's opposition. We know today that the question on which Galileo took his stand, the correctness of the idea that the earth rotates around the sun rather than the sun around the earth, is largely an unnecessary question. The two descriptions are equivalent, according to general relativity, although the first is simpler. And yet we honor Galileo for his pioneering courage and determination in deciding what he really thought was right and speaking out. This was important to his own integrity and to the development of the scientific and religious views of the time, out of which has grown our own better understanding of the problems he faced.

The authority of religion seemed more crucial in Galileo's Italy than it usually does today, and science more fresh and simple. We tend to think of ourselves as now more sophisticated, and science and religion as both more complicated so that our position can be less clear cut. Yet if we accept the assumption of either one, that truth exists, surely each of us should undertake the same kind of task as Galileo, or long before him, Gautama. For ourselves and for mankind, we must use our best wisdom and instincts, the evidence of history and wisdom of the ages, the experience and revelations of our friends, saints, and heroes in order to get as close as possible to truth and meaning. Furthermore, we must be willing to live and act on our conclusions.

The Christian reader may be left to decide for himself if this is a fair challenge, and should it be so, whether he is prepared to accept it.

8. Charles H. Townes, *THINK Magazine,* Spring, 1966.

5. Is Christianity Enough?[1]

"I realize that patriotism is not enough. I must have no hatred or bitterness towards anyone." With this statement Nurse Edith Cavell, a heroine of the First World War, met her death on October 12, 1915. Only a little adaptation, it seems to me, is needed for these words to be applied to the position of Christians today: I realize at least that my kind of Christianity is not enough; I must have no sense of superiority or exclusiveness toward anyone. For perhaps the first time in its history the Church has the opportunity to reflect on itself calmly, to discover its identity. Expansionist missionary endeavor appears to be in abeyance; at home, controversial churchmen are hard put to find anyone to argue with, the old-time hostilities have given place to indifference. Since its beginnings the Church has propagated itself from the highest motives, largely by self-serving declarations, insisting, so to speak, on its own necessity. Now when an individual is engaged in proclaiming his own worth or defending himself against attack, he may be doing what is necessary to advance his interests or preserve his life, but he is unlikely to gain much in terms of luminous self-knowledge. So it may be with institutional Christianity: at last the opportunity has come for a corporate observance of the Socratic maxim that the unexamined life is not worth living. The self-scrutiny that is called for should be made all the easier by the fact that the Church—including by that term the various Christian communions and denominations—is being left more or less alone to debate with itself.

The first generic description of the Christian religion is probably

1. Though integral to these "explorations," this chapter was written partly with an eye to its being read as a paper at a local ecumenical conference, convened to discuss "The Crisis of Belief." Accordingly, it may stimulate thoughts reaching beyond the bounds of current Christian orthodoxy. That the reader is being confronted throughout this book with no more than a personal viewpoint should perhaps again be stressed.

that which is found in the Acts of Apostles (19:9), where it is referred to as "the Way." The context there shows St. Paul in the synagogue at Ephesus speaking of the "Kingdom of God," that is to say, the imminently expected messianic kingdom, which in fact did not arrive. The "Way," then, presumably means the Christian faith and practice that fits one to be a member of the kingdom when it comes. As we have seen, however, the apocalyptic standpoint of the earliest Christian communities gave place within a century to the realization that the Church must come to terms with the world of the Roman Empire and settle down to an indefinite existence within the historic process. In a profound sense it is undoubtedly still true that here "we have no lasting city" (Hebrews 13:14). But some of our cities—Jerusalem, Athens, and Rome, to name but three—have lasted quite a time, rather longer than the tradition behind Mark's Gospel, for example, may have given grounds for expecting. But what was to be the fate of these concretely existing cities is not really to the point. The initial proclamation of Jesus, I am persuaded, was understood to be a message of crisis, of imminent judgment. What happens when the crisis has passed?

The easy answer, of course, is that Christians should conduct their lives in a climate of crisis, as if death and judgment were just round the corner. But there is not much evidence that this is the way the faithful, even the devout, do in fact behave. They hope and make plans for a normal life span for themselves, their children, and more than likely, their children's children. There are few who appear to share the Pauline desire "to depart and be with Christ" (Philippians 1:23). In other words, for all practical purposes, Christians act as if they were involved in and even enjoying an earthly city, a way of life that is here to stay. Now it seems to me, though the point is controversial, that the manner in which a large number of reasonably clear-headed and well-intentioned people act is a pretty clear indication of how they should be acting. And this leads us to the question: In what measure does the Christian religion, as it has so far developed, provide for this situation? Put more pointedly: Does Christianity as it has hitherto existed afford truly adequate guidance, a philosophy of life, for people living in the late twentieth-century world? Can it even be said that it claims to do so?

The common assumption among practicing Christians is that these two questions are to be answered with an emphatic yes.

Christianity, wrote G. K. Chesterton in his most slapdash manner, has not been tried and failed; it has never been tried. That seems to me patently untrue, at least if it means that very many generations of people have not seriously attempted to base their lives on Christian standards, whatever those standards may be and however they are to be conceived. The question to be examined, then, is not the always pertinent one of how we are to live up to the Christian ideal but the much more radical problem of whether there is a distinctively Christian ideal and if so in what sense we are meant to be living up to it. Though here it is worth noting that the word "ideal" does not appear in the New Testament or anywhere in the Hebrew Bible, and that in itself suggests ground for reflection. "Ideal" and its source word "idea" are Platonic rather than biblical notions, though there is no reason why they should not have been taken over by the Church. There are hints of just such a movement of thought as early as the writing of the Epistle to the Hebrews, where the manner of earthly worship is to be modeled on that of heaven, "according to the pattern which was shown you on the mountain" (Hebrews 8:5).

At a time like the present, when organized Christianity is on the defensive, neither believers nor seekers can be satisfied with operations in ecclesiastical face lifting. There is a certain pathos about efforts to make the existing Church more "relevant" to the moods and fashions of the hour. Rather, what is called for, it seems to me, is a discriminating survey with a view to disentangling what is permanent from what is obsolete, what was intended for all time from what was temporary, what corresponds to the abiding human condition from the needs of an emergency situation, what holds possibilities of growth and development from what is lifeless in the Christian tradition as it has come down to us. Such an inquiry should not begin, as some have naïvely thought, with the demolition of the Church's corporate structure. Truth cannot be conveniently sought in a vacuum; to get to where we want to go we have to start from where we are. The ecclesiastical framework, therefore, should be held together until the need for structural alterations becomes decisively apparent. But those responsible for preserving the general fabric should regard themselves precisely in that capacity as supervisors and maintenance men rather than as architects, designers, or even interior decorators.

The survey I have in mind would need to begin not with the creeds of the second and subsequent centuries but with the New Testament itself. One of the first things we notice there is the seeming vindication of Julius Wellhausen's famous paradox: "Jesus was not a Christian; he was a Jew." In the light of the Resurrection faith he was recognized as the Christ (i.e., the Messiah). But the circle of his first disciples did not regard themselves as a Christ party; they waited for the arrival of the kingdom of which he had warned them (Acts 1:6), and they continued as before to worship daily in the Jerusalem temple (Acts 2:46). The author of Acts goes out of his way to make the point that the term "Christian" was first applied to the faithful not at Jerusalem—the community where Peter and the Lord's own kinsman, James, were active—but at Syrian Antioch, as it fell within Paul's sphere of activity (Acts 11:26).[2] Here it may be remarked that perhaps the official Church would be wise to take rather more seriously than in the past the efforts of Christian scholars to disengage from the records what Jesus thought and taught about himself from what even his earliest and most inspired interpreters thought and taught about him. By opening our eyes to what could prove at first sight disturbing possibilities, the cause of truth might be better served, the ecumenical dialogue extended and enriched, and nothing of what is essential to Christianity lost.

Without entering into the controversies of the early Church and the absorbing problem of the emphasis in the belief of the first Palestinian communities compared with that of the Hellenistic circles that form the background to the Pauline Epistles, it seems to me that one point can be made with confidence. The Christian religion is on its own admission not enough: not enough for those who believe—perhaps wrongly, as many a devout Christian would doubtless say—that this present life is to be enjoyed and lived to the full. Christianity in its origins was eschatological, that is to say, focused on the future, on the end of the existing world order and of human life as the first believers knew it. The primitive Church was the congregation of "the end of days." And that is still the message, emphasized by the Second Vatican Council and in the revised Liturgy. The committed Christian nowadays is no more allowed to be noneschatological than he can afford to be nonexistential. In fact, according to Rudolf Bult-

2. Only twice elsewhere in the New Testament does the term "Christian" appear: Acts 26:28 and 1 Peter 4:16.

mann—who, for all his learning and apparent skepticism, echoes many of the Lutheran positions—faith is nothing other than "eschatological existence." Not only the early Christians but Christians today are members of a pilgrim Church, wayfarers, looking forward to the coming of Christ in glory.

Let all the intended truth and its full practical value be conceded to this doctrine; it can safely be said that it is not the whole story. C. S. Lewis could be right in his suggestion that after a mere 2,000 years we are still early Christians. A much longer time and a wider experience of the world as a whole, with its varying religious traditions (some of them much older than Christianity), may be needed to draw out the Church's full spiritual resources. Moreover, it must not be forgotten that for the typical audience to whom the Christian message was first preached—the poor and oppressed in Galilee and Judea, the unprivileged populations of the Roman world—life in the present was scarcely worth living; they lived for the future. They wanted to hear that a good time was coming of which they and not their oppressors would be the beneficiaries—and that was the good news they did in fact hear from Jesus and the first missionaries.

Original Christianity, though it had the seeds of long life within it, appeared as something of an emergency measure; it was a religion to meet a crisis. Thus Albert Schweitzer's point that Jesus' teaching on conduct could be interpreted as an "interim ethic" still has a measure of validity. The spirit of the Sermon on the Mount and the critique of an oppressive legalism in religion were for all time; but the specifics of how to act in a long-continuing workaday world were hardly there. Similarly, the Pauline teaching on faith, the very heart of his message, could serve Paul himself as an adequate guide to conduct, but not those influenced by him, as his letters to the Corinthians clearly show. Recourse was had in the early days, for want of something better, to the Old Testament decalogue (itself the product of its time and place), which was reduced by Jesus to loving God and one's neighbor (Matthew 22:40). St. Paul more or less repudiated it in favor of a life determined by faith in Christ and aimed at producing the truly admirable qualities designated the "fruit of the spirit" (Galatians 5:22, 23), though the Ten Commandments are still regarded as providing a satisfactory pattern of behavior by perhaps the majority of Christians. The truth appears to be that the primitive Church had no consistently thought-out ethical system comparable, for example, to that of Buddhism—in which the initial vision produced simultaneously from within itself a carefully articulated method for living indefinitely a life of Buddhist virtue. Comparing for a moment the Judaic tradition with that of Hinduism, in the whole of biblical literature I can think of nothing to compare —for an ethical ideal expressed with succinctness, clarity, and precision—to Krishna's counsel to Arjuna at the opening of the sixteenth chapter of the Bhagavad-Gita.[3]

What we find, and what was to be expected in the period of religious syncretism which saw the birth of Christianity, is that the Church made its own the best available ethical teaching of the Hellenistic world. The ground was already prepared for this by what had been going on among the Jews outside Palestine as early as the second century B.C. Embodied in the Roman Catholic canon of the Old Testament is a book emanating from Alexandria, originally written not in Hebrew but in Greek, known as *The Wisdom of Solomon.* Wisdom, personified as feminine, is closely associated with God.

> She reaches mightily from one end
> of the earth to the other,
> and she orders all things well.
>
> I loved her and sought her from my youth,
> and I desired to take her for my bride,
> and I became enamoured of her beauty.
>
> And if any one loves righteousness,
> her labours are virtues;
> for she teaches self-control and prudence,
> justice and courage;
> nothing in life is more profitable for men than these.
>   (8: 1, 2, 7)

In the verse quoted last are enumerated what were later to be called the four cardinal virtues: prudence, justice, courage, and self-restraint. The source for these, it need hardly be said, is not the existential excitement of "salvation history," but the coolly rational *Republic* of Plato. We can detect hints of what could be interpreted as the broader Platonic outlook even in St. Paul, as he gets more and more involved with his converts in Greece. For instance, 2 Corinthi-

3. See pp. 136–137.

ans 4:18: "... we look not to the things that are seen but to the things that are unseen; for the things that are seen are transient, but the things that are unseen are eternal."

Again, the links between early Christianity and the Stoic philosophy are recognized by all scholars. St. Paul's speeches at Lystra (Acts 14:15ff.) and Athens (Acts 17:22ff.) are probably typical of Jewish and Christian preaching to the pagan world, owing much to Old Testament thought but with an admixture of those ideas that could be shared by the Stoics. Official Platonism was out of fashion when the Church was first establishing itself, but the Platonic contribution remained, to be revived and modified by the Neoplatonists, from whom St. Augustine was to learn so much. Later, in the thirteenth century, Plato's thought, qualified but not obliterated by Aristotle, was to enter the theological synthesis of St. Thomas. When the latter works out his conception of how human life should be lived, the underlying inspiration is neither the Old nor the New Testament, but Plato's four key virtues as elaborated by Aristotle in his *Nicomachean Ethics*, though here the same psychology is extended and applied by St. Thomas to the specifically Christian virtues of faith, hope, and love. Aquinas's debt to Stoicism is no less apparent: the concept of natural law reflecting an eternal law, from which the primary ethical axiom—"good must be done and evil avoided"—derives, is easily traceable in Stoic and pre-Stoic sources.

Today Platonism is not much regarded by academic philosophers. It is the custom to smile indulgently at Alfred Whitehead's dictum that Plato founded Western philosophy single-handed, that its subsequent history amounts to little more than a monumental series of footnotes on the original work. Whatever the merits of that particular controversy, it may be confidently asserted that the Christian Church wisely exchanged the apocalyptic urgency of its primitive tradition, where the end might come at any moment "like a thief in the night" (1 Thessalonians 5:2), for a calmer atmosphere and longer views. Consider, for example, the seventeenth-century thoughts of St. François de Sales on the subject of death: "The consolations of this life appear in a moment, and another moment carries them off ... Go, dear friend, go into that eternal existence, at the time fixed by the King of eternity; we shall go thither after you. ... You will not be separated or divided, for all will go away, and

all will stay." [4] Do we not almost catch an echo of the Platonic Socrates? "And now it is time to go, I to die, and you to live; but which
of us goes to a better thing is unknown to all but God."

Here we touch on a matter that seems to me crucial in current
ecumenical discussions. Did the Hellenization of primitive Christianity tend to pervert or to perfect the original message of Jesus? If the
process was a perversion, then the familiar appeal, "Back to Christ,"
should once more be listened to, and this line of thought has some vocal and extremely able expositors today. But if the work of elucidation arising, as we have seen, from the controversies with Gnosticism
was the providential means of saving the Christian Church from extinction, then certain further consequences seem to follow. Among
the first of these consequences, I suggest, is the necessity for the current dialogue between the Catholic and Protestant traditions within
Christianity to be conducted at a more radical level than at present
appears to be the case. Let good will and charity prevail, but they do
not require that basic differences be disregarded. The Protestant outlook, if I understand it aright, is much more biblical than the Catholic, though Catholic theologians nowadays seem unwilling to be out-
done in this respect by their Protestant confreres. The genius of
Catholicism, I submit, while repudiating such aberrations as those of
Marcion and his Gnostic associates, is more universalist and open-
ended than the Bible-based piety of much of the tradition emphasized by the reformers. Thus I find it hard to resist the force of the
following observation.

Protestant versions of the Christian faith tend to lean more heavily
than the Catholic on the family-cult theology of the Old Testament,
which when seriously considered as an appropriate base for a proper
world religion is constitutionally ineligible, since it is finally but the over-
interpreted parochial history and manufactured genealogy of a single
sub-race of a southwest Asian strain, late to appear and, though of great
and noble influence, by no means what its own version of the history
of the human race sets it up to be.[5]

Another consequence of the Hellenization of Christianity was
that it made contact with Greek mysticism. Insofar as mysticism is

4. *The Spiritual Maxims of St. Francis de Sales,* edited with an introduction
by C. F. Kelley (London: Longmans, Green & Co., 1954), pp. 75–77.
5. Campbell, *The Masks of God,* p. 366.

linked with hidden mysteries and ecstatic experiences, its benefits to religion are questionable. Here there may be some point in the clever comment that mysticism is a phenomenon that begins in mist, is centered on I, and ends in schism. But if the projection outward of the Deity and its activity is withdrawn so that they are recognized as operating within one's own spirit, then the experience can be as rewarding, I would think, as anything made available by the externals of religion. Could it be that institutional Christianity as it now exists is not enough, is still incomplete in terms of *inwardness?* This is the burden of much of the criticism of the Church today, particularly by the young: priests and ministers may be kindly and agreeable, but they don't have much to offer that enlightens the spirit or satisfies the mind. Western religion seeks to be rightly related to a transcendent God; it is outward-, or rather, upward-looking to the Creator and Redeemer. (And God's transcendence, be it noted, is not ontologically changed by the fact of the Incarnation, at least as this was interpreted by the Council of Chalcedon.) From the beginning the Church looked outward: outward to the coming of the Kingdom; then, progressively, to adjusting its relations with the Roman Empire; to meeting persecution; to organizing its official hierarchy; to conducting its ritual; to converting the heathen; to dealing with heresies; to political maneuvering as an established religion; and now, still outward, to interdenominational dialogue.

Has the moment perhaps come for the Church to look inward upon itself—not with reference to its structure and organization and how they are to be preserved, with which its officials have been much too preoccupied, but in terms of a radical self-scrutiny? Such a scrutiny would have to include an examination of a good many assumptions that underlie the Roman Church's understanding of itself as set forth in the Dogmatic Constitution on the Church (*Lumen Gentium*)[6] of Vatican II. More is called for than the private meditation of individuals, which has always gone on. What is being suggested is a sustained act of corporate self-examination in which institutional Christianity evaluates itself, helped by its ablest and most thoughtful representatives from each of its communions, with an eye to the ultimate demands of religion.

6. For some remarks on the character of this document, see "The Constitution on the Nature of the Church," *Ampleforth Journal,* Summer 1970, Vol. LXXV, part 2.

St. Augustine, commenting on the Fourth Gospel, gives some advice to the individual; it could fittingly be taken to heart by the members of the Church collectively. "Recognize in yourself something within, within yourself. Leave aside the externals of life (*relinque foris et vestem tuam et carnem tuam*); descend into yourself; go to that hidden apartment, your mind. If you are far from your own self, how can you draw near to God? Not in the body, but in the mind was man made in the image of God. In his own likeness let us seek God; in his own image recognize the Creator." [7] Catholicism takes account of the fact that God is immanent as well as transcendent, though Church authority has not always been very happy about the divine immanence. Things are really much simpler to handle if people would only be content to go to Mass instead of wanting to sit quietly in meditation. Augustine could not be prevented from saying that God is more inward to man than is man's own spirit; but professional churchmen get restive when the point is made as boldly as it is, for instance, by Eckhart: "The knower and the known are one. Simple people imagine that they should see God, as if He stood there and they here. This is not so. God and I, we are one in knowledge."

Eckhart and those who think like him do not by any means have all the answers—and some of their answers may be wrong—but the fact remains that you are more likely to find their works on the bookshelves of the thoughtful and religious-minded among the rising generation than the documents of Vatican II or the latest Papal encyclical. Christianity as it stands today, I submit, is no more than potentially "enough." "When the Spirit of truth comes, he will guide you into all the truth" (John 16:13). The Church, it seems, has still some distance to go before that promise is fully realized. This should be kept particularly in mind when we strive to impart what are admittedly "the unsearchable riches of Christ" (Ephesians 3:8) to the peoples of India and the Far East. Like Paul to his pagan audience, we are bringing the truth, but if we are sufficiently receptive, we shall also be finding it. "He who begins by loving Christianity better than truth," wrote the poet Coleridge, "will proceed by loving his own sect of church better than Christianity, and end by loving himself better than all." Might we not take that as a pointer to a wider ecumenism than most Western Christians, understandably enough, are yet ready to consider?

7. St. Augustine, *In Joannis Evangelium*, xxiii, 10.

6. Promptings from India

i. Preliminary

"It only goes to show, doesn't it, Father, how right Kipling was when he said, 'East is East and West is West, and never the twain shall meet'?" The occasion for this remark was a small gathering, composed chiefly of nuns, to which I had been invited to give an informal account of my travels shortly after returning to England from India and the Far East. The Sister, on a sightseeing visit to the monastery and school at Ampleforth, was assured and happy in her religious vocation. Clearly devoted to her chosen way of life, she was pleased and excited at the more positive results of the Second Vatican Council. What unkindly impulse was it that caused me to wonder if she could have recited some other lines, less unrelated to my recent experience, from the poet she had quoted?

> Ship me somewhere east of Suez, where the best is like the worst,
> Where there aren't no Ten Commandments, an' a man can raise
>   a thirst:
> For the temple-bells are callin', an' it's there that I would be—
> By the old Moulmein Pagoda, looking lazy at the sea.

Let me not be unfair: she was making a valid point. The barrier between the Eastern approach to religion and that of the West, insofar as it corresponds to what divides the non-Semitic and the Semitic traditions respectively, has hardly begun to be surmounted. Nor is there any widespread desire, as far as I can see, to change the situation. As recently as January, 1970, I watched Malcolm Muggeridge engaging in a half-hour discussion on British television with a Christian bishop in Madras. The theme was entitled "To Dwell Together in Unity." Roughly ninety-seven per cent of the Indian population are non-Christian, yet not by so much as a phrase was any other religion than Christianity touched on. The Christian way of life is difficult enough to practice, it has been put to me quite seriously, why complicate matters with the pagan religions? Perhaps this will always be the way of it for those to whom the emphasis in religion lies in attaining salvation, that is to say, finding security, rather than seeking out the truth. And when one subscribes to a form of Christian belief that already "has" the truth, or had until recently, then of course no such dilemma arises. Only those who see the situation rather differently, for whom truth is something we are possessed by rather than possess, who are attracted by what has been called the "wisdom of insecurity"—only they, it could be, among Western Christians, are prepared to explore beyond the boundaries of their inherited or chosen institutional framework. Though a willingness to embark on such adventures is much more evident in the United States than in Britain, where theological insularity still largely prevails.

I was already far east of Suez, having flown from Bangkok to New Delhi, when I first set foot in India late in the evening of November 20, 1967. Here I was met by my host and his wife. It was in their roomy, comfortable house, surrounded by the warmest hospitality, that my companion and I were to make our headquarters during the next four months. The rule of not mentioning personal friends by name in these pages is a token of a greater rather than less sense of indebtedness to them. The obtrusion of private faces into public places is almost as great an anomaly as the invasion of private places by public faces. My host, who proved to be also an invaluable mentor, was an American citizen and a Catholic, though unhappy with most of the goings-on in the Church since Vatican II. Hearing of my project, he had most kindly invited me to be his guest. We had never met, but having read one or two essays of mine, he shared my interest in trying to penetrate to the heart of religion. He had been profoundly influenced by the writings of Ananda Coomaraswamy and particularly René Guénon, from whom he had acquired a deep understanding of Sufism. He and his wife gave me their generous help in innumerable ways. Should they chance upon these remarks, may they be accepted as an acknowledgment of lasting appreciation.

Not that my investigations were confined to the area of Delhi. Between November and March, a period of over four months, during which the Indian weather is most favorable to Westerners, I made a two-week visit to Madras and the surrounding country.

Further south, in the beautiful island of Ceylon, I was able to renew acquaintance, begun three months earlier in Thailand, with the southern school of Buddhism. Returning to Hindu-dominated India, I made my way, with several pauses, notably in Bombay and Calcutta, to India's holiest city—Banaras (Varanasi), where I stayed long enough to absorb something of its indescribably impressive religious atmosphere and to learn much from the authorities at the Hindu University. Before leaving India I had the happy experience of fairly lengthy contacts with Tibetan Buddhism in the Himalayan foothills—at Dharmsala, Darjeeling, and, provided with the needed permit by the Indian government, in Sikkim, on the borders of Chinese-occupied Tibet. Of these encounters—with the aid of a personal journal, much expanded by my companion with his tape recorder—I was able to keep a fairly comprehensive record.

At this point the reader may welcome some indication of how I intend to proceed. In the first place, we are not concerned either with a travelogue or a study in comparative religion. While in India I took part in a number of rewarding conversations with recognized authorities on the Hindu-Buddhist tradition. These discussions generally took the form of questions raised by me and answered by my interlocutor. It is not my intention to reproduce these dialogues at length;[1] we shall confine our attention to carefully selected extracts. I shall edit the material as a whole and supply the necessary background, so that the meaning is clear to a reader with no specialized knowledge of Eastern religions. Professional scholarship in these areas I cannot aspire to. For this reason, and also to make life easier for the printer, there are no diacritical marks to the occasional Sanskrit or Pali word. Even in their transliteration there may be an occasional inconsistency or deviation from the accepted norms, but where such terms are used, I believe that their meaning has been rendered correctly, if not exhaustively. No more is claimed for the result than that, so far as it goes, it is accurate, up-to-date, and a reflection of my own interest and experience. Anything here reported verbatim was spoken in English, so that the hazards of translation

1. As proved to be practicable in the case of a parallel series in Japan, because of the continuity of the subject matter and a fairly consistent use of Buddhist terminology, making possible an adequate glossary for the benefit of the general reader. See my *Conversations: Christian and Buddhist* (New York: Harcourt, Brace & World, 1968; London: William Collins Sons & Co., 1969).

have been avoided. Those with whom I conversed were kind enough to allow me to make a tape recording of what was said. In the text I have cited them by initials, or designated their office; but in an appendix (see pp. 267–268) they are identified by name, together with an expression of my gratitude for their generosity in giving me the benefit of their wisdom and learning.

The phrase "Hindu-Buddhist tradition" in the preceding paragraph could well appear unsatisfactory to some readers. After all, there are substantial differences between Hinduism and Buddhism, and the Buddhist faith, though originating in India, now flourishes outside rather than inside that country. But I soon discovered, what I had long suspected, that the Hindu attitude to Gautama the Buddha, like that of the Jews to Jesus of Nazareth, is ambivalent. The Buddha is rejected outright by some as a "heretic" for his repudiation of the Vedas, Hinduism's inspired writings; he is revered by others as an avatar, a manifestation or incarnation of the Hindu god Vishnu, and regarded, as he was by Nehru, as the greatest of Indians. Buddhism, since it allegedly denies the Supreme Being, Brahman,[2] is repudiated by many of the devout as "atheistic," whereas by others, the Mahayana,[3] i.e., the more liberal form of Buddhism, is considered virtually indistinguishable from the Vedanta.[4] These factors will be kept in mind in what follows, but for our present purposes it would not be helpful to treat Hinduism and Buddhism as entirely separate and distinct religions.

And what, it may be asked after these preliminaries, are our present purposes? They do not include an outline survey of Hinduism and Buddhism, or even a general comparison between these religions and Christianity. A good deal of scholarly work of this kind is

2. For the sake of convenience I shall use "Brahman" as representing the Hindu Absolute, or Ultimate Reality, and "Brahma" as representing the Absolute as personified, the "Immense Being," often in association with the other two members of the Hindu Trinity, Vishnu and Shiva, while admitting that this procedure would not quite satisfy Sanskrit scholars. See Alain Daniélou, *Hindu Polytheism*, Bollingen Series LXXIII (New York: Pantheon Books, 1964), p. 23.

3. The "greater vehicle," or "greater way," the more highly elaborated and speculative form of Buddhism, originating in India, and taking root notably in Tibet, China, Korea, and Japan.

4. The end of the Vedas (i.e., the original source books of the religion of India), "end" meaning the highest and final point of the teaching given in the Vedas.

already available,[5] and I have no wish to compete with it. Instead I shall take in order a number of doctrinal points that interest me as a Catholic and examine whether any light on them can be derived from the Hindu-Buddhist tradition, having regard to my modest studies and recent direct contact with it *in situ*. We shall therefore be concerned chiefly with matters of record, their inspiration deriving mainly from India, but also to some extent from Thailand, where I spent a month. Comments, suggestions, tentative conclusions, should any occur, are in principle reserved for a later page. Such as are implied in the course of our discussions, like those that come more explicitly in their proper place, obviously carry no more weight than the voice of an individual inquirer. It must be confessed that when facing the richness and depth of the religion of India I lacked any missionary zeal. Having long since happily retired from office as a "dogmatic theologian," and being even more happily without ec-clesiastical responsibilities, I can now assume the most congenial of all roles, which of course is no role at all—that of a mere human be-ing, observing and trying to understand.

The sadly familiar squalor, disease, and heart-breaking poverty, the scientific and technological backwardness, the blind fatalism and superstition to be found in large areas of India, are unfortunately most of what is known of that ancient country to many Westerners. These deficiencies have been more than adequately described by visiting publicists from Europe and America—in the hope, no doubt, of focusing attention on the need to alleviate so much seemingly pointless suffering: even though this may just possibly be less baffling to those who endure than to those who observe it. What is not so well understood is a rich spirituality which, in its serene depths, of-ten leaves the parallel contribution of the West appearing meager and superficial. It is with this aspect of India's legacy to the world that we shall now be concerned.

ii. Hinduism and the Gods

The term "Hindu" originally meant a geographical area that lay around and was contiguous with what is now known as the river

5. As, for instance, the work of Professor R. C. Zaehner, whose writings are much commended in Catholic circles in India.

Indus (from which "Hindu" is derived) in northwest India. In the course of time the word came to denote the whole of that vast country. Accordingly, "Hindu" signifies all the various beliefs and practices to be found in the far-spreading and variegated stretch of land known as India. Thus when Gautama the Buddha appeared on the northeast Indian scene in what is now Nepal in the sixth century B.C. to challenge certain contemporary beliefs and establish his characteristic way of life, his criticism was directed not at Hinduism (the term did not then exist) in general but at the practices and underlying assumptions of the Brahmin priestly caste. By contrast with Buddhism, Christianity, and Islam, Hinduism has no historic founder and it does not acknowledge any governing hierarchy competent to declare what is and what is not orthodox doctrine. It has been well described as "a federation of different kinds of approach to the Reality that is behind life."

"God is one, but men call him by many names." This piece of theological wisdom from the Rig-Veda—as much inspired scripture for the Hindu as is anything in the Bible for a Christian—should be kept in mind by Westerners who tend to be put off by Hinduism's multiple deities. Shortly after my arrival, a learned Indian Jesuit, Father Sebastian Kappen, then resident at the Indian Social Institute in New Delhi, kindly gave me the opportunity to discuss with him aspects of the religious situation.

A.G.: Well, let us go to the Hindu situation, particularly your own field. . . .

JESUIT: Actually we have two traditions in Hinduism. We have the mystical tradition and the devotional tradition. According to the mystical tradition there is identity between atman and Brahman,[6] that is, identity between the ultimate ground of my empirical existence, ego, and the ultimate ground of the objective universe. These are the same. This is the mystical trend. Then we have the devotional trend, which is represented by the bhakti school. Bhakti actually means devotion. The bhakti school admits distinction between God and man, and God is conceived as a person, a person who knows and loves, who is gracious to the devotees, who confers his grace on them. So, in the bhakti school we have interper-

---

6. Atma or atman: the true self, in contrast with the false self of individuality, which each man commonly thinks himself to be. Brahman is the ultimate ground of the objective world.

sonal relationship between God and man. . . . But the dominant trend in Hinduism is perhaps the monistic mystical trend, dominant as a philosophy. But if you take the masses, the common people, bhakti has a greater hold than Advaita.[7] Advaita is too philosophical, too abstract.

A.G.: Advaita is nondualism, isn't that right?

JESUIT: Nondualism, yes. Now, coming to the point of Hindu atheism, we already have in the Rig-Veda a form of agnosticism. That is, the Rig-Vedic poets give expression to a certain doubt regarding the ultimate ground of being, of the universe. So we have texts where this doubt regarding the ultimate ground, the Absolute, is given expression, for example, in the "Creation Hymn" in the Rig-Veda. In the Rig-Veda we also find a sort of naturalism: a certain naturalism in the earliest Indian thought, a certain emphasis on things of this world and optimism concerning the realities of this world. That is the earliest phase, so to speak, of atheism in India, the Rig-Vedic atheism. It is more agnosticism than atheism. And this trend to some extent continues throughout India; a certain agnostic trend persists in Indian history.

A.G.: And that was taken up by the Buddha, wasn't it?

JESUIT: Yes, we find a reaffirmation of it in Buddhism. Even among contemporary Hindus, you will find many who are agnostics.

The passage from the "Creation Hymn" alluded to in this conversation is worth noting. After an account of the Creator's work, comparable in certain respects to the opening passage of the Book of Genesis, comes the anticlimax.

> But, after all, who knows, and who can say
>   whence it all came, and how creation happened?
> The gods themselves are later than creation,
>   so who knows truly whence it has arisen?
> Whence all creation had its origin,
>   he, whether he fashioned it or whether he did not,
> he, who surveys it all from highest heaven,
>   he knows—or maybe even he does not know.[8]

---

7. Advaita, a term that will often occur in these discussions, means literally "nondual," that to which there is no second. This is one of the themes of the Upanishads (i.e., certain books attached to and forming a portion of the Vedas) —that Ultimate Reality is "One without a second."

8. Rig-Veda, X, 129, 6–7, quoted from Mircea Eliade, *From Primitives to Zen* (New York: Harper & Row, 1967), p. 110.

Hindu scholars point out that there are in fact three strata of development to be found in the thought of the Vedic hymns not easy to keep separate: naturalistic polytheism, monotheism, and monism. The last of these strata, monism—a Western term, usually applied to any system of thought that seems to eliminate a duality between God and man—is of dominating importance in any approach to Indian religion. The topic came up in one way or another in almost all my discussions. By way of placing it in focus I shall present a statement of the underlying doctrine. What follows is an extract from the Chandogya Upanishad, which the thoughtful reader should find rewarding. Like a New Testament parable, it is full of meaning, yet with all the charm of an appealing story well told.

When Svetaketu was twelve years old, his father Uddalaka said to him, "Svetaketu, you must now go to school and study. None of our family, my child, is ignorant of Brahman."

Thereupon Svetaketu went to a teacher and studied for twelve years. After committing to memory all the Vedas, he returned home full of pride in his learning.

His father, noticing the young man's conceit, said to him: "Svetaketu, have you asked for that knowledge by which we hear the unhearable, by which we perceive the unperceivable, by which we know the unknowable?"

"What is this knowledge, sir?" asked Svetaketu.

"My child, as by knowing one lump of clay, all things made of clay are known, the difference being only in name and arising from speech, and the truth being that all are clay; as by knowing a nugget of gold, all things made of gold are known, the difference being only in name and arising from speech, and the truth being that all are gold—exactly so is that knowledge, knowing which we know all."

"But surely those venerable teachers of mine are ignorant of this knowledge; for if they had possessed it, they would have taught it to me. Do you therefore, sir, give me that knowledge."

"Be it so," said Uddalaka, and continued thus:

"In the beginning there was Existence, One only, without a second. Some say that in the beginning there was non-existence only, and that out of that the universe was born. But how could such a thing be? How could existence be born of non-existence? No, my son, in the beginning there was Existence alone—One only, without a second. He, the One, thought to himself: Let me be many, let me grow forth. Thus out of himself he projected the universe; and having projected out of himself the universe, he entered into every being. All that is has its self in him alone. Of all things he is the subtle essence. He is the truth. He is the Self. And that, Svetaketu, THAT ART THOU."

"Please, sir, tell me more about this Self."

"Be it so, my child:

"As the bees make honey by gathering juices from many flowering plants and trees, and as these juices reduced to one honey do not know from what flowers they severally come, similarly, my son, all creatures, when they are merged into that one Existence, whether in dreamless sleep or in death, know nothing of their past or present state, because of the ignorance enveloping them—know not that they are merged in him and that from him they came.

"Whatever these creatures are, whether a lion, or a tiger, or a boar, or a worm, or a gnat, or a mosquito, that they remain after they come back from dreamless sleep.

"All these have their self in him alone. He is the truth. He is the subtle essence of all. He is the Self. And that, Svetaketu, THAT ART THOU." [9]

"That art thou," or, in the original Sanskrit, *tat tvam asi;* in one way or another, this is what Hinduism is all about. Again and again the phrase was to come up in my subsequent discussions. "Please, sir, tell me more about this Self (atman)." The Chandogya Upanishad continues the refrain, but the nonduality between "thou" and "that," atman and Brahman, cannot be told; it has to be experienced, or, more accurately, *realized.* I pursued the matter further with my Jesuit friend, who, being an Indian, was thoroughly familiar with the Upanishadic teaching. Employing spatial metaphors, we were discussing the difference between the linear or horizontal view of the life process on the one hand and the vertical standpoint on the other.

JESUIT: As for Hinduism, I think nirvana, or samadhi, for instance, is more in the vertical line, whereas samsara is in the horizontal line, where we have various cycles coming one after another, the eternally repeating cyclic system, samsara.[10] And somehow you

9. I have taken this celebrated passage from the Chandogya Upanishad in the most readable translation I can find: *The Upanishads—Breath of the Eternal,* trans. Swami Prabhavananda and Frederick Manchester (New York: New American Library [a Mentor Book, by arrangement with the Vedanta Society of Southern California], 1957), pp. 68–69.

10. Nirvana is more properly a Buddhist rather than a Hindu term, and its meaning will become clearer in our discussions on Buddhism. Still, the term does occur in the Hindu scriptures, where it appears to mean either intimate union or actual identity with Brahman, which is its meaning here. Samadhi:

get out of this by meditation and mystical experience. Therefore, meditation is precisely the process through which you relinquish the samsaric cycle of existences and you vertically reach the Absolute. Now I accept the positive element contained there, namely the desire to reach union with the ground of all existence, objective and subjective; that is something good which I can accept. But what I cannot accept and understand is the idea that we have to withdraw from the world and look into ourselves in order to reach the Absolute.

A.G.: Well, I have yet to find out more about Hindu meditation, but the form I'm most familiar with, at least theoretically, is the Zen Buddhist, and I think a Zen Buddhist would say that the point of interest, to use your spatial analogy, would be the intersection between the horizontal and the vertical. And when you get to that, that is liberation, that is enlightenment. So that you live on two levels at the same time.

JESUIT: Yes, I would accept that point of view. I would even say that it is an authentically Christian approach to reality.

A.G.: Yes, I would think so. . . . But now let's take the *tat tvam asi* doctrine: Does this mean "that thou art the Ultimate, thou art the Supreme Being?" Or does it mean also "thou art . . ." I can say, "you are me and I am you." Does it mean that?

JESUIT: Well, *tat tvam asi* means "thou art that." *Tat* means "that"; *tvam* means "you"; *asi* means "art," or "are." "That" refers to the ultimate ground of the objective world. *Tvam* refers not so much to the empirical "you" as to the ultimate ground of the empirical ego, the empirical you. Therefore the ultimate ground of the empirical ego in me is the same as the ultimate ground of the universe.

A.G.: And the ultimate ground in all of us, therefore, is the same.

JESUIT: Exactly.

A.G.: And that's the brotherhood of man, isn't that right?

JESUIT: Yes, exactly. So that at the deepest level all men are the same. We are all absolute at that level, paramatma.[11] In fact, many Hindus are trying to build up a new ethic based on this idea.

---

contemplation of reality—"the state of evenmindedness, when the dualism caused by thought has ceased to ruffle the surface of the ocean of Truth." Samsara: the cycle of birth and death, the world of flux, change, and ceaseless becoming in which we habitually live.   11. The supreme self.

A.G.: I mean, couldn't one say when you see a defect or fault in somebody else or something that you dislike, isn't it true to say that thou art that, too?

JESUIT: Perhaps it wouldn't be quite correct because these observable phenomena, actions, defects, and so on would be part of his empirical ego, which is not identical with the Absolute. The deepest stratum in him, the root of his being, is identical with the Absolute. The identity will be at the deepest level. At that level we are all the same. Here, of course, identity is emphasized. But what value have these differences—between one man and another man? Advaita, nondualism, does not recognize any value. That is why the dignity of the person as unique, unrepeatable, is not fully recognized by the Advaitins (i.e., adherents of Advaita). What is recognized is the full dignity of the substratum, the deepest ground in each human being.

A.G.: That's very important, very significant. I don't know how true it is, though. I've been deeply impregnated with Buddhism, you see, and the Buddhist doctrine of the impermanence of the ego, or the unreality of the ego, that it's to some extent an illusion, is very interesting, to say the least.

JESUIT: Some Indologists say that Shankara[12] was influenced by Buddhism. And many call him a Buddhist himself: Shankara, the great Advaitin.

Let us turn now to my visit to Dr. Lokesh Chandra, at the International Academy of Indian Culture. An expert in both Hinduism and Tibetan Buddhism, he was kind enough to give me much of his time.

A.G.: I would be interested in hearing if there is perhaps a Hindu critique of Buddhism. What was the point of departure of the Buddha himself from Hinduism? Why is he regarded, as I understand he is, as a heretic, as out on his own perhaps? Could you say something about that, do you think?

DR. C.: According to Hinduism, the Vedas constitute the primary source of our religion. Though they constitute the prime source,

---

12. Shankara: one of the most celebrated Hindu theologians. He lived in India, possibly in the eighth century A.D., and commented on the Upanishads and the Bhagavad-Gita (i.e., "The Song of God," one of India's holiest books, being a portion of the epic, the Mahabharata).

they are followed by a vast ancillary literature. And we have
freedom to interpret them. In the Vedic tradition the meanings
are not rigidly fixed, and we are free to interpret the Vedic tradition, and not only the Vedas. So far as practicing Hinduism is
concerned, we can always effect changes in the interpretation,
and they may be effective mutations from the original wording.
In our way of life we believe that every individual has a right to
evolve his own personal salvation. In our terms we would say
that each individual can find his way through sadhana,[13] through
self-realization. And it is not necessary to have any mediator. But
then the Buddha comes, and he does not accept the authority of
the Vedic tradition. There is a point of departure. And the second
point of departure is that he does not accept God as such, a supreme power. He does not accept these two fundamentals. But
then Hinduism and Buddhism, as they were lived, are a different
matter. As they have been lived by us throughout the ages, Buddhism shares with us all the concepts of life, all the constants of
India's life. There have been variables and constants. The variants were the philosophical interpretations of the Ultimate Reality,
or man's relationship to that Ultimate Reality. And here we could
differ; even within the different schools of Hinduism you find vast
divergences. You see, you can accept a dualistic conception of the
Ultimate, you can have a monistic conception, and you can have
a qualified monistic system; so there are many ways to Hinduism.
As far as life is concerned, there, of course, Hindus and Buddhists
have the same language, the same soil where the religion took its
birth, the same ceremonies and rites. And the strange thing is
that when Buddhism moves away from India, it comes closer and
closer to Hindu practices. . . . And present-day Hinduism owes
so much to Buddhism that we really cannot differentiate between
them.

I asked if the *tat tvam asi,* the doctrine that Brahman and atman are
the same, played much part in the life of the ordinary Hindu. He
replied: "It may not play a direct part in the daily life of a Hindu,
but it forms so fundamental a part of our conceptual make-up that I
think we are separated from the other religions, the Semitic religions,

13. Sadhana: a practice that is a means or method to achieve self-realization.

which means Judaism and Christianity, by that very basis, that we accept the divinity of man. Christianity says that man is born in sin; he is conceived in sin. In our way of understanding the Ultimate, we think that man is part of the divine and that he himself is divine basically."

He explained that the opposition between the good and the bad does not exist for Hinduism. "In Christianity, and I think in European thought generally, you have only good and bad." The Hindu view is to be understood on the basis of the "three gunas." These are three qualities of nature: tamas, rajas, and sattwa. Tamas has been called "static inertia": it is a natural quality or power which paradoxically causes things to maintain themselves in existence and yet leads to their final disintegration. It is seen in man in the form of sluggishness of mind or body, emotional apathy, and mental prejudice. Rajas, by contrast, is "dynamic inertia," a natural force that causes things to continue their tendencies or habits of motion. In man it shows itself as restlessness of body, excitability of the emotions and the flow of old ideas. Sattwa means "orderliness," a natural quality that causes things to retain their mutual relations or reactions, once these are established. In man it shows itself in the quiet and orderly functioning of the breathing, circulation of the blood, digestion, and the natural functions generally. Dr. Chandra deplored the fact that Christianity lacked this key psychology of the gunas. "No rajas, while life itself is run on the basis of rajas. Life is not a matter of extreme good or extreme bad but something in between. Wickedness or evil is simply a part of human nature, just as goodness is. The question is, how are they proportioned?"

Before concluding, Dr. Chandra touched again on the *tat tvam asi* doctrine: "*Tat tvam asi* means that man is part of the divine. If you accept that man is conceived in sin, then many other things follow. But if we accept that man is fundamentally a part of the divine and has strayed from the divine path, he has been soiled by the maya[14] that envelops him, so he is just shipwrecked."

According to the Hindu view of life, mankind is not progressing

14. Maya is a fundamental Hindu and Buddhist conception. It is usually translated as "illusion," which is not to be confused with "delusion." Delusion would mean that we see what is not there; illusion implies that we see what is there but see it wrongly, either because we do not penetrate to the *reality* and see it as it is, or because we ascribe to what we see notions that do not belong to it.

to some end foreseen by God, the climax of history. Rather, we are caught up in a cyclic process, like the ebb and flow of the tide or the movement of the planets. No more than they does the human race have a final goal; there is no "one far-off divine event to which the whole creation moves." Eschatology, which occupied our attention earlier in these pages, makes little sense to the Hindu or Buddhist. For him the procession of birth, life, death, and rebirth is to be accepted as something given, like the weather or the annual sequence of the seasons. Release, if release is desired, from the wheel of birth and death, is achieved by the *experience* of either nondualistic identity, or dualistic union, with God (Brahman), according to Hinduism, or according to the Buddhist viewpoint, by the attainment of nirvana.

Presiding over this process—for the Hindu, if not for the Buddhist—are a multiplicity of gods and goddesses. For Hinduism, unlike Judaism and much of Christianity, has an affectionate respect for the feminine element in any dealings with the divine. The earliest seers had observed that within the Hindu pantheon no god was left without his appropriate consort. We may note in passing that something of the same sensitivity can be seen in Catholicism, where the veneration shown to the Virgin Mary is at least the equal of the honor given to all the goddesses of antiquity. According to the Brihadaranyaka Upanishad, which quotes as its authority the "Hymn to All the Gods," the number of the gods is "three hundred and three, and three thousand and three" (3,306). Then within the text there follows a reduction of the numerous gods to the unitary Brahman:

"Yes," said he, "but just how many gods are there, Yajnavalkya?"
"One . . ."
"Which is the one god?"
"Breath," [15] said he. "They call him *Brahman,* the Yon." [16]

As we have already noted (p. 106), Brahman is the impersonal Absolute, linked with Brahma, "Immense Being," as the Godhead, i.e., Divine Essence is with God.[17] Personified as originator of the world,

15. Compare Genesis 2:7, where "breath" signifies an emanation of the divine into man.
16. Quoted from *A Source Book in Indian Philosophy,* ed. Radhakrishnan and Moore, p. 86.
17. For an interesting parallel in distinguishing, if only verbally, between the Divine Essence and God, see St. Thomas Aquinas, *Summa Theologica,* 1, 39, 5.

Brahma is known as Ishvara and as such is the focus of much popular Hindu worship.

The Hindu Trinity—Brahma, Vishnu, and Shiva—is mythological, but like any myth that answers to the needs of mind and heart, it may operate more powerfully than realities of whose historical existence we are assured but which lack imaginative appeal.[18] Brahma can be considered as the all-inclusive divinity; he is the source, the seed, of all that is. He presides over the universe, preserving like Vishnu, destroying like Shiva. But in later, popular Hinduism Brahma is overshadowed, his powers as creator being taken over by Vishnu and Shiva. Brahma yields place to his female counterpart, Shakti. She represents divine power, or energy, and it is under this feminine form that the Creator remains the chief object of worship and ritual among large sections of Hindus. They even claim that the worship of Shakti—defined as energy resulting from the union of opposing principles, i.e., the complementary aspects of Vishnu and Shiva—"is the only religion suited to the conditions of the modern age." [19]

Vishnu is the *pervader* of the cosmos: the centripetal tendency that holds the universe together, the inner cohesion through which everything exists. Vishnu dwells in everything, owns everything, is the positive force that defeats the powers of destruction. All religion is of Vishnu. Thus Krishna, who dominates India's best-known poem, the Bhagavad-Gita, is an incarnation of Vishnu; so also is Rama, hero of the Ramayana, who was Gandhi's favorite among the gods. Hindus are ready to regard the Buddha, and even Jesus, as manifestations of Vishnu. Vishnu is the key to Hinduism's capacity to absorb every religion into itself, while not being itself absorbed by any.

According to Hindu thought, all that has a beginning of necessity has an end, all that comes into existence must cease to exist. Thus everything tends inevitably toward disintegration. The power of destruction is the nearest thing to nonexistence, to the "Qualityless Immensity" into which all must return. The universal power of destruction by which all existence ends and from which it rises again is known as Shiva, the lord of sleep, whence, according to the Tait-

18. I have had it put to me, not entirely in jest, that the Christian Church would be much less uninteresting to Hindus and Mahayana Buddhists if it could allow its abstruse masculine Trinity to fall into the background and bring forward a much more appealing one—Father, Mother, and Child.

19. Daniélou, *Hindu Polytheism*, p. 234.

tiriya Upanishad, "all these elements came forth, by which once born they exist, into which they enter and dissolve." Shiva is the embodiment of tamas, the centrifugal inertia, the tendency toward eventual dispersion, disintegration, and annihilation. In the world process of coming to be and passing away Shiva is both creative and destructive. He is often depicted as dancing—but the dance may show forth either the sheer joy of creation or the mad frenzy of destruction. He creates and he destroys. Sometimes he obscures by his power of illusion (maya); sometimes he offers grace to the suffering world. The phallic emblem, the linga, symbol of the creative power of Shiva, is the most widely venerated cult object in Shiva worship. "When the Hindus worship the linga, they do not deify a physical feature; they merely recognize the divine, eternal form manifest in the microcosm. It is the human phallus, which is a divine emblem of the eternal causal form, the all-pervading *linga*." [20] How many worlds away does this bring us from the Judaeo-Christian tradition? Though perhaps we are not quite so far: Alain Daniélou, in the work just cited (p. 24), develops the thought that there may be links between the Hindu Trinity and its later Christian counterpart. "In the notion of 'God the Father' the person of the procreator has been substituted for the symbol of procreation."

Sleep, dream, and awareness—so I learned in the course of my travels through India—are the three conditions corresponding to the deities just considered. Thus Shiva is experienced in the emptiness of dreamless sleep, Vishnu in the vision of a dream, and Brahma in the state of awareness. I was also reminded that even children and uneducated villagers somehow realize that the many gods and goddesses are but aspects and manifestations of the one Absolute. Each individual is free to choose the god or goddess that appeals to him most. Gandhi, for example, was heard to cry "O Rama!" at the moment he was shot. A guru will often assign a suitable deity to those who are in doubt.

In practice, while one particular god or goddess: Shiva or Kali, Rama or Krishna, or any other deity, is singled out for special worship according to the caste, tribe, family or private likes and dislikes of the individual worshipper, all the other gods are also given some respect and attention; special favours are asked from this or that god or goddess, special prac-

20. *Ibid.*, p. 227.

tices are observed in honour of various devatas (i.e., divine beings), according to the rites to be performed or the feasts of the calendar. Where religion is deep and sincere, monotheism asserts itself in spite of this baffling multiplicity; where superstition prevails, an *endless fragmentation of the Divine is the sad result of this mythology* [italics in original].[21]

At the deepest level there is a vital tendency in Hinduism to leave aside all myths and anthropomorphic conceptions in order to concentrate on the formless and nameless spirit. We find this expressed in the Mundaka Upanishad.

> Not by sight is It grasped, not even by speech,
> Not by any other sense-organ, austerity, or work.
> By the peace of knowledge, one's nature purified—
> In that way, however, by meditating, one does behold Him
> who is without parts. (III, i, 8)

This message came home to me again and again during my discussions in India. The Advaita Vedanta—though as remote from popular Hinduism as is the *Summa Theologica* from everyday Catholicism—appealed to me as reaching to the heart of the matter. It seemed to provide grounds for the Hindu's claim, made without any sense of proprietorship, that his is "eternal religion," sanatana dharma. So the point had been made by my learned Hindu friend in New Delhi.

DR. C.: All that the Europeans have done during the last hundred years of their studies is to distort our cultural fabric and to split it. They have understood the external details, the point at which a particular thing happened, how a particular thing has been expressed, but not its living aspect. There is a current of life flowing in it; it is not only a thought which belongs to the second century B.C. or five hundred A.D. It is not restricted in time. We call it the sanatana dharma or the "Eternal Religion." So to understand India's thought you have to give up Christian conceptions. And the moment you try to fit them in you are nowhere, because there are basic differences. We do not necessarily accept unitary concepts even for a single Scripture or teacher. It is an intellectual dictatorship to insist on only one book and teacher through whom you can approach God.

21. Jesuit scholars, *Religious Hinduism*, pp. 83–84.

A similar approach was indicated in an informative discussion with a no less well-qualified Hindu authority in Banaras (Varanasi), Dr. T. R. V. Murti, author of the magisterial volume *The Central Philosophy of Buddhism*. Our talk ranged from the Vedanta, over revelation, grace, sacraments, and some comparisons between Hinduism and Catholicism.

A.G.: I was particularly interested in your opening remark at your lecture at the university the other day, in which you said, if I recollect aright, that truth was something you couldn't, as it were, get at directly, that it was a process of removing the false.

DR. T.M.: Yes.

A.G.: Is that your own position? Or is it the traditional Hindu view of the situation?

DR. T.M.: It is the Vedantic position.

A.G.: I understand the Vedas are considered to be a revelation. Is that correct?

DR. T.M.: Yes.

A.G.: And so would that be a removing . . . would that process as applied to the Vedas be a removing of false conceptions? I'm particularly interested because I think it's the heart of the matter, and I want to try to get it across to the Christian West when I go back. Would our understanding of Divine Revelation, so called, be a progressive removing of false notions, would you say?

DR. T.M.: Look, the world itself is a false appearance. And what the Veda says is: "Behind the world is Brahman." So in that sense the Veda is a revelation in the sense that it removes the veil of appearance and asks you to see through, see beyond the appearance, and see Brahman behind the things that form the world. And *tat tvam asi*, "that thou art," is the last word of the Vedas, as of the Vedanta. The Vedanta means the end of the Vedas. The Vedanta means primarily the Upanishads, as being the end portion or quintessence of the Vedas. And it tells you that the world is an appearance and you are Brahman. And in spite of the fact that you and God are so disparate, at heart you and Ishvara, God, are really Brahman.

A.G.: Well, then, all the Hindu gods, all the avatars, to some extent conceal the truth.

DR. T.M.: Yes, they conceal the truth. They conceal the truth; they also reveal it in fact. They progressively reveal also.

A.G.: That is the Christian way of seeing it, too, as I understand it, that there's a progressive revelation, so far as we are concerned, and that everything that reveals at the same time conceals.

DR. T.M.: Yes.

A.G.: When we come to religions as they actually exist, however, isn't it true that you always have to have some institutional element there? And institutions are to some extent falsifications, but they're necessary. Harnack made the point in his *History of Dogma* with regard to Christianity. He said that the formulations of the Church, the early creeds and so on, falsify the doctrine of Christ, but they preserved it. Without those formulations the doctrine would have been lost.

DR. T.M.: I agree with you absolutely.

A.G.: If the doctrine hadn't been formulated, we wouldn't have had it. And that's the antinomy, that's the difficulty, isn't it?

DR. T.M.: That's the difficulty of all existence itself. In a way it reveals; it also falsifies. And to the extent it falsifies, you have to reject, you have to see through it. And to the extent it throws light you have to welcome it.

A.G.: That's right. And so we have to work out, don't you think, some kind of *levels* of religious thought? I don't know if that has been done.

DR. T.M.: That is Hinduism, actually. People are on different levels. And Hinduism does not apply or appeal to all persons in an equal manner. To the man in the street you would prescribe a certain philosophy, and then as the capacity to understand rose, higher and higher. The Vedanta is actually meant for the highest level.

A.G.: There's the active approach and the bhakti (devotional) approach, and then this Advaitist (nondual), I suppose.

DR. T.M.: The bhakti approach is also available in the Vedanta. In fact it is only through the grace of God that you can reach the Advaita itself. Vedanta is misunderstood. It is taken as an atheistic creed. Actually, it is not. In fact, Vedanta means the revelation given us through the Veda. Veda is the spoken word of God, and without his grace you can't know that there is Brahman . . . Not only can't you receive the ultimate truth, but in your treading of the path, I mean achieving salvation itself, you have to depend upon God. You have to have bhakti toward him, devotion to him, so that your mind can be purified and you are able to receive that knowledge. But it is by knowledge alone that you can ultimately win salvation or achieve Brahman.

A.G.: What would a Hindu mean by, or how would he define, God's grace?

DR. T.M.: Grace is not something deserved.

A.G.: What is it? Is it a quality? Is it an activity?

DR. T.M.: It's an activity. It's an activity which would express itself in many ways. It may even be that it supplies some favors to you. But the real activity, real grace, is that the god comes to you in some form or other, in the form of a guru, for instance, and takes hold of you actually and converts you and transmutes you. Therefore, we even say that the god comes to us in the form of a guru, and the guru is even in a sense greater than the god. Because the god is some remote being, whereas the guru is somebody who actually comes into your life and takes hold of you, sometimes even in spite of yourself, and then brings about a transmutation in your whole life.

A.G.: Of course, grace is fundamental to Christianity, too. But I wonder if you would think that the doctrine of grace is vulnerable to criticism, in as much as it tends to substitute the sacraments for real insight or the modifying of character for the better.

DR. T.M.: Sacraments also have a place.

A.G.: Yes, indeed, they do have their place, as long as they're seen as symbols and signs of the divine and not as . . .

DR. T.M.: They are that by which you can appropriate yourself to the divine. You can assimilate yourself to the divine only through sacraments.

A.G.: Yes. What would be the Hindu sacraments? For instance, we saw the people bathing themselves in the Ganges the other morning.

DR. T.M.: Yes, that's a sacrament. And their throwing flowers on the image of the god is a sacrament, and their performance of certain ceremonies on occasions with mantra (i.e., a sacred sound) and oblations is a sacrament. In fact, our whole life is a sacrament in the sense that all our rites and rituals are sacraments. They remind us of the divine, and through this act of appropriation the sacrament gives you assimilation, that sense of nearness to God, intimacy with God.

A.G.: But does anything actually ontologically happen to you when, say, you bathe yourself in the Ganges? Does anything happen to you other than water flowing over you?

DR. T.M.: No, that is the external way. But actually it is the belief, the intention, that matters.

A.G.: You see, a Christian would say that when he is baptized something ontologically happens.

DR. T.M.: It also happens here.

A.G.: In other words, a new quality . . .

DR. T.M.: New life has entered, a new outlook. His whole life is changed in a way.

A.G.: Yes, but that change, that second birth, to be really effective, doesn't it have to take place existentially and not just symbolically?

DR. T.M.: It is through symbol that it is done, but the effect is existential. The symbol does it, but in an existential way. That is, you will actually see the effect in your life itself.

A.G.: To become a fully enlightened or fully realized person, do you think sacraments and the bhakti approach are necessary?

DR. T.M.: I think in the initial stages sacraments are necessary. I was struck by the Catholic performance of the sacraments.

A.G.: Oh, yes. They play a very important part in Catholic life.

DR. T.M.: And I believe it is all derived from the Hindu. You see, you could trace it from Hinduism, though the links may be missing. But we could say that it was from the East that you got it. Jesus himself does not say anything about sacraments, does he? [22]

22. "To be remarked further is the astonishing point-for-point correspondence of the forms and paraphernalia of the rites performed in temple and cathedral. As Sir John Woodroffe has pointed out in his fundamental work, *The Principles of the Tantra*, the following statement from the Roman Catholic Council of Trent (1545–1563) can be readily annotated in Sanskrit to indicate the Indian parallels, viz.: 'The Catholic Church, rich with the experience of the ages and clothed with their splendor, has introduced mystic benediction (*mantra*), incense (*dhupa*), water (*acamana, padya*, etc.), lights (*dipa*), bells (*ghanta*), flowers (*puspa*), vestments and all the magnificence of its ceremonies in order to excite the spirit of religion to the contemplation of the profound mysteries which they reveal. As are its faithful, the Church is composed of both body (*deha*) and soul (*atman*). It therefore renders to the Lord (*ishvara*) a double worship, exterior (*vahya-puja*) and interior (*manasa-puja*), the latter being the prayer (*vadana*) of the faithful, the breviary of its priest, and the voice of Him ever interceding in our favor, and the former the outward motions of the liturgy.' The use of the rosary, too, might be mentioned, which entered Europe in the course of the late Middle Ages. Further, both the form and the sense of the main service in both religious precincts is the same. A priest con-

A.G.: Well, baptism and the Eucharist are there in the New Testament. It is not easy to say just what was the part played by Jesus himself and how much was legitimate development.

DR. T.M.: What about the Mass?

A.G.: That certainly comes from the Last Supper.

DR. T.M.: That has got a powerful influence upon the mind.

A.G.: Oh, very much so. And it's the central act of Catholic worship. But my observation is, over a good many years now, that Catholicism and Christianity in general need to be invigorated by something of the Hindu-Buddhist meditation tradition, and the importance of knowledge and insight. Christianity tends to substitute good intentions and good will for knowledge and insight.

DR. T.M.: Yes, you are right there.

iii. Creation

"What does orthodox Hinduism have to say about Creation?" I asked a learned authority at a peace foundation in honor of Mahatma Gandhi. I received a succinct reply without a moment's hesitation: "Creation has neither beginning nor end. Like the life of a tree creation is a cycle. Creation means '*the Unmanifest becomes Manifest.*' It is continuously going on; it has no beginning. Here is how the cycle is represented: Brahma stands for creation; Vishnu stands for preservation; Shiva stands for destruction. Nara Raja (i.e., king of men) is the Dancing Shiva. It is the dance of destroying what has been created. Out of that chaos a new harmony emerges."

Our basic religious attitude is determined by the manner in which we conceive our relationship to the ultimate reality we call God. The three religions with which we are here chiefly concerned—Hinduism, Buddhism, and Christianity—are agreed that man as a conscious being is completely subordinate to a transcendent "Supreme"; but the nature of that subordination, as of the Supreme it-

---

ducts the rite, opening with preliminary prayers and, on high occasions, intoned chants. An offering—bread and wine in the West; in India, milk or butter, fruits, an animal or a human being—is consecrated, symbolically or actually immolated, and in part consumed in communion; after which, prayers of thanksgiving are offered and the company is dismissed" (Campbell, *The Masks of God*, pp. 168–169).

self, is conceived differently. Christianity speaks of "creation," Hinduism of "manifestation," Buddhism of "dependent origination"; and these three concepts are by no means one. Not only do they represent different cosmic processes by which man and his world are held to have come into being; they produce, according to my limited observation, a distinctive spirituality in those who adhere respectively to one or other of these beliefs.

Orthodox Christianity's position on the matter, it seems to me, might well at some future time be subject to review. Israel, like India, had its myths about how the world originated. God was depicted as the master workman, forming the earth and everything on it out of pre-existent matter. Earlier myths lie behind the creation stories in Genesis 1 and 2. According to Genesis 2:7, God "formed" man out of the dust. The later creation story in Genesis 1 is based on the notion that God creates the world out of primeval matter, "chaos," by separating the mingled elements and rearranging them to suit his purpose. But there is little attempt to describe the process of creation for its own sake. God speaks the word, and it is done. "And God said, 'Let there be light'; and there was light" . . . "And God said, 'Let the earth put forth vegetation. . . .' And it was so." . . . "And God said, 'Let there be lights in the firmament of the heavens. . . .' And it was so." (Genesis 1:3, 11, 14–15). The myth has faded into the background before the conception of God as the omnipotent Ruler, who calls into existence that which is by a mere fiat.

It followed that Israel never developed a mythology along the lines of the Greek *arché*. The world is not conceived after the analogy of a craftman's product; the concept is that of sheer power operating in a vacuum. The problem of the relation between form and matter, which so much exercised the Greek mind, as it was later to exercise the mind of Thomas Aquinas, is conspicuously absent from the Old Testament. There is no conception of the cosmos as harmonious structure, or of "nature" or the "law of nature."

The world is never objectified as a natural order whose eternal laws are open to intellectual apprehension. There is no natural science or physics. The Greek saw the divine power in the cosmic law whose existence he had apprehended by reason. In this way he brought the deity into relation with the universe. The Bible on the other hand regards God as transcending the world. He "has established his throne in the heavens, and his kingdom rules over all" (Ps. 103: 19). The transcendence of God receives its classical expression in the doctrine of *creatio ex nihilo* (creation out of nothing), a notion utterly inconceivable to the Greek mind, though a logical development from the premises of Biblical thought (Jubil. 12:4; 2 Macc. 7:28, etc.)." [23]

The idea of "creation out of nothing," it was brought home to me, is equally unacceptable to the Hindu mind. In New Delhi my kind informant Dr. Chandra was telling me of his recent visit to the United States and of his discussions with young people, including "hippies."

DR. C.: I have talked with some of your younger people. They are not able to express what their problem is, but so far as I can see from a distance and from my short experience of about a fortnight in the U.S.A., you have an undercurrent which is democratic, and which is basically linked to the classical tradition, to the Hellenic tradition, with its polytheism and with its fundamental urges for freedom of inquiry, whether it is an inquiry into the natural sciences or a quest for spiritual realization.

A.G.: Seeing that you have touched on that, do you know what links there are, do you believe there are links between the Hellenic tradition and the Indian?

DR. C.: Oh, yes.

A.G.: Can you refer to any work on that?

DR. C.: Well, there is no good work. You see a multiplicity of gods in the Indian tradition and the classic Hellenic tradition; this is a very visible expression of those traditions. Then the freedom to change the dogma—if there ever was any dogma in the Indian and Hellenic traditions. I don't think there was at any time a dogma in the Aryan tradition. The dogma—fixation, centralization—is a condition peculiar to the Semitic peoples.

A.G.: I think that the Semitic-Christian idea of history as some kind of progress, that we can make the situation better, has point. The feeling that there is going to be some climax to it all—do you think that that makes any sense?

DR. C.: What you are speaking of is not a system of progress; it is simply a system of finality. It is a system which wants to congeal the conditions of a particular time into eternity.

23. Rudolf Bultmann, *Primitive Christianity in Its Contemporary Setting* (London and New York: Thames and Hudson, 1956), p. 17.

Again, it was at Banaras that I was able to obtain a more precise statement concerning man's relation to God, as it is understood in Hinduism. I was given the opportunity to talk to Dr. R. S. Misra, head of the Department of Indian Philosophy and Religion at the Hindu University.

A.G.: Do all Hindu thinkers agree, or would they disagree, that enlightenment consists in realizing the identity between atman and Brahman?

DR. M.: That is true from the Advaita point of view.

A.G.: But only from that point of view?

DR. M.: Yes. But so far as the other schools of Vedanta are concerned, to them enlightenment means the attainment of union with Brahman or Ishvara by the individual soul.

A.G.: That is the same as the Christian, pretty well—a kind of Beatific Vision.

DR. M.: Very much the same, though according to me there's some difference.

A.G.: What would be the difference?

DR. M.: The main difference, according to me, is that in Christianity the soul is something created. It is not beginningless and eternal. The soul is created, and after creation it can enjoy immortality. But it is something which was not there, and it came into existence by an act of God. In Hinduism the soul is never created. This is a basic difference. And then, in Christianity ultimately, in the state of salvation the individual enjoys eternal communion with God, fellowship with God; he finds himself in the eternal presence of God, but I don't think that in Christianity the soul enjoys an integral union with God. I call it communion in order to distinguish it from union. By union I mean that the soul realizes itself as an integral part of God, in the state of liberation.

A.G.: Well, according to your view, is the soul the same as God or not?

DR. M.: I will say that in one respect or according to one approach, it is the same; according to another approach, it is a portion of God. But it is never different from God. According to Christianity, the soul, being created, is certainly different from God, the Creator and Lord. This difference does not exist in Hinduism: the soul is a portion of God; it is not something created. And this also has significance for salvation.

A.G.: Well, according to the Christian view, or according to Thomas Aquinas's view, for instance, he would say that to ascribe portions or parts to God is to posit imperfection in God. Wouldn't that be Shankara's view? Shankara and Aquinas, it seems to me, are very much kindred spirits.

DR. M.: Yes. This criticism has been leveled also by the Advaitins against the other schools of Vedanta, who call the soul a portion of God. But then they explain it in other ways: they say that this relationship should not be looked at from the point of view of physical objects. God can't be divided into parts. So it may be taken as just an analogy. It only shows that the soul is not different from God, it is within God, it is part and parcel of God; the soul is something eternal which is not different from God, it is an individual center of the Divine.

A.G.: You mentioned creation: would what you say about the noncreation of the soul apply also to the noncreation of the phenomenal world? Is all this world noncreated?

DR. M.: The thing is that Hinduism does not believe in any original creation. You have this doctrine of original creation in Semitic religions. But Hinduism does not believe in any such doctrine. According to it, the world process is beginningless and, as you know, the Hindu view is the cyclic view. There is creation; there is dissolution. This process of creation—dissolution—creation—dissolution is going on. So there is no original or first creation; and it is better to call it manifestation rather than creation. The world actually is not created, it is manifested out of prakriti, the power of Ishvara,[24] and it goes back to its original source. The Hindu view does not believe in any such development as the "fulfillment of history," along the lines of Judaism and Christianity. There the whole creation is heading ultimately toward an end. One thing you will find: the Hindu view conceives a destiny for the soul and not for the world. And this is a basic difference between the Hindu view and the Christian view—or the Semitic view, we may say. Zoroastrianism also comes very close to the Semitic religions in conceiving a destiny for history or for the world process. But according to Hinduism, it is the souls which attain destiny, not the world itself.

24. Prakriti, literally, "forth-made," from *pra* (forth) and *kriti* (something made): the material or manifest side of the universe, the substratum of objective reality.

The Hindu viewpoint becomes slightly more qualified and perhaps a shade nearer to Catholicism's current orthodoxy at the hands of Professor Murti, whom we have already met in Banaras. Here is the conclusion of my companion-secretary's transcript.

A.G.: I'd just like a few words on the Hindu doctrine of creation. You see, the Christian view is that God was in his eternity and suddenly he said that he would make the world—"Let there be light." And immediately there was light. Now how would you say the Hindu view differs from that? The Buddhist doctrine is that of "dependent origination"—everything depending on everything else, as I understand it. According to the Hindu view, can it be said at all that God creates the world or the cosmos out of nothing?

DR. T.M.: We don't say creation out of nothing; it's out of himself. The substance of the world is of the same nature as the substance of God. But with a difference: there is a transcendent aspect of God which is not exhausted in this world. That is why we say that it is an "appearance" of Brahman. Just as a snake—in the example of perceiving the "rope snake"—is not anything apart from the rope; yet you can't say that the rope has transformed itself into the snake.[25] There is a one-sided dependence, as it were. The world depends on God because it's made of the same stuff. But God does not depend on the world. So in that sense your Biblical saying that God created the world out of nothing is substantiated. He does not coin himself, does not transform himself into the world.

A.G.: Well, that is the same as the Christian view, or Aquinas's view, that the world is related to God but God is not related to the world.[26]

25. The allusion here is to a passage from Shankara's treatise *On the Nature of Brahman*, 1, 4, 6: "A man may, in the dark, mistake a piece of rope lying on the ground for a snake and run away from it, frightened and trembling; thereon another man may tell him, 'Do not be afraid, it is only a rope, not a snake'; and he may then dismiss the fear caused by the imagined snake, and stop running. But all the while the presence and subsequent absence of his erroneous notion, as to the rope being a snake, make no difference whatever in the rope itself. Exactly analogous is the case of the individual soul (*atma*) which in reality is one with the highest soul (*paramatma* = Brahman), although ignorance (*avidya*) makes it appear different." Quoted from Eliade, *From Primitives to Zen*, p. 615.

26. For St. Thomas Aquinas's point, that the relation between God and

DR. T.M.: Yes. One-sided.

A.G.: Yes. That's correct.

DR. T.M.: That is, identical—but identical understood not of oneness, the world being dependent on God but God not being dependent on the world. Because if God depended on the world, like the Hegelian Absolute, there could not have been any God before creation. It could not have been said, "Let there be a world," because then God should have existed before the world. So was he God before the world came into existence?

A.G.: But does God know what goes on in the world?

DR. T.M.: Yes.

A.G.: But then, I thought you said earlier that he didn't.

DR. T.M.: Brahman and God are different; also identical.

A.G.: Oh, you're talking about God under the aspect of Ishvara?

DR. T.M.: Yes, yes.

A.G.(laughing): Let's stop there.

More than once in the course of the preceding discussions I have alluded to the Buddhist doctrine of "dependent origination" (pratityasamutpada). The impression may have been conveyed that it supplies a cosmological theory about the origin of the world, comparable to, or contrasting with, the Hindu or the Christian. This would be a mistake. The Buddha did not encourage the holding of "views," and he was reluctant to discuss the metaphysical questions we have been examining, because he believed that salvation lay in experiencing, rather than talking about, enlightenment. He probably shared up to a point the Hindu understanding of the relation of "the Manifest to the Unmanifest." But his followers could hardly fail to draw certain deductions from Gautama's teaching, which derived from the unique experience whereby he became the Buddha, the all-enlightened one.

Central to the Buddhist psychology is the affirmation that what we regard as our personal "self" is a transitory composite of perception, feeling, volitions or emotional reactions, consciousness, and form or body. These are known as the five skandhas (i.e., heaps, aggregates), which together make up the personality as it exists in

creation is unilateral, being real only on the side of creation, see *Summa Theologica*, 1, 45, 3, 1.

the sphere of samsara, that is, the everyday world. The skandhas are interrelated and are the result of karma, i.e., causal activity deriving from all the influences, past and present, that bear upon us. These aggregates are collectively and individually in a state of flux; they are quintessentially impermanent. Illusion lies in supposing that they have a permanent substratum, an abiding, unchanging *self*.

Now it is through the skandhas that our experience of the world is mediated. Through them is shown the "chain of causation," which indicates the middle way between the opposing illusions, on the one hand that "things have being," and on the other that "things have no being." The classical text for the doctrine of dependent origination is the Samyutta-nikaya, 22, 90.[27] The two paragraphs that follow paraphrase, but only slightly.

The fact that we are involved in karma—the chain of past actions causing our present state—is because we are not fully enlightened and are ignorant of our true situation. Karma, however, entails a limited degree of awareness or consciousness. This awareness causes us to interpret what we experience in terms of name and form. These last give rise to the various sense organs, which in turn bring us into contact with their objects and so cause sensation. From sensation emerges desire and hence attachment or craving. Attachment is what gives reality to existence. On existence, rooted in attachment, depends birth. And on birth depend old age and death, sorrow, lamentation, misery, grief, and despair. In this way the sum and substance of unhappiness arise.

But on the complete fading out and cessation of ignorance karma ceases. When karma ceases, so does our limited awareness, and with its cessation name and form disappear. When these have gone, so also go the various sense organs. Hence there is no contact with their objects and thus no sensation. With the absence of sensation desire also ceases. If there is no desire, then gone is the reality of existence and with it the need for birth. When birth is no longer, then old age and death, sorrow, lamentation, misery, grief and despair cease. In this way all the causes of unhappiness have ceased.

This, in brief outline, is a statement of the Buddhist doctrine of dependent origination. Many of its assumptions are no doubt highly questionable, perhaps even unintelligible, to a Western mind. They

27. In *A Source Book in Indian Philosophy*, ed. Radhakrishnan and Moore, pp. 278–79.

are by no means all accepted by the Hinduism we have been discussing. The account just given of the chain of causation, it will be noted, does not bear upon a succession of realities existing in a world outside the mind but upon an order of *experience*. Thus, for example, it is not existence that causes attachment, but attachment that gives rise to an illusory conception of existence. Accordingly, it may be said that Buddhism has no doctrine of creation (or "manifestation"), only of how what these terms apply to is experienced. The position may become clearer when we consider Buddhism more explicitly in Sections (v) to (vii) of the present chapter. Meanwhile, those best qualified to inform us insist that Buddhism is not, despite appearances to the contrary, a philosophy of annihilation or even negation. It points to a path, the treading of which calls for highly positive generosity, that leads to a goal of unalloyed bliss.

iv. Morality

It would hardly be possible to outline the pattern of morality characteristic of India without entering into the varieties of conduct that Hindus consider appropriate to the several stages of life, and even the caste system, legally abolished, but in practice still a force to be reckoned with. However, I did have an opportunity to form some impressions of the differences and similarities between the Indian and Christian conceptions of sin and its remedy, the goal of the religious quest, and the opportunities available to Indians for learning about their religion. Let us take the last item first.

One day, late in February, 1968, I traveled by car ninety miles or so from Banaras to Buddh Gaya—the historic site of Gautama's Enlightenment, whereby he became the Buddha, the all-enlightened one. A pilgrimage from Ceylon, numbering several hundred people, was there, reverencing the bodhi tree, under which the Buddha had sat in deep meditation until his goal was achieved. The pilgrims then walked in procession to the central shrine. I stood aside as they passed up the middle aisle, singing hymns and carrying garlands of marigolds to be placed at the foot of the immense Buddha image. As they slowly walked by, a number of the pilgrims held out their garlands in an appealing gesture to the bystanders, including me, that we might touch them lightly and so have a part in their ceremony.

It was on the return journey to Banaras that a pleasing incident occurred. We stopped at a small Indian town, broken-down and poverty-stricken, like so many Indian villages. An old man, his face kindly and humorous, was sitting in the open air near the door of his house with a huge volume open on his knees. He invited me to drink tea with him. We could not talk much, but I asked him, with the help of our driver, what he was reading. He said it was the Rama-yana. This famous epic, which plays a most significant part in Indian religious life, came into a discussion the next day with Professor Misra at the Hindu University of Banaras.

A.G.: Are Hindu children taught at school that Vishnu and Shiva, Krishna and Rama, and the gods generally are, as it were, mani-festations of Brahman? Are they invited to go beyond. . . ?

DR. M.: In our schools this religious education is not usually given. You know, ours is a secular state, and here religious education is not given in educational institutions. Even from the British days, this has been the practice here—no religious education.

A.G.: Where do they get their instruction? At home?

DR. M.: Yes. And these days even homes are not generally able to impart that kind of education, because many parents don't know much about the Scriptures.

A.G.: Wouldn't that seem to imply that Hinduism is dying out?

DR. M.: I wouldn't say that, because in Hinduism, you know, there are, as happens elsewhere also, different expressions of religious faith. For example, we may conceive it at different levels: there is religion as expressed in the observances and in the form of fasts and the performance of religious rituals and ceremonies, and then temple-going and taking baths in the holy rivers. Many peo-ple do it, and especially on certain auspicious days large numbers of people make the fast and observe these things. And then, so far as systematic religious education is concerned, I have to say that our children are not getting that kind of instruction. And that is why you may meet college students—you just put them simple questions about the Upanishads or the Bhagavad-Gita, and they won't generally be able to answer. I will tell you one thing: there is one work, the Ramayana. It is a great religious work. We have the Ramayana in Sanskrit as well as in Hindi; and in South In-dian languages you have different Ramayanas. But in North

India I can say that it is the Ramayana of Tulasidas which is very
popular. It has done a great deal not only in spreading and incul-
cating religious faith, but in explaining the basic doctrines of
Hinduism. Tulasidas was a saint of the medieval period. His
work has attained a popularity and sale like that of the Bible in
North India. You will find the Ramayana in every home. It is
widely read by the people, even those who are uneducated. They
also know the contents of the Ramayana, because it is recited in
almost all the villages of India, in the cities also. I think the main
source of religious education today happens to be the Ramayana.

A.G.: More so than the Mahabharata?

DR. M.: The Mahabharata, including the Bhagavad-Gita, is not known
to all. Though the characters of the Mahabharata are very popular among the masses—like Krishna and Arjuna. But the Ramayana is widely read and recited.

A.G: And throughout Southeast Asia as well?

DR. M.: Yes. You will find one strange thing here: even the most illit-
erate villager in India has some understanding of the higher
truths of religion. He will have some answer regarding what is
meant by karma, what is meant by rebirth, by bondage and
moksha (liberation). He will give you an intelligent answer, not
like a scholar, but you will be able to know that he knows these
things.

In view of the Hindu's belief in the ultimate divinity of man it
follows that his conception of good and evil, virtue and vice, will
have a different emphasis from that of the Christian. For the latter,
moral obligation lies in his conformity to a law, God-given and
therefore external to himself, whereas for Hinduism the goal is to
realize the self (atman) within—which is identical, or has a close
affinity, with God (Brahman). Broadly speaking, a Christian considers himself as failing through a lack of moral energy or good will, not
because of his ignorance. Thus St. Paul knows what he wants to do but
complains that he has not the strength to do it: "For I do not do the
good I want, but the evil I do not want is what I do" (Romans 7:19).
A Hindu saint, on the other hand, would say that the root of the
difficulty lies in ignorance (avidya); we are enveloped by illusion
(maya), and perhaps never more so than when we are confident that
we are acting rightly. Here it is worth remarking that Hindu and
Buddhist scholars claim to detect in the Judaeo-Christian tradition a

thread of profoundly irreligious self-righteousness. It arises, they point out, from the fact that many dedicated Westerners conceive religion in terms of offering the self-conscious individual ego to God. Whereas the real situation, according to Hinduism, is that, provided we are freed of ignorance—the "knot of the heart"—God, who is the true "Self," manifests himself so luminously that he reveals the self-conscious ego as being itself the most deep-seated illusion. So we find it stated in the Mundaka Upanishad:

The Self, who understands all, who knows all, and whose glory is manifest in the universe, lives within the lotus of the heart, the bright throne of Brahman.

By the pure in heart is he known. The Self exists in man, within the lotus of the heart, and is the master of his life and of his body.

With mind illumined by the power of meditation, the wise know him, the blissful, the immortal.

The *knot of the heart* [italics added], which is ignorance, is loosed, all doubts are dissolved, all evil effects of deeds are destroyed, when he who is both personal and impersonal is realized.

In the effulgent lotus of the heart dwells Brahman, who is passionless and indivisible. He is pure, he is the light of lights. Him the knowers of the Self attain.[28]

Sin, according to the Upanishads, is the consequence of ignorance, which in its turn entails desire and craving. The remedy for sin is not the confession of guilt, praiseworthy though this may be, or the practice of austerity, but the removal of ignorance by the attainment of true knowledge. A Hindu scholar has pointed out the contrast between the Christian and Hindu view of the origin of sin: "We have noted that Adam's Fall lies in the eating of 'the tree of the *knowledge* of good and evil', whereas in Hinduism the soul's bondage comes about by its association with the principle of *ignorance*. Whereas Christianity considers man's attempt to be God as the main cause of his fall, in Hinduism it is man's forgetfulness of his divinity that is regarded as his bondage."[29] The point came up in a discussion with Professor Murti in Banaras:

28. Quoted from *The Upanishads*, trans. Prabhavananda and Manchester, p. 46.
29. S. C. Thakur, *Christian and Hindu Ethics* (London: George Allen and Unwin, 1969), p. 98.

A.G.: There's another point, isn't there? What does Hinduism have to say about original sin?

DR. T.M.: We have original sin in the sense that we have original ignorance. We think of it as a defect of the mind. Moreover, ignorance is beginninglessness.

A.G.: So sin comes in later. It is not original?

DR. T.M.: It is original in this sense: How have *you* committed sin? You have not committed sin in the sense that Adam has committed sin, but because you are heir to Adam by some mystic thing. Actually, that is an admission of original sin.

A.G.: But, according to you, if ignorance is cleared away, then you have your original nature, isn't that right? You realize your own true basic being?

DR. T.M.: Yes.

A.G.: Now, is God's grace required to remove that ignorance?

DR. T.M.: Yes. As I said, it is through God's grace that you can *know* that there is Brahman, that your real self is this. You can't do it by yourself.

The key term in Hindu ethical teaching is "dharma"—a word that has come to be equated with "religion" in modern Indian languages. Its classical meaning is "righteousness," or good moral conduct according to the prescriptions handed down from age to age by the virtuous ancestors. Dharma puts one on one's guard against the three chief moral pitfalls: lust, covetousness, and anger. Here, according to the Gautama Dharma Sutra are the eight good qualities of the soul: "They are, compassion for all creatures, patience, freedom from discontent, purity, earnest endeavour, auspicious thought, freedom from avarice, freedom from envy." In a passage from the Bhagavad-Gita, the Lord Krishna explains to Arjuna, whose "birthright is divine," what qualities are to be looked for in such a man.

A man who is born with tendencies towards the Divine, is fearless and pure in heart. He perseveres in that path to union with Brahman (= God) which the scriptures and his teachers have taught him. He is charitable. He can control his passions. He studies the scriptures regularly, and obeys their directions. He practices spiritual disciplines. He is straightforward, truthful and of even temper. He harms no one. He renounces the things of this world. He has a tranquil mind and an unmalicious tongue. He is compassionate towards all. He is not greedy.

He is gentle and modest. He abstains from useless activity. He has faith
in the strength of his higher nature. He can forgive and endure. He is
clean in thought and act. He is free from hatred and from pride. Such
qualities are his birthright.[30]

First among the qualities listed in this passage is fearlessness.
Hindu religious thought is emphatic on the need to eliminate fear,
for fear, which is a kind of negative sensuality, constricts the spirit
and blocks the path to liberation (moksha). Visiting the great memorial to Mahatma Gandhi at New Delhi, I recall seeing one of his
aphorisms (the precise wording escapes me) engraved in stone near
the entrance. Its message was to the effect that so long as we have
fear there can be no growth in the life of the spirit. The Hindu ideal
of fearlessness, along with several related topics, came into a discussion held in Madras with Dr. Venkatarama Raghavan, professor of
Sanskrit at the university. We were speaking of the now familiar *tat
tvam asi* doctrine.

A.G.: Would *tat tvam asi* be applicable in interpersonal relations? Or
does it just apply to the divine? Can one say basically that we are
one another?

DR. R.: Yes, we all basically represent several modes or forms of the
same divine principle, the divine self.

A.G.: And that would be the basis for love, to see the divine in everybody else?

DR. R.: Yes. "The moment you make a distinction, fear pursues you."
That is what the Upanishad says. Fear arises when you are confronted by something other than yourself. That is the source of
fear. And if you know that everything is yourself, what is there to
dislike, what is there to hate, what is there to loathe? That is the
basis for the ethical outcome of this philosophical doctrine. It is
not a school of thought without any ethics, but it transcends ethics.
Ethics is a very necessary step.

A.G.: Isn't that a great doctrine of Mahatma Gandhi: elimination of
fear?

DR. R.: Yes. Any Hindu who becomes a monk must take some Hindu
religious vows, the chief one of which is that you will afford security to every living being: no one has anything to fear from me.

30. Bhagavad-Gita, 16, trans. Swami Prabhavananda and Christopher Isher-
wood (New York: New American Library, Mentor Books, 1954), p. 114.

Such a one can say, I have reached the stage of fearlessness. Not only am I not afraid of anybody, but also I am no longer the source of fear to anybody.

A.G.: Have you given any thought to Christianity at all? I'm going back to the West, and I'm wondering if there is anything from your knowledge and experience you think Western Christians need to know about?

DR. R.: The Western Christians must understand one important principle, that is, they should come around to our Vedantic idea that Christianity alone is not the sole path of salvation, that it is not correct to say that everybody will have to become a Christian before he can be saved. That we cannot accept. I think that even in the West this is an old outworn idea. Each religion is a path by itself, and you can approach the Ultimate by that path. In that sense I also believe that Christianity is a path—one of the true paths. All these paths lead to the Ultimate Reality. Conversion is of no use. If you convert twenty Brahmins in Madras, they will not practice Christianity as the Pope does in Rome or as the Anglican Archbishop does in Canterbury. They will do it in their own way, and they will think that Christ is a guru or a form of the Godhead (Avatara). They will have his picture and perform yoga. The whole thing will take a new turn. This is how it happened historically with Buddhism also. Buddhism started as a nihilistic religion; it was rather agnostic; it did not believe in any ultimate reality. But by the beginning of the Christian era the Mahayana had really developed as a duplication of the Hindu Vedantic type of personal religious devotion. Buddha became a center of worship, and they developed a mythology. They had several Bodhisattvas (Buddhas of Compassion) who were also worshiped. They began to sing sutras (sayings of the Buddha) or hymns about Buddha. So this is again Buddhism coming to terms with the world and adjusting itself, fully aware that there are different approaches. Hinduism is so diverse that the same path is not prescribed for everybody. Intellectuals and thinkers will take the path of knowledge or gnosis. A practical, actively minded person who wants to serve his fellow men will take the path of action. By concentrating on rituals he will attain a certain purity which will ultimately lead him to knowledge. Or again, if he is a very emotional person full of impulses, and he is given to adoring things, he will cling to an image or idol, go to some shrine, and there pour out his love. He takes the path of bhakti (devotion). Ultimate self is one; the paths to it are diverse. There are three paths to suit the different types of mind: the purely intellectual, the active, and the emotional and impulsive. These are ideas which the Christians must imbibe. There is another question which is at present disturbing Christian missionaries and the scientists brought up in that tradition: they are trying to discover by means of scientific enquiry if there is an afterlife or if there was a previous birth. Hinduism strongly believes that you can be the architect of your own destiny and that whatever you are now is the result of your own action. The Bhagavad-Gita says that you must lift yourself up by your own exertion. For that the karma theory is absolutely necessary.

A.G.: But wouldn't one's parents' or one's grandparents' actions have anything to do with the position you and I are in now?

DR. R.: They may have some effect by modifying your own mind.

A.G.: What would you say about the part of a guru in spiritual discipline?

DR. R.: In the technique of spiritual effort you must have a personal guide. All messiahs, great teachers, and writers are gurus. Guru means an elder or a revered person—a "dispeller of darkness."

A.G.: And the ultimate guru is God, isn't it?

DR. R.: God is the prototype of all gurus. They are only interpreting him. . . . But you must remember what Shankara says: the final certitude, the final ground of reference and verification is your own experience.

It is worth mentioning that this conversation was being carried on amid a great deal of turmoil and disturbance. Dr. Raghavan had to deal with some urgent administrative duties while we talked: his telephone was constantly ringing, and people were coming into his room to consult or ask him for a decision. Despite all this he had invited me to visit him and seemed glad to talk.

A.G.: I'm grateful to you for sparing this time.

DR. R.: Well, we seekers can come together. Life and the supreme self—two sides of the coin. So in the midst of all the turmoil, if you can have an anchor for your soul, you are able to face anything. You simply brush it aside. When a porcupine is faced with an attacking animal, it has sharp pins and it just shrugs its body and shivers: everything is thrown a furlong off. So if two people like you come together and ask about Brahman, all the outside distractions simply fly off.

A.G.: One final question: Is there any place in Hinduism for what Christians call faith? A kind of belief in the unseen without any real knowledge of it.

DR. R.: There is sraddha. Sraddha is the first step. For example, when I talk to you I must have faith in what I say; you must have faith that I am worth talking to. *Srad* means "heart"; *dha* means "to put into": "that which you have firmly put into your heart." Sraddha is faith.

At another discussion in Madras the subject of yoga was touched on. What seems to interest Westerners most—yoga with the aid of ordered breathing and certain physical postures—is only one of yoga's forms: hatha-yoga. But it was not of this that the celebrated Dr. Sarvepalli Radhakrishnan, former President of the Republic of India, chose to talk when we broached the subject.

DR. S. R.: The hippies and the Beatles! "Transcendental meditation," as it is called! You see, if you open a classic work on yoga, it only tells you that man as he is, is full of discord. His mind goes one way; his heart goes another way. You should try to bring both, and everything else, into harmony. Yoga is merely the method by which you examine yourself practically every day for a few minutes. Investigate your own nature and ask yourself the question: What is wrong with me? How can I harmonize the different sides of my nature to make the outward and the inward coincide? That's the purpose of yoga as you find it in the classical books. Look at the Yoga Sutra. It starts like that. It tells you that your body, your mind, and everything else are meant to harmonize. That's the meaning of yoga—not the sort of thing that's happening today. . . . Or take the word "Zen"; it is the Japanese equivalent of *dhyana*, a Sanskrit word meaning "meditation." It merely tells you that you have to penetrate beyond the layers of your body, mind, and all the rest; you have to concentrate deeply until you are able to reach that universal light, or spirit, or whatever you call it, which is your nature. If you are able to reach that and allow it to penetrate every aspect of your being, then you are an integrated, a harmonized, individual. To become integrated involves constant practice; it's not by mere talk, not merely by chanting mantras or hymns or things like that, but by a kind of self-examination, scrutiny. That is what is essential to develop into any kind of integrated being. After all, the purpose of religion is the integration of the personality. Let your depth penetrate into your surface; then the two will coincide.

A.G.: Do you think, sir, that that can be done without a guru?

DR. S.R.: It can be done without a guru.

A.G.: Is there perhaps an Eternal Guru?

DR. S.R.: God, the guide for us all. He is the Everlasting Guru. He is always behind us, supporting us, helping us—and if we follow, take hold of him, we shall always have God for our perpetual guide.

A.G.: You know, I was brought up in the Christian tradition. . . .

DR. S.R.: I always say that Christianity, or any religion for that matter, involves the transformation of your consciousness—metanoia, as you call it; the noetic sense has to transcend itself, become different from what it is. Unless you are born again you can't enter the Kingdom of God. That rebirth—that's the essence of religion. To be reborn, to be remade, that's the essence of all religion. Christianity emphasizes it much more than any other religion. You find a statement like that when Nicodemus went up to the Master: "Unless a man be born again . . ." And elsewhere: "Go, sell all that thou hast. . . ." That was too much for him. It is too much for us all. You see, for us all, the Cross symbolizes material death and spiritual victory, properly speaking. But today we are concerned with material survival, whatever may become of spiritual values. We are surrendering spiritual values for the sake of possessing ourselves of this world. I mean, all the wars that are fought are fought for material survival. And we don't care about the sort of things that happen. We use religion for gaining our own earthly ends.

A.G.: Yes, as a sort of *instrumentum regni.*

DR. S.R.: The real religion is different. Take a man like Gandhi: you find in him a very different religious voice. When he was asked here what we should do, he said that truth and love are the things by which we should live; we must practice those things if we wish to gain our freedom. Then somebody said, "History testifies that no country has ever gained freedom by the practice of truth and love. It is by the practice of deceit and cunning that countries have gained their freedom." And Gandhi's answer was: "Let my country perish if that is the only way it can gain its freedom." There you find the true voice of religion.

A.G.: Yes. We visited Gandhi's tomb in New Delhi the other day. I was very struck by the inscription at the entrance, on the need to eliminate fear. Wherever you have fear there can be no true spirituality. It was very noteworthy.

DR. S.R.: Gandhi was not a Hindu in any narrow sense of the word. He said, "If untouchability is a part of Hinduism, I will discard Hinduism." That's what he said; a number of times he said that. In other words, he refined Hinduism, so to say, and tried to abolish whatever was inimical to the true spirit of religion. When Gandhi was in South Africa, one of his enemies came and bit off a mass of flesh from his shoulder. And Andrews[31] said, file a suit, complain. But Gandhi's reply was: "No use to complain to a magistrate. May this blood be the cementing bond between my enemy and me." While he was there, the Zulus were all thrown out, and some of them contracted leprosy. Andrews was there, his man, and Gandhi was wiping the leper's sores with his own clothes and doing the work of a nurse. And Andrews said, "My ideas of hygiene and sanitation prevented me from doing what this man, a heathen so to say, was doing out of utter unconscious love for humanity." He was doing that of his own, not from any deliberate effort, but because he felt the call of somebody's suffering. He went there and wiped their sores and did the work, because the white nurses in South Africa had refused to touch them. There you find the true spirit of religion. Not by their beliefs but by their deeds shall you judge them.

A.G.: That was wonderful. . . . Would you say, sir, that in order to lead the sort of life that Gandhi led there must be a deep-down conviction, that it wasn't just a question of deeds?

DR. S.R.: No, no. There was a burning conviction. It is not a question of intellectual propositions, but a burning conviction that trans-

31. Charles Freer Andrews, a British disciple of the Mahatma and a Christian missionary.

forms one's whole nature. That must be there. Otherwise one
can't act in that way. It's impossible. I believe that for every man,
if his life is to be complete, religion is essential. There is an order
of reality higher than the phenomenal and the spatial. What we
see and hear and touch is not all. We must get behind that and
take hold of it; you must have faith in that if you want to be
a religious man.

A.G.: Yes. And as you say, we must get beyond verbal propositions
and statements. Catholicism has been very much caught up in
that sort of thing.

DR. S.R.: Yes, I know. Scholasticism must cease; we must go beyond
it.

A.G.: Beyond name and form, as you Hindus say. Though we need
name and form, don't we?

DR. S.R.: Yes, indeed. We live in this world, so we have to have name
and form. But understand that names and forms are all halting,
imperfect expressions of one Supreme. You can never do justice
to the work of the Supreme, its majesty and greatness. Incompar-
ably great. Many people speak nowadays of "the God beyond
God." It is Paul Tillich's expression. We have heard it earlier.
There is a God beyond all Gods. That mode of expression comes
from the Upanishads. There is a reality behind the flow of the
universe. You must have a grip on it if you want to be a truly
religious man. And by meditation, self-discipline, self-scrutiny,
you are trying to get a stronger hold on that ultimate reality. That
is what we have to do, at any rate, what we are attempting to do
to the best of our ability.

A.G.: Could you say something, sir, about the devotion of individuals
—particularly, so I understand, among the Buddhists—to a particular guru? My feeling is that you must get beyond that, very
much so.

DR. S.R.: As for gurus, sometimes they're good, sometimes they themselves are misleading the people, and then you go astray. Nothing
except the highest Guru, the Divine Spirit: that is the one Guru
you have to trust.

A.G.: The Buddhists attach some importance to the guru. I wonder if
you could say something of the difference between the Mahayana, which interests me most, and Hinduism at its deepest level.

DR. S.R.: The Buddha never assumed spiritual airs. He said, test everything that I say; test it by reason, by the experience of life, and see if your mind is satisfied. If you are satisfied, accept what I say. Otherwise not—not out of regard for me. That's what the Buddha said. Buddha was a man of very great intelligence who condemned superstitions. He said somewhere, "What harm has your hair done that you should want to shave it off. Cut off the defects in your heart. If your mind is full of defects, what is the use of putting on the orange robe of a monk? Cleanse your heart and mind, then all will be well."

A.G.: As for his attitude to the divine, what would you say? The doctrine of sunyata (emptiness), so far as I understand it, seems suggestive. Is that a part of Hinduism?

DR. S.R.: Sunyata is there. The Upanishads say that we can't describe the Ultimate. *"Neti, Neti"*: "Not this, not that." Then you say that it is sunyata. You can't use the empirical categories to describe the transempirical. So you must see it that way: what you call sunyata, emptiness, is the plenitude of being—only it is not being in the sense that tables and chairs in the space-time world are. That is what is being said.

A.G.: Yes, that is how I understand it.

DR. S.R.: You are right.

A.G.: So that it is absurd to speak of the Buddha as being atheistic.

DR. S.R.: Atheist or agnostic or even annihilationist: "Nirvana as a night of nothingness." If you talk like that you are unfair to the Buddha, you are unfair to the environment in which he lived, where he was able to make such a tremendous appeal to the people round about him. An atheist could never have made the appeal which he made during his lifetime. . . . You see, the Buddha . . . the real trouble was that he kept silent on the ultimate metaphysical issues, with the result that in the first century after the Buddha, eighteen different schools emerged. That shows that the human mind wants something positive. The Buddha had said, "I am keeping silent on these metaphysical issues, because they do not help you to solve the problems of daily life." But this was not enough for his followers. Some of them said, "To imitate the life of the Buddha is the greatest thing." Others said, "Buddha is the Saviour who has come to save us." The Hinayana creed on the one hand and the Mahanaya on the other. The first thought that the ideal of the arhat (the disciplined soul, the worthy one) was the best; the second preferred the ideal of the Bodhisattva (to become a "Buddha of compassion," one who renounces nirvana in order to help humanity on its pilgrimage). These developments, along with the Bhagavad-Gita, actually brought the Saviour concept into Buddhism. You see, you may try to keep silent and not commit yourself, but when these ideas are passed on to others, they will translate them into their own idiom. That sort of thing happens. The ideas of the Bhagavad-Gita were all familiar at the time it was written here in India. Zen Buddhism grew up outside, in China and Japan.

A.G.: Is it established when the Gita was written? Was it before or after the Buddha's time?

DR. S.R.: I don't know. Maybe about the same time. That was a conservative development. Buddha was a radical. There was confusion in the country at his time: people trying to do all sorts of useless things in the name of religion. Buddha said, Don't do any of that. The Gita said, I will sublimate all that. The latter is conservative; the former is a more radical protest.

A.G.: I've heard it said by someone in Delhi, sir, that if the Buddha saw Hinduism as it is practiced today, he would find no grounds for protest.

DR. S.R.: I don't know. It is also practiced today in a bad way. Why do you think it is practiced in a noble and dignified manner? The actual practice in some of the villages, where you may still go about, is not that. In some places they still sacrifice buffaloes and so on, cocks and so on. Or again: untouchability is rejected legally, but still many people practice it. Because it is repudiated by law, it does not mean that in our lives we repudiate it. That will take some time; men have to be educated. There is improvement, no doubt. The Buddha is regarded by Hinduism as an avatar, a manifestation of Vishnu, because he did something to fulfill our religion; he did not merely cast it aside. . . . Tell me, where is your monastery in England?

A.G.: At Ampleforth in Yorkshire. I shall be going back there, and I hope to try to throw some light on Catholicism from this viewpoint, from what I have learned, from the standpoint, so to speak, of "eternal religion." It seems to me that this was understood in the Middle Ages and that the tradition somehow got lost. René Guénon and others have pointed this out. Is there anything

that strikes you as particularly worthwhile pointing out to Christians today?

DR. S.R.: We have a ceremony, upanayana, "initiation." You are born
into the world by a necessity of nature; you must be reborn into
the world of spiritual freedom. That is the meaning of initiation.
My feeling is that if you penetrate into the meaning of any religious scripture, you will always find there the fundamental note
that you are incomplete; you have to complete yourself. You are
born in . . . you may call it sin, or ignorance. We say, men are
not born wicked; they are born imperfect, unfortunate. But
slowly man can raise himself—by practice, by austerities, by discipline. Man can become naturalized in the atmosphere of divine
reality, soaked, so to say, in the Spirit of God. You feel that you
are there. You may not be able to live up to all the obligations it
imposes; you are aware that you are falling short of the ideal. But
you may be able to raise yourself so as to see that the deviation is
not much. That is what you should attempt to do. And you will
find the same situation in Christianity. So far as I am concerned,
if I talk about Christianity, it is in terms of that kind of spiritual
rebirth. And I would say that Jesus was one who exemplified it in
a magnificent way. He was there; he grew, as you say, in wisdom
and stature. That is, it was not a gift which he had, but he grew;
and what happened to him may happen to others also. We
should all try; we should all put forth an effort. This is the way in
which I look on Christianity.

A.G.: A Christian would say, I think, that he feels the need for some
kind of outside help; prayer is called for. What would you say
about that? Is there anything corresponding to divine grace in
the Hindu tradition?

DR. S.R.: Yes, I think it is there. The Bhagavad-Gita has got enough
scope for that. When you ask for a thing urgently, seriously, and
fully, you will get a response. The world is not a dead one; it is a
live universe. If you ask for something, there will be a response,
but you must ask for it seriously, honestly, and with all your heart
and mind. But it depends on your own earnestness and effort if
you are to get a response.

A.G.: Well, I feel we have been taking a lot of your time.

DR. S.R.: Oh, no, not yet . . . You see, what the world needs today is
for the two traditions to get together. Look at the whole growth

of Christianity from its beginnings to today (I told His Holiness the Pope this when he came to Bombay): Jesus gave the ideas; then they were taken into the Graeco-Roman environment. Greek thought gave all the concepts, the *Logos* and other ideas, and the Roman organization gave you *Ecclesia*. The Jewish soul, the Greek brain, and the Roman body—the three together produced Catholicism. Then much later you find Aquinas saying, we want to reconcile Christianity with Aristotelian thought. That was the peak of contemporary culture then. He wanted to bring the two things together. A similar process has been going on throughout history, whether it is in Christianity, Hinduism, or Buddhism, because you have to reckon with the environment in which you are placed. At the birth of Christianity, the environment was Graeco-Roman; today the whole world is the environment. So there is needed the same kind of absorption or assimilation of what is valuable and the discarding of whatever happens not to be valuable. That sort of thing goes on perpetually: so long as the human mind is active, that is the sort of thing that happens.

A.G.: Would you care to comment on the Christian missionary effort here in India?

DR. S.R.: People are taking to this religion or that religion as their mind dictates. They keep their minds open. Conversion, real conversion, is that re-bornness I have been speaking of. Rebirth is the only conversion. Whether you are once born or twice born makes all the difference: between what we are and what we should be. And that is the only true kind of conversion that can take place.

Now let us turn more explicitly to the contribution linked with the name of Siddhartha Gautama, the "Enlightened One," the Buddha—or rather, to be accurate, my very fallible impressions of that contribution. Through previous reading and discussion, supported by three months' direct experience in Japan, I had learned something of Mahayana Buddhism. Already in Thailand, and then in Ceylon, the Hinayana or Theravada[32] emphasis in the Buddha's mes-

32. Some readers may welcome a reminder of the meaning of these three terms: Mahayana = the school of the "great vehicle" of salvation, also called the Northern School, as it embraces Tibet, Mongolia, China, Korea, and Japan. Hinayana = the school of the "lesser vehicle" of salvation, also called the

sage occupied my attention. I use the word "emphasis" because, coming in contact with Buddhist personalities of the various schools, I sensed a similar underlying spirit. There is less distinctiveness of ethos, I would guess, between the Mahayana and Theravada, than there is between Catholicism and Protestantism in Christianity.

v. The All-Enlightened One

Among the most pleasing of my encounters with Buddhism, as it is lived and practiced, was an experience in Ceylon early in January, 1968. Ceylon is the oldest existing center of the southern, Theravada tradition, and although my stay was too brief and the time unpropitious to allow of any lengthy discussions there, I was rewarded by one charming and unexpected insight. My companion and I put up at a hotel overlooking the sea within a few miles of Colombo. The island was disturbed by political strife and labor unrest, from which it resulted that the normal services of the hotel were disrupted. The waiters were on strike.

However, the management contrived to keep the essential facilities going, with the help of a score of teen-age boys, still on holiday from school. They were, I suspected, sons of the absent waiter staff, striking under pressure from the labor unions rather than out of personal conviction. These children more than compensated for their inexpertness by their interest in the guests, whom they served with concern and attentiveness. Each afternoon I would sit out on the terrace, where it was warm and sunny, and read or just gaze idly westward over the Indian Ocean, its green-blue waves wallowing under the wind, across to Africa, two thousand miles away. Most of the guests were elsewhere, so that when tea was brought, it was usually by a small company of these Singhalese youngsters. Several of them spoke fluent, idiomatic English, which they would air unabashedly, my presence supplying them with an opportunity that left them in no hurry to depart. A group would often stand around

---

Southern School, embracing Ceylon, Burma, and Thailand. This term was applied by the Mahayana school to those who did not accept its more liberal developments and is somewhat discourteous. To be preferred is the term Theravada (practically equivalent, for practical purposes, to Hinayana), which means the "way of the elders."

my table, volatile and voluble, happily unaware of what a pleasant sight they made, clad uniformly in sandals, khaki shorts, and clean white shirts.

They would ask me questions about where I came from, pressing me to tell them of the way people lived in England and America. This catechizing was reciprocal, and they proved ready enough to tell me anything they knew of what went on in Ceylon. I asked them about school, to which they were shortly to return from the holidays, more specifically touching the topic of the religious instruction they received. On this they were about as coherent as Christian children are apt to be when faced with similar questions. However, it slowly emerged that they learned about the holy truths and noble path taught long ago by "the Lord." Rather hesitantly, I asked them who the Lord was. The leader of the group looked at me in surprise, startled at my ignorance. "Our Lord Buddha, of course," he said.

It still seems almost inconceivable to many Christians that roughly 170 million of our fellow men regard the Buddha in much the same light as we look on Jesus of Nazareth. Yet not only is this a fact, but recent New Testament scholarship has detected parallels between the Buddhist and the Christian scriptures, even possible areas of dependence of the latter on the former. "There are also some extraordinarily instructive analogies to the history of the synoptic tradition in the history of the Jataka[33] collection in the Buddhist canon." [34] More specifically, it is suggested that the relationship of Mark 12:41–44 to a story in the Buddhist tradition is so close that the conclusion of actual dependence on it is hard to avoid. Both the narrative of the Presentation in the Temple and that of the Temptations of Jesus have parallels in the historically earlier story of the Buddha. The following, offered without comment, may be allowed to speak for itself.

Most notable is a Buddhist parallel to Matt. 14:28–31 (the text is in J. Aufhauser, *Jesus und Buddha*, Kl. Texte, no. 157, p. 12). It tells of a disciple "who wanted to visit Buddha one evening and on his way found that the ferry was missing from the bank of the river Aciravati. In faithful trust in Buddha he stepped on to the water and went as if

33. Jataka means "a birth story." The "collection" is a work of the Theravada canon containing stories of the former lives of the Buddha.

34. Rudolf Bultmann, *The History of the Synoptic Tradition* (New York: Harper & Row, 1963), p. 7.

on dry land to the very middle of the stream. Then he came out of his contented meditation on Buddha in which he had lost himself, and saw the waves and was frightened, and his feet began to sink. But he forced himself to become wrapt in his meditation again and by its power he reached the far bank safely and reached his master." (Garbe, pp. 56f. and *Buddhist. Maerchen,* pp. 46f.) Garbe thinks that the gospel story was borrowed from the Buddhist tradition.[35]

Siddhartha Gautama, later to become the Buddha (i.e., the "Enlightened") lived in northern India probably between 560 and 480 B.C. The stories of the birth and early years of the Buddha[36] are legendary, but like most legends that survive the test of time, they embody important elements of truth. What emerges clearly is that the young Gautama's observation of the inevitability of sickness, decrepitude, and death taught him to despair of finding life's fulfillment on the merely physical plane. "Life is subject to age and death. Where is the realm of life in which there is neither age nor death?" He resolved to become a truth seeker and, cost what it may, discover the secret of human existence.

Following the Hindu custom for those who wish to embark on such a life he put on the yellow robe of a monk, began to live alone in the forest, and devoted himself to profound meditation. For six years he pursued his search, encountering all its difficulties. "How hard it is to live the life of a lonely forest-dweller . . . to rejoice in solitude. Verily, the silent groves must bear heavily upon the monk who has not yet won fixity of mind." He sought wisdom from the Hindu masters of his day, and practiced raja-yoga, that is, the yoga

35. *Ibid.,* p. 237.
36. For easily accessible and readable accounts of the Buddha and Buddhism, the reader may refer to: E. H. Brewster, *The Life of Gotama the Buddha —Compiled Exclusively from the Pali Canon* (London: Routledge & Kegan Paul, 1926); Edward Conze, *Buddhism: Its Essence and Development* (Oxford: Bruno Cassirer, 1951; New York: Harper Torchbook, 1959); Edward Conze, ed. and trans., *Buddhist Scriptures* (Baltimore: Penguin Books, 1959); Ananda Coomaraswamy, *Buddha and the Gospel of Buddhism* (Bombay: Asia Publishing House, 1956); Dwight Goddard, *A Buddhist Bible* (London: George G. Harrap & Co., 1956); Christmas Humphreys, *Buddhism* (Baltimore: Penguin Books, 1955); Bhikshu Sangharakshita, *A Survey of Buddhism* (Bangalore: Indian Institute of World Culture, 1957); Guy Richard Welbon, *The Buddhist Nirvana and Its Western Interpreters* (Chicago: University of Chicago Press, 1968); N. Wilson Ross, *Three Ways of Asian Wisdom* (New York: Simon & Schuster, 1966); John Blofeld, *The Way of Power: A Practical Guide to the Tantric Mysticism of Tibet* (London: George Allen & Unwin, 1970).

of meditation and contemplation. He gave himself up to extreme asceticism, so that he nearly died, but to no purpose. From this experience he concluded that austerity was futile; he evolved the doctrine of the "middle way," a course of life between extreme asceticism on the one hand and mere self-indulgence on the other. He returned, his mind now at a deeper level, to his life as a yogi[37]—a life of rigorous thought and concentration.

We approach the event that for the Buddhist world holds a comparable place to that held by the Crucifixion and Resurrection in Christianity. One evening near Gaya in northeast India Gautama sat in deep meditation beneath a fig tree—afterward to become known as the Bo (short for Bodhi, i.e., "enlightenment") tree. The place has since been named the Immovable Spot, for tradition relates that Gautama, sensing that he was on the brink of enlightenment, seated himself that epoch-making evening with the vow not to rise until his illumination was achieved. Then came the tempter, Mara, to play a role analogous to that of Satan five centuries later, as a prelude to the ministry of Jesus. The Evil One, realizing that his antagonist's success was imminent, rushed to the spot to disrupt his concentration. He attacked first in the form of desire, parading three voluptuous goddesses with their enticing retinues. When the Buddha-to-be remained impassive, the Tempter assumed the guise of Death. His powerful hosts assailed the aspirant with hurricanes, torrential rains, showers of flaming rocks that splashed boiling mud, and finally a great darkness. Then followed the encounter often depicted in Buddhist iconography, where the Buddha is shown seated in meditation and resting one hand on the ground. Mara, accusing him of presumption, challenged his right to be doing what he was. Buddha touched the earth with his right fingertip, whereupon the earth responded, thundering, "I bear you witness, with a hundred, a thousand, and a hundred thousand roars." Mara's army of evil spirits withdrew defeated, and the gods of heaven descended, transported with rapture, to wait upon the victor with garlands and perfumes. The legend continues:

While the Bo tree rained red blossoms that full-mooned May night, Gautama's meditation deepened through watch after watch until, as the

---

37. One who practices yoga. The word "yoga" means literally "union"— so that for a Christian to practice yoga should mean that he is striving for union with God.

morning star glistened in the transparent skies of the east, his mind pierced at last the bubble of the universe and shattered it to nothing (sunyata)—only, wonder of wonders, to find it restored to his gaze with all the reality that could be claimed for it, the effulgence of true being. The Great Awakening had taken place. Gautama's being was transformed, and he emerged the Buddha. The event was of cosmic import. All created things filled the morning air with their rejoicings and the earth quaked six ways with wonder. Ten thousand galaxies shuddered in awe as lotuses bloomed on every tree, turning the entire universe into "a bouquet of flowers sent whirling through the air." The bliss of this vast experience kept the Buddha rooted to the spot for seven entire days. On the eighth day he tried to rise but was lost again in bliss. For a total of forty-nine days he was deep in rapture, after which his "glorious glance" opened again onto the world.[38]

His public ministry was to last forty-five years until he died at the age of eighty. He strove to communicate to others through the inadequate medium of words what "enlightenment" amounted to. All he could feel confident of was that "there will be some who will understand." Those who would understand, in part at least, were his first disciples, who made up the beginnings of the *sangha*, the "congregation of the initiated," the oldest monastic order in the world. To a small group of these, in a deer park at Sarnath near Banaras, was preached the Buddha's first sermon,[39] by which he "set in motion the Wheel of the Law." [40] The sermon—which, according to T. S. Eliot, "corresponds in importance to the Sermon on the Mount"—consists of three parts: (1) the Middle Way of the Tathagata[41]—that is, midway between austerity and indulgence, which "brings clear vision,

38. Huston Smith, *The Religions of Man* (New York: Harper & Row, 1958), p. 84 (with some slight modification of wording). This brief account, by way of background to my own experience of Buddhism as it exists today, owes much to Professor Huston Smith's admirable Chapter III—informative, unacademic, lively, and extremely readable—in the work just cited.

39. The text can be found in *The Buddhist Tradition in India, China and Japan*, ed. William Theodore de Bary (New York: Random House, 1969), pp. 15–17.

40. This celebrated phrase, signalizing the start of the Buddhist movement, refers to the chariot wheel, which in ancient India symbolized empire. The phrase has been paraphrased as "embarked on his expedition of conquest on behalf of the Kingdom of Righteousness."

41. Tathagata (Sanskrit): a title of the Buddha used by his followers and also by him when speaking of himself. It means one who has attained full realization of suchness (Tatha-ta), i.e., become one with the Absolute, so that he "neither comes from anywhere nor goes to anywhere."

makes for wisdom, leads to peace, insight, enlightenment and Nirvana";[42] (2) the Four Noble Truths, concerning the nature, origin, term, and cure of all human distress; (3), the Noble Eightfold Path, the cure, whose stages are "Right Views, Right Resolve, Right Speech, Right Conduct, Right Livelihood, Right Effort, Right Mindfulness, and Right Concentration."

The Buddha manifested to a supreme degree that rare combination—a cool head and a warm heart. He was free from sentimentality on the one hand and from indifference or aloofness on the other. His early disciples regarded him as "omniscience incarnate," and he is reported to have said that "it is not possible that in disputation with anyone, I could be thrown into confusion or embarrassment." Yet his concern for "all sentient beings" was so great that the story is told of his risking his life in order to free a goat caught in brambles on a mountainside. The extraordinary power of his mind was balanced by a tenderness so remarkable that his message has been characterized as "a religion of infinite compassion." Finally, and what made him perhaps unique among charismatic personalities, was his nonauthoritarianism. This quality, which he shares with Socrates, accounts for much of the interest in Buddhism among the more thoughtful in the West today. Contrasting his own openness with the professional secrecy of the Brahmins, he pointed out that "the Tathagata has no such thing as the closed fist of a teacher." He challenged each individual to make his own existential decision about religion: "Look not for assistance to anyone besides yourselves . . . Hold fast to the truth as a lamp . . . Seek salvation alone in the truth . . .

42. Nirvana (Sanskrit) Nibbana (Pali): this term must inevitably recur in any discussion of Buddhism. So as to eliminate the need for further explanation, here is Mr. Christmas Humphreys' careful elucidation: "The supreme Goal of Buddhist endeavour; release from the limitations of existence. The word is derived from a root meaning extinguished through lack of fuel, and since rebirth is the result of desire, freedom from rebirth is attained by the extinguishing of all such desire. Nirvana is, therefore, a state attainable in this life by right aspiration, purity of life, and the elimination of egoism. This is cessation of existence, as we know existence: the Buddha speaks of it as 'unborn, unoriginated, uncreated, unformed,' contrasting it with the born, originated, created and formed phenomenal world." For an account of the complexity of the Nirvana concept, and the variety of ways in which it has been understood, see Guy Richard Welbon, *The Buddhist Nirvana and Its Western Interpreters.* On page 219 the author makes a tantalizing observation: "Many students cease to be shocked about nirvana, not because they find it obviously a positive goal, but because its moral implications are so modern." *A Popular Dictionary of Buddhism* (New York: Citadel Press, 1962), p. 138.

Those who, either now or after I am dead, shall be a lamp unto themselves, relying upon themselves only and not relying upon any external help, but holding fast to the truth as their lamp, and seeking their salvation in the truth alone, shall not look for assistance to anyone besides themselves. . . . It is they who shall reach the very topmost height! But they must be anxious to learn. . . ."[43]

Such doctrine appears at first sight the very antithesis of Christianity with its emphasis on self-distrust and the need for God's grace. This position does in fact reveal what is acknowledged to be the central paradox of Buddhism: for combined with the stress on self-reliance and self-effort is what is known as the *anatta* (nonego) doctrine. This is the belief that the "self" is an illusion, that what we take to be the self is merely a conscious identification with such changing phenomena as the body, feelings, perceptions, impulses, and emotions. Salvation lies in piercing through this illusion—not intellectually, for it cannot be done that way, but experientially—as the Buddha did at his Enlightenment. So that far from encouraging self-assertiveness, Buddhism is a religion of selflessness, or rather, of nonself. We have here the chief point on which Gautama departed from the Brahminism of his day, and where the Buddhist tradition differs from Hinduism, as expounded by its leading doctors and saints. For the self (atman) which Shankara taught as ultimately identical with—and Ramanuja as separate from, but to be finally united with—Brahman, the Buddha held not really to exist at all. But to pursue the matter further would involve us in the metaphysics of the Buddhist experience—only remotely to be expressed in words —of emptiness[44] (sunyata). As it is, I think the reader should now be in a position to share with me some of my merely verbal experiences in places where Buddhism is part of the natural scene.

At the end of October, 1967, in Thailand, I had my first meeting with a Buddhist monk, or Bhikkhu (the Pali spelling; in Sanskrit, Bhikshu) of the Theravada tradition. Visiting Wat Bovoranives in Bangkok, I was received in friendly fashion by the dedicated and highly knowledgeable Bhikkhu Khantipalo. He was learned and

43. E. A. Burtt, *The Teachings of the Compassionate Buddha* (New York: Mentor Books, 1955), pp. 49–50.

44. This doctrine, fundamental to the proper understanding of Buddhism, was elaborated by the Buddhist philosopher Nagarjuna in India during the second century A.D. See Frederick J. Streng, *Emptiness—A Study in Religious Meaning* (Nashville: Abingdon Press, 1967).

more than willing to give me the benefit of his knowledge. Being
English himself, in fact at one time a member of the Anglican Communion, he was acquainted with the Western mentality. After some
comparisons between the Buddhist and Christian forms of the monastic life, our discussion took a wider turn.

A.G.: But to go back to the Buddhist philosophy or message, what is
the goal, what is the objective, according to the Theravada?

BHIKKHU: Well, now, as we go through our life, the sufferings that
we experience, most of them we can trace to our own wrong
grasp of circumstances, to our wrong dealing with situations.
When a situation is presented and while one has to deal with it,
most people may "instinctively," to use that word, be greedy for
something attractive in the situation, or they may be averse from
something that is painful in that situation, or they may be dull
and stupid with the situation, not understanding it properly. Now
these three, greed meaning desire for, and aversion meaning not
wanting to experience, and dullness, or stupidity, meaning ignorance, not knowing, not wanting to know—these three are responsible for the troubles that one has in one's life. If one reacted with
a mind which was free from these things, there would be no
dukkha (discomfort, disharmony with environment)—unsatisfactory experience, pain or anguish to the slightest degree or the
greatest degree, physically or mentally, all of which is covered by
the word "dukkha." So this dukkha, which really all of us suffer
all of the time to some degree, is there. Now if we take ourselves
in hand, so to speak—and there are methods for doing this—then
the causes which produce dukkha, namely, greed, envy, aversion,
delusion, can be removed from the mind, or dissolved in the
mind, and the causes of goodness, of nobility of conduct can be
cultivated. Now these two processes, that is, the destruction or
limitation of unwholesome impulses and the growth of wholesome ones, these go on side by side to start with. But when the
unwholesome impulses become very weak, as they will do if one
follows the way consistently, then it is very easy for the mind to
drop into a state of calm tranquillity, of quiet absorption, samadhi (collectedness of heart and mind); but this can't happen while
the unwholesome tendencies are very strong. Then it is not possible. That's why all the Buddhist systems emphasize lots of disci-

pline to start with. And then after the discipline has been going on for some time, perhaps a long time, there is a natural attainment of this samadhi. It's not a thing which can be forced; it just happens naturally owing to the conditions that are there, which one has brought about. Now this samadhi then becomes the basis for the development of prajna (transcendental wisdom). Wisdom in this sense, prajna, means seeing clearly, understanding thoroughly, the nature of oneself. Because when we understand thoroughly the nature of ourselves, we are no longer in any sort of trouble. All the troubles that we formerly had with the world, we are at peace with them, we don't come into contact with these things. Of course, this is a way of solving the personal approach to religion; it's not a way of solving the world's social problems. But it is especially the path that is taken by the monk and to some extent by dedicated lay people.

A.G.: That is a very impressive exposition of it. Samadhi is, as I understand it, a state which is achievable in and compatible with normal, everyday existence, is that right?

BHIKKHU: Yes. There are lay people in Bangkok who lead busy lives and who attain samadhi in the early morning, seated in a quiet place. It has been compared to taking a bath in the morning. This is an inner bath; it's very refreshing, and usually the effect of deep samadhi during the day is such that one won't become angry easily and one will have generally restrained appetites—not greedy.

A.G.: Is it possible to say something on the topic of nirvana? A lot has been said—perhaps the best thing is to say nothing?

BHIKKHU: It has been truly said that those who haven't discovered nirvana can't really say anything about it, except what is already in the books, and those who have can't say anything about it either. There is a very famous verse which tells of one Brahmin wanderer going to ask a question of the Buddha: "Those who have reached the goal: Are they annihilated or do they live forever free from ill? Please tell me the answer to this question, for I am sure that you know what the answer is." To which the Buddha replied: "Of the person who has reached the goal, there is no measure. When all the dhammas[45] have been destroyed, de-

---

45. Dhamma, the Pali spelling, of which the Sanskrit is dharma. The meaning of this multipurpose word in the present context is explained by the Bhikkhu.

stroyed are all the ways of telling, too." Now the dhammas here are the eye and sight objects, the ear and sound objects, the nose and smell objects, the tongue and taste objects, the body and contact objects, the mind and mental objects. These are called the twelve ayatana (spheres of experience). They form another comprehensive category like the skandhas (aggregates; see pp. 130–131). When you come to think about it, there is nothing that we know outside these twelve categories, called the dhammas here.[46] When these things are not any more, then what would you say? But the Buddha was very firm on many occasions: to the effect that those who accused him of being an annihilationist —one life here, and then "finished"—people like this were quite wrong. The only things he was concerned to annihilate were *greed, aversion,* and *delusion.*

A.G.: Very good; most interesting.

BHIKKHU: In other words, you must get on with the work you've got here, which is with this mind and body. And that goal will take care of itself. When you are ripe, ready to receive this experience, then it will take place, then it will happen.

A.G.: What would be the comment from your background, training, and experience on what I take to be the Zen view, that what they call satori, or enlightenment, can be achieved, is achieved after a period of discipline, and that its signs are recognizable? There are such people, enlightened people, who have received, or have achieved, enlightenment?

BHIKKHU: Certainly, there are such people.

A.G.: And that's it? There's nothing more for them to do except carry on their enlightened lives?

BHIKKHU: They are, so to speak, the torch bearers; their students are the next generation. With these sort of teachings—in any age, but

46. Behind the Buddhist position here being unfolded by the Bhikkhu lies a classical statement of it in the Udana ("Solemn Utterances of the Buddha"): "There is a stage (ayatana) where there is neither earth nor water, nor fire nor wind, nor the stage of the infinity of space, nor the stage of the infinity of consciousness, nor the stage of nothingness, nor the stage of neither consciousness nor nonconsciousness. There is not this world nor the other world, not sun nor moon. That I call neither coming nor going nor staying nor passing away nor arising; without support or going on or basis is it. This is the end of pain. There is an unborn, an unbecome, an unmade, an uncompounded; if there were not, there would be no escape from the born, the become, the made and the compounded." Udana, viii, 1–4. Quoted from Radhakrishnan and Moore, eds., *A Source Book in Indian Philosophy,* p. 635.

I think particularly in the present age—this very deep heart of religion is not possible for ordinary people to comprehend; it is too profound for most people. They require some symbolic way of representing it. I mean, this is a thing of experience. They may not come near this experience; they may not have the ability. So I think that this deep heart of religion is for a few people always.

A.G.: But don't you feel that it should be held up as the goal, as it were, to all people? And that somebody, or individuals, should try to get it understood that anything short of that is *not* the heart of religion? I suppose it would be true, would it, speaking in terms of the heart of religion—a person wouldn't really aspire to experience anything, would he?

BHIKKHU: How do you mean?

A.G.: Well, if you aspired toward something, wouldn't that be a form of clinging or projecting some idea? What I'm hinting at is the sunyata, emptiness doctrine, of which we heard a great deal in Japan.

BHIKKHU: By cultivating the right path one becomes a person with more desire for good than desire for evil. And eventually the desire for good becomes very strong, and they really are not desires. It's more that one's habitual practice is to do beneficial deeds and to be friendly and helpful; it becomes part of one's character. Now wisdom, or prajna, is the factor which permits one to go beyond good and evil—yes, the "void," sunyata, comes in there. But not before. One has to make allowance for the fact that most people have a considerable degree of defilement of mind, so their progress is step by step. As the Buddha said in his teaching, the doctrine (dhamma) does not suddenly become deep; it's like the ocean which shelves out gradually to become deeper and deeper. That's why monks may sit around in a Zen monastery for twenty years or so, because they are being matured, they are ripening. The ways are various, and the speed is not the same for everybody. So the deepest levels of wisdom, voidness, can be discovered only by the people who have become ripe. The deeper levels of the ripening process, the samadhi, usually require a teacher, because in meditation all sorts of strange things can happen, as well as the more expected things.

A.G.: That seems to be the common experience. So the saying, "Do not say good, do not say bad" is not merely a Zen saying, but a Buddhist saying at the prajna level, presumably.

BHIKKHU: The thing about Zen, and the trouble with it as far as the West goes, is that people don't realize that many of the words of the Zen masters *are* at the highest level, and when they were spoken they had a real significance for those people who heard them. But if somebody comes along, a college student or some such, buys a book on Zen and reads these things, supposing he's not a very spiritually advanced person, well, then, he's likely to get it all mixed up.

A.G.: Yes, he's liable to think he's got carte blanche to do whatever he likes.

H.T. (my friend-companion-secretary): Perhaps that's one reason why the negative theology in Christianity is so little adverted to publicly: because if you get the idea that nothing can be attributed to God, that qualities like good and evil are anthropomorphic modes of speaking, then people will stop thinking and talking about God—until they learned that that was speaking on a very high level, which is difficult for the mind to attain.

A.G.: But could it be that the time is coming when an effort must be made to get that understood? Because I think in the West people are pretty fed up with anthropomorphic gods.

H.T.: Back to the college student reading Zen and getting it, understandably, mixed up because he doesn't realize at what level it was spoken of: I have a feeling that those college students in the West may be somehow more capable of getting things back in focus than they would have been perhaps a generation or two ago. I think there's something there that they're looking for.

BHIKKHU: Certainly, they're looking for something.

Later, in Bangkok, I met a Western scientist, a layman, Dr. Robert Exell, who had become a Buddhist. We discussed the Buddhist view of Christianity and the recurring question: whether Buddhism was or was not atheistic.

A.G.: Could you volunteer any insights concerning the similarities or contrasts between Buddhism and Christianity?

DR. R.E.: Well, from what I've gradually learned and developed in my own mind, I would think that at the beginning Buddhism makes less demands on one's belief. I feel that Christianity says you must believe this and you must believe that before you can do anything. Faith seems to be the fundamental requirement. In

Buddhism on the other hand, again the way I have discovered it, it seems that faith is only a kind of inducement, it's not the real thing. And Buddhism tends to say, well, as for doctrine, you can investigate it yourself. Take it or leave it; you're not required to believe it. There is a sermon delivered by the Buddha, which was a response to a number of lay people who went to him. They lived in a town where there were many religious teachers all teaching different things. The Buddha was asked, since all these teachers teach different doctrines, how can we tell which one is correct? And the Buddha said, you shouldn't rely on tradition or ancient texts, or simply because you have some kind of personal respect or faith in him; you should rely on experience, rely on your own observations. If what a person teaches is in accordance with the facts, then you can accept that doctrine. If it isn't, then you can reject it. And since I've been trained as a scientist, that's very appealing. Whereas in Christianity you're expected to believe things which seemed to be improbable, and in any case there didn't seem to be any way of verifying them. This is originally what made me go toward Buddhism rather than Christianity. I wouldn't say I entirely agree with this now. At a later stage I think one's philosophical views change and one can derive something of value from both. But I think that at the beginning, at least for me, the faith approach was not the right one. The try-it-for-yourself Buddhist approach I found more appealing.

A.G.: So you would repudiate the idea that Buddhism is atheistic, would you?

DR. R.E.: Well, now, if you're going to say that God is the Almighty Creator upon which the whole of the universe depends, as in Christianity, then I think you would say that Buddhism is atheistic, because Buddhism does not say that there is such a God. But if you're going to regard gods as heavenly beings, rather like the Greek gods, who don't have the absolute qualities of the Christian God, then I'd say it was theistic.

A.G.: Do you think that the Buddha himself was perhaps more an agnostic than an atheist? Would he perhaps just have said, we don't know? "I preach suffering and the way to deliverance from suffering; work out your salvation with diligence. Be a light unto yourselves." And so on. Couldn't he have said, God may or may not exist, but we just don't know if he does or not? What we do

know is the fact of unhappiness, the impermanence of all that
exists, and how to deal with those problems. Couldn't that have
been his way of putting it, or something like that?

DR. R.E.: Well, I think that if one accepts that the Buddha is enlightened, as Buddhists do, then it would not be correct to say that it's
not knowable. That is to say that although perhaps the ordinary
person would not know, I don't think that could be applied to the
Buddha.

A.G.: On the Buddhist premises, I think that that is a very fair reply:
he would not be agnostic about what was knowable.

DR. R.E.: Buddha himself would not be agnostic, but I think he
would tend to avoid such questions, avoid discussing that kind of
problem on the whole. It would depend very much on who he
was talking to, what that person's particular religious problems
were. Some people would ask him these philosophical questions,
whether the world was finite or infinite, and so on. There may
have been someone who asked him whether there was an almighty God or not, although I can't remember that. But in any
instance I know, the god has always been regarded as deficient in
some way compared with the Christian idea of God. If there
were some question, philosophical or religious, the Buddha
would always know better than any god. In fact there are stories
about dialogues between Buddha and a god, or between Buddha
and some human being who asks about the gods.

While in Thailand, I had the privilege of a long conversation
with Mr. John Blofeld—yet another Westerner become Buddhist, an
author and recognized authority on the religious situation in China
and Tibet. We began with a reference to several Chinese Buddhist
temples of the Mahayana school, which existed in and around Bangkok. He alluded to one in particular, which we afterward visited
together, since he wished me to meet the Abbot. He "really is a
highly spiritual man, a most admirable person and someone whom
one likes to be with, one of those quiet people whose quietness you
can actually feel." Later the same day I met this monk, and he made
just such an impression on me. Mr. Blofeld acted as interpreter, but
the conversation was rather halting because, as he pointed out, "He
speaks to me in Cantonese, which I don't understand very well, and
I speak to him in Mandarin, which he doesn't understand very well."

The Abbot was most welcoming. It appeared that in China Catholicism is known as the "Lord of Heaven religion," and that once a year Chinese Buddhists have a festal day on which they worship "Heaven"; in consequence, I was being received as a "within man" rather than a "without man." This spirit of a deeper ecumenism made its presence felt again and again throughout my visit to India and Thailand. Both Hindus and Buddhists would offer freely, when invited and when they had any, their impressions of Christianity, but with no suggestion that their own religion was better, or that they in some unique way "possessed" the truth. Doctrinal formulations and distinctive modes of worship, I found, were considered hardly worth discussion. The interest of those I met with was in *practice*, particularly meditative and contemplative practice. When you reach the level of deep meditation, I was repeatedly told, human beings discover their unity; the differences between religious beliefs scarcely matter. It is usually better to leave the externals of each religion undisturbed, for these are probably the best means for those accustomed to them to reach the depths of the spiritual life. "Beneath all sorts of differences among people following the great religions," said the Chinese Abbot, "the essential thing is the heart, the mind. The higher the level of spiritual attainment the less fundamental difference there is between the various groups and religions."

Apart from meeting this most reassuring personality, relaxed and at one with himself, I was grateful to have been able to experience at least once in my journey a living contact with China. At Hong Kong I had touched the barbed-wire fence, the only barrier separating the British colony from the mainland, and gazed in fascination at the borders of that proud and ancient country. Traveling by sea southwest to Macau, I watched the coastline, and in the town itself, where Portuguese control is no more than nominal, I found myself for a few hours virtually inside Communist China. For me, however, this was not "Red China," but the civilization that had produced, six centuries before Christ, Confucius and Lao Tzu. Chairman Mao—whose education until he was twenty-six was Confucian—could have pondered in his youth such observations of the sage as, "The superior man is not absolutely for or against anything in the world. He supports only what is right." He is "not partisan but for all." He preserves his openness. "When he does not understand something, he is reticent." He is "firm in character, but not obstinate," "congenial without stooping to vulgarity," "self-confident but not self-righteous."

Or Lao Tzu: "Be humble; you will remain yourself. Be flexible, bend, and you will be straight. Be ever receptive and you will be satisfied . . . Thus the truly wise seek Unity, they embrace oneness, and become examples for all the world. Not revealing themselves, they shine; not self-righteous, they are distinguished; not self-centered, they are famous; not seeking glory, they are leaders. Because they are not quarrelsome no one quarrels with them. Thus it is as the ancients said: 'To yield is to retain Unity.' The truly wise have Unity, and the world respects them." Who knows but that Mao Tse-tung's remote ancestors, reclining on silken cushions, surrounded by the long-cherished decorum of ancient China, could have read these words when freshly minted—while my own forebears in faraway Britain, adorned with blue paint and clad in animal skins, were emerging from their mud huts to greet the barbarian day?

During my stay in Bangkok I was particularly impressed by a young Bhikkhu in his late twenties, who acted as interpreter at a conference in which I was involved. Though he had never been outside Asia, he spoke English extremely well and discharged his task without faltering throughout a somewhat intricate discussion. Moreover he was suffering some discomfort, having had a recent operation on one eye, which was shaded. Yet his manner exhibited in an indescribable way, to a degree unique in my experience, the Buddhist quality of metta—friendliness, loving-kindness. His demeanor was curiously dispassionate and unemotional, yet he appeared as amiability personified. He had "the festal air, the radiant look" which now and again one observes in a Western monk or religious. Its source, I think, does not lie in extraordinary virtue or exceptional continence—though both are more than likely to be there—but in being attuned to what is real in all its depth and fluidity, a happy willingness to sit down quietly before whoever comes one's way, to observe with interest, to respond and felicitate.

During the conference we had established an immediate rapport, so that when the formalities were over, we lingered as if by mutual consent. I asked him gently if he believed in God. He said that he did not believe in any one Creator of the universe, and he referred to the Buddhist doctrine of dependent origination. I asked him what he thought of Christ. He said that all he knew of him was that he held much the same place for Christians as the Lord Buddha did for Buddhists. He added that he had sometimes seen a crucifix; it caused him distress and he thought it a very repellent religious emblem.[47] I asked him if he believed in personal immortality. He smiled and said that he was not sure but that he was prepared to wait and see.

As he had set aside the three basic truths around which center the hopes and fears of the majority of Christians, I asked him if he could tell me what it was that made him so evidently happy. He said that when one is striving to remove from oneself the sole cause of suffering, namely, the triple fires of hatred, lust, and illusion—then you are on the way to nirvana (he gave it the Pali pronunciation, nibbana), and therefore you could not fail to be happy. "And what," I asked, "is nibbana?" Again he seemed mildly amused. "The word means a blowing out (of fire), an extinction through lack of fuel. Much more than that I cannot say, but I'm not worried about it." Then he took down a book from its shelf and showed me, in English, the following text from the Dhammapada, the "Way of Righteousness":

"He insulted me, he struck me,
     He defeated me, he robbed me!"
Those who harbour such thoughts
     Are never appeased in their hatred . . .
But those who do not harbour them
     Are quickly appeased.

Never in this world is hate
     Appeased by hatred;
It is only appeased by love—
     This is the eternal law.

Victory breeds hatred,
     For the defeated lie down in sorrow.
Above victory or defeat,
     The calm man dwells in peace.

47. This sentiment was expressed to me several times when I was in the East. The depiction of an almost naked human being nailed to a cross as an object to be revered is unintelligible, with its presentation of barbarous cruelty, to a devout Buddhist, who is predisposed to regard violent death in any form as the result of "bad karma."

vi. The Tantra

The Tantra is a risky subject for a Westerner to tackle; it is also one that is intriguing and challenging. Besides, we may discover that it has some fruitful implications for Christianity and that the word "obscene," which slips so easily from the pens of Western scholars when they are alluding to it—or for that matter in their discussions of certain aspects of Indian religion in general—does not quite meet the situation. It cannot be repeated too often that to impose Judaeo-Christian moral categories upon the Hindu-Buddhist tradition is to preclude any real understanding of it. Tantra came up several times in the course of various discussions, and it occurred to me that we might then be touching all too briefly on the heart of the matter. This is certainly the standpoint of Tibetan Buddhism, which regards the Hinayana, the Mahayana, and the Tantrayana[48] as successive stages on the path to enlightenment. Therefore, I shall here reproduce what was said about it in the course of my travels, then outline my own certainly inadequate understanding of its nature and background, adding perhaps one or two quite tentative conclusions.

Leading into the discussion of Tantric practice, Mr. John Blofeld, one of my kind instructors in Bangkok began with the mandala, that is, a diagram used—particularly among the Tibetans and also in the Shingon school of Japanese Buddhism—in invocations, meditation, and temple services. It was my young companion, Harold Talbott, who more than once, and much to my satisfaction, would raise the topic of the Tantra, typically expressing the interests of his generation. We spoke first of the actual appearance of mandala.

H.T.: I understand a mandala is square, is that correct?

J.B.: A mandala is square on the outside, and then it's usually a series of concentric circles within. But it's always based on a cross

48. The nonspecialist reader may care to be reminded that "yana" signifies career, vehicle, or means of progress. In the context it connotes a vehicle of salvation from the round of samsara (i.e., daily life, the world of flux, change, and ceaseless becoming in which we live). Thus for these three terms read successively: "the small vehicle" (of salvation); "the great vehicle"; "the vehicle of the Tantra." "Tantra" means thread, loom, or warp, and so implies in practice "obtaining the inner essence."

shape, because you have what are called the five primordial Buddhas or what Westerners (following a purely Nepalese tradition) call Adibuddhas, which are aspects of wisdom, or you can say aspects of reality, or in Christian terms, of God. You see, the central one is the dharmakaya[49] form or pure unadulterated spirit, and then there are four to north, south, east, and west, which have their appropriate colors and significances. And these form the center of a typical mandala. It's sometimes expressed in the form of five dots •••• and then perhaps there will be some minor figures •••• but, then, the mandala can be without figures at all.

H.T.: What is the depiction then?

J.B.: A kind of geometrical design.

H.T.: With the implication of those five Adibuddhas, five aspects of the Absolute?

J.B.: Yes, but then you see, when one goes more deeply into this division of, shall we say, pure unadulterated reality into five, we find that it is reflected in everything. I mean that every single force or object in the universe is also divisible into five, and then again and beyond that. So that what is in a sense a form of divinity or Buddhahood, looked at another way is true of you or me or of this table.

A.G.: All have the Buddha—in the sense of Absolute—nature?

J.B.: Yes, in this philosophy there is no distinction, I mean no ultimate distinction between this and that or I and you. These are all temporary rather than arbitrary distinctions . . . Mandalas are fascinating things. Take C. J. Jung in Switzerland dealing with odd people, I mean Swiss maidservants and people like that, who couldn't possibly have had any connection with Tibet. Very often during the course of treatment, he'd get them to draw things that they'd visualized, and what they drew very often had the perfect characteristics of the Tibetan mandala, which is extremely interesting because it shows that it is not, as one might think, that the Tibetans had certain deities or aspects of the Buddha which they then decided arbitrarily to place in a certain form, but rather that there is some spiritual experience common to man which when expressed in visual form is like that.

49. Dharmakaya: dharma body, the underlying principle of Mahayana Buddhism; the Buddha considered as the Absolute.

A.G.: And what is supposed to happen, or what does happen, as one contemplates the mandala in the right spirit?

J.B.: If you contemplate it, normally with the teaching associated with it, which is often quite complicated and which will vary a bit according to the mandala and also to the person who is being taught, it helps one to achieve spiritual states, which certainly can be achieved without the mandala. But it is one of those things which I suppose you find in all religions—what I like to call the equivalent of ropes and climbing boots and that sort of thing, to get to the top of the mountain. Some people can do it without, but if you have them it's easier.

A.G.: And the state is what? Is it samadhi, deep objectless awareness?

J.B.: Yes, but samadhi not in the sense of blankness necessarily, although one aspect may be like that; rather it's a state in which you intuitively perceive the nature of reality and how from *one* all things are built up into *many*. There are many, many states, and by contemplating the mandala you may go deeper and deeper. It's very interesting.

A.G.: I'm sure it is. And so that is part of the devotional life of individuals, is that it?

J.B.: Oh, yes. But very rarely in Thailand. Most of all in Tibet, then Mongolia, and formerly at least in China. But these mandalas—it's not a matter of just seeing them, so to speak, by chance in your meditation, but rather of using them before you start your meditation.

A.G.: Does this have a link with the Tantric form. . . ?

J.B.: This is Tantric, yes.

A.G.: What does the word "Tantric" mean?

J.B.: Well, this is very difficult. Nobody seems to know exactly the origin of it, but I think I can explain it to you roughly. It's got a bad name in England, well, in the West generally I would say, so much so that when people ask me what kind of Buddhism I follow, I prefer to say Vajrayana,[50] because if I say Tantric, they'll

50. "The Vajrayana is the *Adamantine Vehicle*. The Vajra is literally the Thunderbolt which Indra, like Zeus and Thor, used with great effect as a weapon. Itself unbreakable, it breaks everything else. In later Buddhist philosophy the word is used to denote a kind of supernatural substance which is as hard as a diamond, as clear as empty space, as irresistible as a thunderbolt. The Vajra is now identified with ultimate reality, with Dharma and enlighten-

think I'm indulging in all sorts of sexual amusements [general laughter at this]. . . . But actually Tantra is a method of employing everything for enlightenment. This may not have been tried by the Zen people, but I'm sure they'll agree with the theory behind it: that you rise above distinctions of good and bad—as in Zen. That doesn't mean that everybody is free to be good or bad as he likes, but at a certain point you reach that freedom.

A.C.: "Do not say good, do not say bad." Isn't that what in point of fact they do say?

J.B.: Now here is a very simple kind of Tantric method which I happen to use myself because it's very easy. It does describe the whole thing at a very low level. When I was in Sikkim I was living on a mountain in a Tibetan monastery, and the Tibetans were producing sound all through the night: vroom vroom vroom vroom—that sort of thing, you know—doing their liturgy and at the same time beating drums. And at the bottom of the mountain there were two torrents that crashed together with a terrific RRrrlllmm sort of noise. Now these sort of noises were very effective, I found. I mean they helped me with my meditation a lot. Then coming back to Bangkok and staying in a house which had an open space outside: every night at about two o'clock in the morning, the drivers of the three-wheeled vehicles (taxis) would use this space to teach new drivers how to drive—all going along in bottom gear, you see, so you get Aaarrraaahhm, you know! So this was about the time that I used to do my meditation, and you can imagine that I found it very tiresome. I mean no sooner had I just got into—you know, taken my seat and so on, when suddenly these dreadful machines started up. And then I remembered the Tantric teaching of one of my teachers who said, "You regard every individual as Buddha and every sound as the sound of a mantra,[51] the sound of the Dharma, and every place as nirvana."

---

ment. The Vajrayana mythologizes the doctrine of Emptiness, and teaches that the adept, through a combination of rites, is reinstated into his true diamond-nature, takes possession of a diamond body, is transformed into a diamond-being (Vajrasattva). The beginnings of the Vajrayana may go back to ca 300 A.D. As it is known to us, the system developed from ca 600 A.D. onward." Conze, *Buddhism: Its Essence and Development*, p. 178.

51. Mantra: a formula or invocation often described as magical, based on a scientific knowledge of the hidden power of sound. The most famous mantra (Tibetan and Vajrayana) is *Om mani padme hum*, which is often rendered in English as "Ah! the jewel is indeed in the lotus."

So I thought, all right, every sound is the sound of a mantra, so in my mind I just converted the noise made by those machines into the remembered sound of the lamas' voices and the drums and the water. It was marvelous.

A.G.: Very remarkable.

J.B.: And this is a case of using a hindrance to make something useful out of something which by itself is tiresome. As for the sexual connotations that Tantra has, among the teachings given, there certainly are some about sex. These include a technique practiced by certain very advanced yogins[52] and another sometimes taught to ordinary married couples. People, I mean laymen, find it difficult to eschew sex. If they find it difficult, no doubt some teaching will be given in individual cases, so that they can at least make some use of it by putting their minds into a certain state during the time that sex is being performed. But I would say that this is only a tiny part of the whole. I would say less than . . .

A.G.: I asked a Bhikkhu the other day whether there was any equivalent in Buddhism to the Christian idea, certain aspects of the Christian idea, not of repudiating sex but of sanctifying it. He didn't think there was. I was just wondering if the Tantra . . .

J.B.: I don't think I would go so far as to say that either technique was sanctifying it; they both make use of it as an instrument for transcending duality, and the second merely makes it less of a nuisance to the spiritual life. I haven't studied the technique, but I'm told that it consists in achieving the skill to meditate on something that helps toward enlightenment at the very moment of orgasm. But this is not the main point. The reason why the Tantra has been given such a bad name in general is because a lot of the treatises or manuals of practice are written in a highly sexual vocabulary. And there's one very good book of Buddhist texts coming from the four main sources: China, Japan, this part of the world [i.e., Southeast Asia], and Tibet. The translator of the Tibetan part was a Catholic Tibetan scholar.

H.T.: Snellgrove?

J.B.: Yes. Well, he knows a lot of Tibetan but, being a Catholic, I wonder if he can get the proper oral teaching because he can't worship the Buddha and go through the initiations and so on. In any case, he translated this section quite literally—something about a young girl being brought before the altar, and so on and

52. A variant of yogi, i.e., one who practices yoga.

so on. You see? But this actually refers to a process which goes on
within the human being himself, and every human being has a
male and female element. For some purposes, this force down
here (pointing to the pelvis), which in this type of meditation
one tries to bring up to the head, is equated with the female
force, and it is intended that it should ultimately come into union
with the male force.[53] But this is such a difficult and possibly dangerous meditation that it should not be undertaken without careful teaching and instruction. Therefore, the books were written in
this form. This has led to a great deal of misunderstanding.

A.G.: They distinguish, don't they, between a right-handed Tantra
and a left-handed Tantra. Is that right?

J.B.: Well, in India there are some Hindu Tantrists, and I'm told
that among the left-handed Tantrists in India there are some of
them who teach that the symbolic language of the books is, at
least on some occasions, to be acted out literally. I have never
come across a case of that among the Tibetans, though I have
heard that some advanced yogins do, after a strictly chaste ap-
prenticeship lasting perhaps twenty years, perform a Yoga involving actual sexual union. I have read books by Englishmen
saying that this is so, but never on very reliable authority. Most
Tantrists do not, I am quite sure, practice that particular Yoga.

H.T.: Vajrayana is not left-handed Tantra?

J.B.: Vajrayana? Well, it includes it all. But left-handed is not and
could not be a Buddhist Tantric term, for it implies dualistic acceptance and rejection. Conze, I think, did wrong by using it in a
Buddhist context. All the Tibetan teachers I have studied under,
most of whom belong to the Nyingma-pa or Red Hat sect, and
are therefore very often married men and not monks, and there-

---

53. Again, Mr. Christmas Humphreys is illuminating on this point: "The
Tantras are writings dating from the sixth century A.D. in India. There are two
types, Hindu and Buddhist. Both are systems of meditation with the use of
ritual, highly cryptic in form, the meaning being handed down from guru to
chela. Both symbolize the basic duality of manifestation in figures, in sculp-
ture or in pictures, composed of some deity or aspect of Reality with a female
partner locked in sexual embrace. In the Hindu Tantras these Shaktis represent
the female 'power' of the god, whereas in the Vajrayana the female represents
Wisdom (*Prajna*), and the male is the active 'use' or compassionate 'skill in
means' of that Wisdom. The ritual to aid meditation involves the use of Mantras, Mudras (= ritual gestures of the hands) and Yantras (= symbolic dia-
grams, i.e., Mandalas)." *A Popular Dictionary of Buddhism*, pp. 192–193.

fore people who would be likely to employ sexual techniques if these were common, have all emphasized chastity as most important for progress, you see? But, failing chastity, well then, controlled sex, which means married life and that sort of thing. They would say that's not a great hindrance. But the idea of mixing up sexual practice with religion as a widespread technique is a notion I've seen only in books by foreigners; I've never heard any such thing from Tibetans. I can't say abuses don't exist, but I'm pretty sure that if sexual intercourse occurs, except as something rare and far removed from sexual gratification, it's one of those minor aberrations. It's not part of the main stream of Tibetan Buddhism.

Some weeks later, when we were in India at Banaras, my companion again raised the question of the Tantra—this time with a Hindu professor whom we have already met, Dr. T. R. V. Murti.

H.T.: I want to ask you about the development in Indian Buddhism of the Tantra. As I understand it, the central doctrine of the Tantra is the nonduality of samsara and nirvana.

DR. T.M.: Yes. You see, Tantra is not a substitute for the philosophy of sunyata ("emptiness"); in fact, it's the basic conception. Only it aims at achieving this by certain techniques, by some shock treatment as it were. How do you achieve the nondualism of reality? By doing away with the apparent duality. That is, it does it through what I would call unorthodox means, or a shock treatment. It brings in certain practices. Suppose your mind is bipolar all the time; suppose it is addicted to "is and is not," "pain and pleasure," "good and bad," "right and wrong," "black and white." Now the Tantrist would say, "You've got to achieve a position beyond this kind of duality. How to do that? You are to do it consciously by abolishing the distinctions." For instance, good and bad: if you eat some food which is bad, very dirty and so on, or if you consort with some female who is forbidden. All these ways . . . these are certain techniques they have evolved, by which the mind is subjected to a kind of shock treatment. It unlearns all it has learned through civilization and culture.

H.T.: Does this follow a period of ascetic discipline? Would a person who was advised to adopt these shock treatments to do away

with the polarity his mind was accustomed to already have had
to practice conventional discipline in a religious setting?

DR. T.M.: Yes, he already has had that. . . . All Tantra, though the
term "right-handed" is used, all Tantra is really left-handed.

A.G.: It sounds as if you don't approve of the Tantra.

DR. T.M.: No, I won't say that I disapprove. But it is not meant for
all. It is not meant for—well, if you can stand the shock and if
you can come out sane, that's all right. But if you can't stand the
shock, then you'll become insane. Your mind will be shattered
actually.

H.T.: That's what the Tibetans themselves say. They say that if you
go along this way it's harder and harder to get back.

DR. T.M.: Not only that. The percentage of success is also very limited.

A.G.: Few people survive?

DR. T.M.: Few people survive, so that it's not safe. So only *vira puru-
sha*, as they say, men of courageous temperament, are chosen for
these Tantric practices, not the creaturely or the ordinary type.
Whereas in the ordinary way you may not achieve as great a
success or as quickly, as thoroughly as you would in the Tantra,
but it is safe. It's a pedestrian way, of course, you don't jump like
a jet, but you are safe. It's a kind of spiritual psychology, the
Tantra. It's a case of treating the mind to certain shock treatment.

A.G.: It must require a very skilled guru.

DR. T.M.: Yes, not only that. He addresses himself to your unconscious processes. A guru sees through to your possibilities, your
potentialities—not what you are, actually speaking, but what you
were and what you could be. He sees through your unconscious.
And that is why a guru is always needed for Tantra, a very realized guru.

H.T.: But the difference between shock treatment, say, and the Tantra is that Tantra is existential whereas shock treatment is something applied from without. It doesn't fundamentally increase vision, but Tantra involves your moral, existential nature.

A.G.: The Hindu Tantra is different from the Buddhist?

DR. T.M.: The same thing, only it puts it a different way. Shiva and
Shakti instead of prajna (wisdom) and karuna (compassion).

As the discussion became rather technical, we may leave it at this
point. In the course of my wanderings among the Tibetan Buddhists,

along the slopes of the Himalayas, from Dharmsala through Darjeeling into Sikkim, I was able to deepen my understanding of the Tantra. Underlying it all is the Buddhist conviction that the polarities and dualisms of everyday life are only apparent; with insight and effort they can be overcome. The result is not a fusion of opposites, but a reaching beyond the opposites so that what gives substance to the opposition disappears. When this happens the realm of sunyata, emptiness, has been reached. Here is the area in which the supreme activities of wisdom (prajna) and compassion (karuna) can come fully into play, for the illusions of daily life lie exposed and the self-centered ego—always a block to complete fellow feeling with others —has become empty (sunya).

Here the Western, and particularly the Christian, reader should reflect that Buddhist thought, as it is concerned with practice, makes little claim to be an *ontology*, that is, to discuss reality in such Aristotelian terms as "being as such." To the assertion that A differs from B, the Creator differs from the creature—a Buddhist, I fancy, would reply: "I don't deny that that is so according to your way of thinking, your conceptualizations; but I'm not concerned with those. I must go by observation and experience." In other words, Buddhist thought is phenomenological rather than ontological, provided it be understood that the phenomena in this case involve not merely the external senses, but the total personality in its deepest experience. Thus, for example, to ask the question of how the Buddhist positions of sunyata, emptiness, and pratityasamutpada, dependent origination, accord with Catholic orthodoxy has no more relevance than to ask the same question about Einstein's theory of relativity—with which, indeed, the Buddhist positions may have some affinity. To apply notions derived from Biblical theology or scholastic philosophy to Buddhism does not illuminate the discussion; it is merely, in the neat academic phrase, to make a "category mistake."

> Since everything is relative (we do not know),
> What is finite and what is infinite?
> What means finite and infinite at once?
> What means negation of both issues?
>
> What is identity, and what is difference?
> What is eternity, what non-eternity?
> What means eternity and non-eternity together?
> What means negation of both issues?

> The bliss consists in the cessation of all thought,
> In the quiescence of plurality.
> No (separate) reality was preached at all,
> Nowhere and none by the Buddha.[54]

These lines from a "Treatise on the Middle Doctrine" were written by the Buddhist philosopher Nagarjuna; they are an expression of the madhyamika ("middle doctrine," i.e., midway between affirmation and negation, school of Mahayana Buddhism), and they bear upon the points of Buddhist doctrine we have just been considering. Before we return explicitly to the Tantra and the Tibetans, a phase in a discussion with Professor Misra at Banaras is worth recording, as he is actually commenting on the somewhat abstruse conceptions of Nagarjuna.

DR. M.: To me it seems that sunyata, as expounded by Nagarjuna, the great exponent of the Madhyamika philosophy, does not posit any Absolute as such; it does not propound any transcendent reality which may be said to be the essence of this world, or the ground of this world. Sunyata is what may be called prajna (wisdom). This is, as I said, awareness of the essencelessness of things, which is another way of expressing nirvana itself. Utter freedom! Sunyata represents that state where man realizes his freedom from karma, from rebirth, from ignorance, from desire. Utter freedom! We may explain it in this way: my point is that sunyata is ultimately utter freedom; it is nirvana. Now, if we say that sunyata is absolute, we are forced to conceive some reality which is there, even though it can't be described. The way some contemporary scholars try to interpret sunyata is, as you say, in the sense that sunyata comes very close to the Advaita (nondualist) view of Brahman (God). These scholars imply that sunyata posits some sort of Absolute, which is very much analogous to Brahman. Here I find difficulty, because Nagarjuna does not convey any idea of such an Absolute.

A.G.: But when one uses a word like "Absolute," the term and the concept, aren't we still in the realm of name and form? And you have to go beyond that.

DR. M.: Yes. But then, even our highest imagination of the Absolute

54. Quoted from Radhakrishnan and Moore, *A Source Book in Indian Philosophy*, p. 345.

does not free us from some sort of concept of *being*. That is, the Absolute has to be posited. It may not, if you like, be character-ized as being, because it transcends being. But "transcendence of being"—what can it mean? If you say that sunyata is Absolute and analogous to Brahman, then you are obliged to call this Ab-solute sat (being) or else you must call it "consciousness," pure consciousness. The Vijnanavadins do say that the Absolute is pure consciousness; they say it, but the Madhyamika school do not say that. They say that we can't describe it in any way, which does not necessarily mean that there is some "It" that can't be described. Both are negated; both knowing subject and known object are utterly negated. But I don't say that this is nihilism-sunyata. It is just realization of freedom. I will put it in two ways: sunyata is the realization of the essencelessness of things, and it is the realization of freedom, utter freedom.

A.G.: Assuming that to be Nagarjuna's position, did not your great Hindu theologian Shankara take it up and refute it?

DR. M.: Now, there is a difference of view in this regard. . . . It appears that the Buddhist dialectic has had some impact on the Vedanta. But then Shankara is very emphatic in affirming the Absolute and saying that the world is only "empirically" real, denying its ultimate reality. . . . As for Enlightenment, or Bud-dhahood, enlightenment *itself* is reality, in my view, not anything about which one is enlightened. And this is, according to me, the basic distinction between the Vedanta and the Madhyamika: that in Vedanta enlightenment is enlightenment of Brahman, the awareness of Brahman as the Absolute, and in Madhyamika en-lightenment, or prajna, does not mean the awareness of any real-ity. It means the awareness that things are essenceless or "sunya" (empty of essence), or the awareness of the relativity of things, and this is freedom. Positively it is freedom; negatively it is the awareness of the relativity of things.

The Tantra may be regarded as the full flowering of Buddhism, while the doctrine has its roots in the actual ministry of Gautama. He himself has entered nirvana, but his followers are in need of "skillful means" (upaya) supplied by the guru in order that they may grasp and apply the message. The Tantra has initiations, the purpose of which is "to introduce you to the true nature of mind." Tantric medi-

tation calls for a degree of concentration so far beyond the capacity
of the average Westerner that he should not attempt it without preliminary consultation and advice, together with actual supervision, at
least in the earlier stages. What is being aimed at is that "you can
concentrate on the object of your concentration with such force that
you lose consciousness of hearing, consciousness of feeling, consciousness of sight." It is in this procedure that the mandala, already
alluded to, comes into play. The end in view is so to concentrate on
the symbols displayed in the mandala that one literally identifies
with that which is symbolized—usually the Buddha himself, or one
or other or several of the multiplicity of his manifestations—and so
realizes emptiness (sunyata).

The suggestion has been made, not by Tibetans but by one familiar with the Christian tradition, that it would be easy to devise Catholic mandalas, which could serve a corresponding purpose. To some
extent, of course, this objective is already brought into effect by
means of the Church's sacred images and pictures. But as for carrying the process further, or developing the technique in any depth,
considering its possible consequences, I have my doubts. Pictorially,
there would be no problem: Christian iconography, centered on a
symbol for God, Jesus, or the Virgin Mary, is rich in possibilities of
adaptation to the structure of a mandala. But the dualistic, subject-
object mode of thought is so linked with Christianity that what is
called for in meditational practice with mandalas might turn out to
be inappropriate. However, the suggestion is not to be brushed aside
lightly at a time when the Church is apparently looking about for
ways—"skillful means" (upaya)—to renew itself.

What should never be lost sight of is that according to Tibetan
Buddhism prajna and karuna, wisdom and compassion, cannot be
separated, since they are complementary aspects of sunyata: the
awareness that all beings, including one's own empirical "self," are
empty of self-essence. In this condition one has achieved the ultimate freedom; one is liberated from "self." The heart of Buddhist
doctrine—or rather of the teaching combined with practice, which is
the meaning of the dharma—lies here, and with it the import of the
Buddha's statement: "Just as the ocean has but one taste, that of salt,
so has the Dharma but one taste, that of freedom." It is this freedom
that enables one to overcome the dualities—of you and me, yours
and mine—and so be as much concerned for other people as one is
for oneself. Such liberation, however, depends on the preceding "en-

lightenment," that is to say, the attainment or bringing into being of prajna. Only a truncated freedom can be exercised without this attainment, with the result that genuine compassion will inevitably be lacking.

Tantric initiations and meditational practices are directed to achieving the state of enlightenment, which can vary very much in degree and then under suitable conditions to exercising or "acting out" the ensuing freedom. Thus, despite the reservations made in an earlier discussion, I am able to state "from an authoritative source" (as the journalists say) that a Tibetan lama will instruct a student of reasonably advanced attainment in breath control to prevent the flow of semen. "Then the union of the yogin and the dakini [his female counterpart considered to be a 'female embodiment of intuitive knowledge as taught in the Tantras'] takes place." As a lighter side to this piece of intelligence it should be added that though the practice has long been considered appropriate for married people between themselves, "the problem is always to have a wife who is as highly attained in Tantric practice as oneself."

For the benefit of those who are disposed to be shocked, and also those who are not, let us try to sort out the moral of the story. As with doctrine, so with ethics; it is irrelevant to apply Western standards to the religions originating in India. Thus whenever the term "antinomian" appears in this context, as it frequently does, one is almost certainly dealing with an unsympathetic Christian writer, since antinomian means "against the law," and by long association, against the law of the Church. Hindu-Buddhist ethical requirements are at least as far-reaching and exacting as our own, in some respects they are more so, but they are basically different. Whether an action is right or wrong is to be determined not with reference to an external law but in terms of whether it helps or hinders the individual's progress to enlightenment and true freedom or, to make the same point in another way, whether the action is an exercise of wisdom (prajna) and compassion (karuna). The latter condition must be fulfilled if the action is to be regarded as right.

The possibilities of self-deception and even moral dissolution in such practices as the one just described must, I tend to think, be many and grave, and it is not in the least my purpose to defend, still less to advocate, them.[55] The suggestion here is merely that in the

---

55. For a brief and on the whole not very favorable account of Tantricism, see De Bary, *The Buddhist Tradition,* pp. 113–115.

West the link between the sex function and the deeper aspects of religion can bear further exploration. After all, it seems not unlikely that the time when man's physical life is pulsating at its highest should also be the moment when, were he sufficiently aware, he is consciously in close contact with life's source. While I was in India the topic came up for discussion more than once. Sometimes I would ask if Hinduism had any equivalent to the Christian concept of sanctifying, making holy, the sexual act. The question caused surprise; the act did not need to be made holy because it was holy already! The requirement was that while sex should be fully enjoyed the act should not be an occasion for mere self-indulgence; it must be appropriately controlled. When sexuality was employed in a strictly religious setting, it should be sublimated to a degree that spiritual awareness is not impaired. This means, according to yogic teaching, that the orgasm is itself spiritualized, with a consequent intensification of blissful feeling, and that there is no spilling of the male seed. How this works out in practice, I cannot say, but it is certainly held that by the properly directed practice of yoga, such control can be achieved, or rather that it happens that way without conscious effort.

It is worth noting also that an ascetic approach to sexuality, as advocated by the Church's teaching authority, is shared to the full by sections of Hinduism. Thus in his *Life of Mahatma Gandhi* Louis Fischer writes: "He always advocated birth control. The birth control he favored, however, was through self-control, through the power of the mind over the body. 'Self-control,' he wrote, 'is the surest and only method of regulating the birth rate.' Without such discipline, he contended, man was no better than a brute. He maintained that abstinence forever or for long periods was neither physically nor psychologically harmful." On the other hand, students of the human condition may care to correlate Gandhi's standpoint on emotional control with his biographer's reference to his family life: "From young manhood, he was sweet and kind toward everybody except his wife and sons. . . . He had an ungandhian coldness toward them. . . . As he was more severe with himself than with anybody else, so he was severest with his own boys."

It should be noted also that Tantric practice for many remains at the symbolic level, as I learned in Thailand. This was the only aspect of the Tantra touched on at the long discussion I was privileged to have with His Holiness the Dalai Lama. As a historian of Buddhism has pointed out: "Many Tantric circles practiced such rites only symbolically, and their teachers often produced works of considerable philosophical subtlety, while the ethical tone of some passages in the Tantricist Saraha's Treasury of Couplets, one of the last Buddhist works produced in India, is of the highest." [56] Here are some verses that throw another light on much that we have learned from the Tantricist just referred to.

> Thought is pure when consigned to the forehead.
> Do not then conceive differences in yourself.
> When there is no distinction between Body, Speech, and Mind,
> Then the true nature of the Innate shines forth.

> See thought as thought, O fool, and leave all false views,
> Gain purification in bliss supreme,
> For here lies final perfection.

> O know this truth,
> That neither at home nor in the forest does enlightenment dwell.
> Be free from prevarication
> In the self-nature of immaculate thought! [57]

Before concluding this section I shall suggest that there exists in the Catholic tradition what might fairly be called a "Christian Tantra." But speaking in general, whether there are any implications in Tantric symbolism that might be adapted to the religion of the West, I must leave to be worked out (should they exist) by a younger generation of theologians and psychologists. The "sexual revolution" of our time could well be nothing more than the old familiar pattern of moral degeneracy. On the other hand, it may indicate a failure on the part of educators, community leaders, and the clergy to face the human situation with the necessary insight, sympathy, and persuasive power. Most people have still to learn how to combine a full acceptance of every aspect of man's sexuality with selfless restraint in its enjoyment. Such restraint could amount, in certain cases, to a sublimation so intense as to become transphysical. How appropriate this is and how far it can be generalized, by means of symbolism and techniques to which the young and the not so young of today can be expected to respond, is precisely the question that needs to be examined.

So far as Church authority is concerned I offer the view that little

56. De Bary, *The Buddhist Tradition*, p. 114.
57. From Saraha's "Treasury of Songs," in Conze, *Buddhist Scriptures*, pp. 176, 178, 179.

is to be gained by wagging an admonitory finger. The stern ascetic can offer no more help to those obsessed by the climactic emotional experience than can the permissive churchman advising others, while being himself under pressure from his as yet unresolved inner personal conflicts. Much thought and discussion, long periods of calm meditation, some risks in experimentation may well be the preliminaries to reaching any assured conclusions of how the ethical traditions we have inherited are to be sifted, and possibly reinterpreted, in the light of all the knowledge available to us today. One point may be made with confidence: those who by their profession have embraced uncritically the Old Testament prophetic moralism based on the ethics deemed appropriate to a nomadic community wandering in the desert, settled though it might be in a pastoral way of life, with that ethics' total incomprehension and therefore abhorrence of the fertility rituals to be found in every primitive agricultural society, are poorly equipped to understand why the religions stemming from India make so great an appeal to the more thoughtful among compulsorily urbanized Western youth, cut off from their roots in nature yet by no means refractory to enlightened and even arduous discipline at the present time. As a corollary it may be said that the inheritors of the Pauline antifeminism, of the residual Manichaeism of Augustine, and of virginity as a supreme ideal cannot expect to be received as the best-qualified guides on how human life is to be conducted at its most vital point.

Finally, since I have raised the question, can we speak with any truth of a "Christian Tantra?" Let it be recalled that the word "Tantra" means "thread, loom or warp," and so implies in practice "reaching to the essence." We have seen that for Hinduism what is involved is transcending the apparent dualism between atman and Brahman and so *realizing* nonduality; for Buddhism it is the liberation of *enlightenment* whereby there is nonduality between samsara and nirvana. Christianity, because of its radical creature-Creator dualism, has no exact equivalent. Perhaps the nearest approximation to it is St. Paul's experience: "It is no longer I who live, but Christ who lives in me" (Galatians 2:20). Christian theology, as it has so far developed, has been insistent on maintaining the dualism between man and his God, and this attitude is reflected throughout the Church's liturgy. The text of 2 Peter 1:4, which refers to our being "partakers of the divine nature," though often referred to in theological trac-

tates on grace, has never been to the forefront of the Church's proclamation. Even in Christ the duality between the human and divine
natures—as we noted at the Council of Chalcedon (see p. 77)—was
emphasized, in the teeth of strong opposition, by the orthodox theologians.

And yet at the devotional level a continuous effort to overcome
this duality is evident. The inclusion of a series of erotic poems,
known as The Song of Solomon, in the Old Testament canon, and its
later interpretation by the Church, have considerable significance.
What might be called a "Tantric strain" is observable, for example, in
Ephesians 5:21ff., where the relationship between Christ and the
Church is compared to that of husband and wife. This passes from
the institutional to the personal and comes to full flowering, with
modes of expression as erotic as anything to be found in Tibetan
Buddhism, with the Catholic mystics—or rather, "realists," as I prefer to designate those who are so preoccupied with the ultimate reality.

> With lance embarbed with love
> He took His aim—
> One with its Maker hence
> My soul became.
>
> No love but His I crave
> Since self to Him I gave,
> For the Beloved is mine own,
> I His alone!

So wrote St. Teresa of Avila in a poem rendered in English as
"The Compact." [58] Nor does the need for any differentiation in sex
trouble so exalted a spirit as St. Bernard of Clairvaux. By way of
commentary on The Song of Solomon we read:

> First of all, I should like to know if to any of you it has been given
> to say with sincerity, "Let Him kiss me with the kiss of His mouth." For
> it is not every man that can speak thus from his heart. But he who has

58. In *Minor Works of St. Teresa*, trans. Benedictines of Stanbrook (London: Thomas Baker, 1913), pp. 17–18. Subsequent to drafting this chapter, I
had occasion to spend ten days in Spain and was able to visit the Monastery of
the Incarnation at Avila. It was a moving experience to stand within the very
convent parlor where Teresa and John of the Cross, though divided by the cus-
tomary grill, had together been transported in ecstasy, so it is related, while dis-
coursing on the Holy Trinity.

even once received this spiritual kiss from the lips of Christ, such a one will surely solicit again what he has learned by experience to relish, and will ask that the favour be repeated. In my opinion, no one can ever know what it is except him who has experienced it.[59]

St. John of the Cross employs a symbolism as emphatic as the Tibetan vajrayana (the vehicle of the thunderbolt), with its celebrated mantra, *Om mani padme hum:* "Ah! The jewel is indeed in the lotus!" —of which the significance is probably sexual, implying that the Bodhisattva has united with his female counterpart.

> Oh flame of love so living,
> How tenderly you force
> To my soul's inmost core your fiery probe!
> Since now you've no misgiving,
> End it, pursue your course
> And for our sweet encounter tear the robe! [60]

It is not, then, only among the "pagans" that religious devotion and sexual symbolism are closely blended. The implications of this state of affairs, as I have suggested, may require a more honest confrontation and closer study than they have so far received from those concerned to maintain the traditional religion of the West. A century, perhaps, will elapse before the Church's teaching on these and other matters achieves the reformulation—or better still, the higher degree of fluidity—toward which it now appears to be tentatively moving. There is no hurry: better that attempts to say the decisive word—if indeed such a word can ever be said—come late instead of early, wisely terminating rather than sharply provoking exhaustive discussion. Meanwhile, by way of emphasizing the fallible character of these remarks, I shall steal a quatrain from one of the favorite poets of my youth, James Elroy Flecker. With its title adapted to our present context, a change of more than half the wording in the first two verses, yet with its distinctive rhythm (I believe) preserved, here —its import being applicable to the entire contents of this book—is how it might read:

59. St. Bernard of Clairvaux, *Sermons on the Canticle of Canticles*, translated by a priest of Mount Melleray (Dublin: Browne & Nolan, 1920), p. 20.
60. St. John of the Cross, "Songs of the Soul in Intimate Communication and Union with the Love of God," in *Poems*, trans. Roy Campbell (Harmondsworth: Penguin Books, 1960), p. 45.

TO A THEOLOGIAN A HUNDRED YEARS HENCE

I who am dead one hundred years,
  And wrote of thoughts that could be wrong,
Send you my words for messengers
  The way I shall not pass along.

vii. His Holiness the Dalai Lama

"On the night of November 23, 1967," I wrote in the travel journal I was keeping, "my companion and I left New Delhi for Pathankot in the Northern Punjab. Arriving there at 7:15 A.M. we were met by a young Tibetan with an army jeep." So started the long prearranged and ever-to-be-remembered visit to the exiled Dalai Lama. The overnight journey by train still left us some ninety miles from Dharmsala.

We traveled by road eastward for exactly three hours, with the foothills and the snow-covered upper slopes of the Himalayas before us almost all the way. The morning was perfect: no clouds, a bright sun, the clearest air. The grandeur of the view confronting us was beyond description. Scenic detail is apt to escape my notice; it was the sheer vastness and bulk of the Himalayan range, only a fraction of which could be seen, that had an overawing effect. On the journey we met no cars, only local buses and army vehicles. This whole area of the Punjab, near the Indian border, is largely occupied by the military. No strangers are admitted without careful inquiry, since the Dalai Lama's person is under the protection of the Indian Government, hosts to the Tibetan government in exile.

The political atmosphere reminded me of the Dalai Lama's visit to Japan, where he was surrounded by a large Japanese military escort and secret-service protection. This was vividly in my mind, as I had happened to be in Tokyo and Kyoto when both those cities were astir with his presence. While I was in Thailand, again it happened that the Dalai Lama came to Bangkok, and was greeted at the airport by King Bhumibol Adulyadej. There was much excitement in this almost entirely Buddhist city, but the Dalai Lama's movements were kept secret for fear of an assassination attempt by the local Chinese Communists.

This whole situation can be understood only by those who recall the flight of the Dalai Lama from Tibet because of the Chinese invasion and persecution in 1959. The story is most readably and touchingly told by the Dalai Lama himself in his autobiography, *My Land and My People,* a book that one would like to see perpetually in print. Although Tibetan Buddhism in its native setting has been virtually destroyed, the Dalai Lama still remains the center of his exiled people's devotion and the head of the Tibetan state, insofar as it may be said to exist. The present Dalai Lama is the fourteenth of his line; he is held to be the living embodiment of the Bodhisattva of Compassion and by reason of what he represents the most revered figure in the Buddhist world. He is treated by his subjects with an honor far surpassing that shown by Catholics to the Pope.

Against this background we arrived at Dharmsala at about 10:15 A.M. and were welcomed at a local guesthouse by the vice president of the Dalai Lama's Council for Religious Affairs. We were presented with gifts of white scarves—the traditional form of greeting and courtesy from Tibetans when meeting those whom they regard as distinguished guests. Later we were informed rather touchingly that we were to be under no expense, since we were the guests of the Dalai Lama and the government of Tibet. At 1:30 P.M. a military jeep arrived to take us to Upper Dharmsala. Already 6,000 feet above sea level not far below the clearly visible Himalayan snow line, we were driven up what must have been another 1,000 feet to Upper Dharmsala and the modest estate of the Dalai Lama. At intervals there were a succession of military checkpoints until we came to the final one, which marked unmistakably the entrance to the Dalai Lama's quarters. Here, despite long-term preliminary arrangements, all particulars were taken by Indian and Tibetan officials: name, address, purpose of visit, passport number, etc. Then we were searched for any concealed weapons. The fear of some attempt on the Dalai Lama's life is ever present in the minds of those responsible for his safety. Only after all precautions had been taken were we allowed to proceed. My companion also made a record of the event, from which he has kindly allowed me to quote.

From the check point at the entrance to the grounds, Dom Aelred and I went on foot up the hill to the compound. Standing on the terrace before an administration building to the right of the residence was a young lama; he came down the steps and shook hands. "I am Tenzin Geyche," he told us, "and I will be your interpreter for your audience with His Holiness." This is the honorific title, by analogy with His Holiness the Pope, invariably used by the Dalai Lama's entourage when referring to him in the presence of English-speaking Westerners. He led us to a reception room, where he left us waiting for perhaps five minutes. On his return we accompanied him across the compound to a lawn in front of the Dalai Lama's residence, nothing more pretentious than a large bungalow—a striking contrast with the Potala he had left behind in Lhasa, "the most magnificent palace in the world, in size, site, and contents." On the porch of the bungalow stood the figure, so well known from photographs, of the fourteenth Dalai Lama. He was dressed in the maroon robes of the Tibetan lama. Standing in profile with a slight smile on his face, he beckoned to us. We walked up to the porch and presented white scarves in the traditional greeting. The Dalai Lama laughed and shook hands after taking each of the scarves and handing them to an attendant. A lama parted a plain curtain, and we followed His Holiness to a glassed-in part of the porch. The room was nearly empty, a few plants standing along the wall opposite the windows, beneath which were four wooden lawn chairs about a small table.

His Holiness shooed a kitten off the farther chair (a Lhasa terrier and another kitten moved in and out during the audience). Tenzin Geyche sat between Dom Aelred and the Dalai Lama, whose chair was hardly differentiated. At once we felt the impact of the personality before us, referred to by the Tibetans among themselves simply as "The Presence." Perhaps it was the aura of the Incarnation of Avalokiteshvara, the leader of a religion and a people in exile. Looking strong and youthful, with powerful eyes and a countenance which reflected the crushing pressure of his preoccupations, the Dalai Lama invited Dom Aelred to begin.

"It is a great privilege to be received by Your Holiness," I said. "I am a Christian monk, and I am wondering if a Benedictine has ever been received by the Dalai Lama before." He expressed much pleasure at our meeting and said that I was the first. He went on to say that although different religions have different systems of belief, we both believed in something beyond what could be seen. He felt that in the present age it was essential to have a closer understanding between the great religions of the world. He would be very happy to give me some idea of the form of Buddhism that is practiced in Tibet. Though he kindly allowed the interview to be recorded, my instinct is that direct quotation would be out of place, in view also of the fact that the discussion became rather abstruse and somewhat technical. Not that any confidences or state secrets were imparted. Looking over the transcripts now before me of what was said in this most rewarding conversation with the Dalai Lama, and later with his senior and junior tutors whom I also met, I can find nothing of substance that has not been disclosed—perhaps to better advantage from the standpoint of the general reader—elsewhere in these pages. "After the tape recorder was turned off," so runs my companion's account,

His Holiness appeared in no hurry to conclude the audience, and the conversation continued for another twenty minutes. We followed him through the curtain onto the porch, where a lama handed him the scarves we had presented. His Holiness returned the scarves to us in the formal Tibetan manner. This act of courtesy was of some significance, in view of the Dalai Lama's own description of a ceremony of the scarves in his autobiography: "The foreign representatives followed and presented scarves to me. These were personally returned by me to the representatives of the highest rank, and to the others by my Chamberlain."

We walked down the steps to the lawn with His Holiness, who had agreed to a photograph being taken with his interpreter, Tenzin Geyche, and ourselves. The hood of Dom Aelred's Benedictine habit was blowing in the wind, a fact which the Dalai Lama noticed. Standing next to him, he leaned over and smilingly adjusted the flowing garment. He thought it important that we should have "a good photograph." After mutual farewells, we walked some distance to the entrance to the compound, noticed the sentry on guard, and climbed back into our jeep. . . .

So ended one of the most memorable personal encounters of my life. It will be in place to give here a brief account of how the Dalai Lama is regarded in Tibet—or rather how he was regarded before the Chinese invasion and is still recognized by his faithful followers both within and outside that country. The word "Dalai" means "great ocean" (i.e., of the Buddhist spirit, dharma). The title is Mongolian; it was given to the first Grand Lama of the Gelugpa School in 1587 by Gusri Kham, a Mongol prince whom the Lama had called into Tibet to help him quash rival attempts for supreme power. The Dalai Lama by whom I was received, the fourteenth, was born in Amdo on June 6, 1935, and was approved, brought to Lhasa and enthroned in 1940. There, from the age of five, he resided at the enormous palace of the Potala, with the exception of a state visit to China and a journey to India, until his self-exile in 1959.

The manner of discovering the Dalai Lama and the doctrinal assumptions behind it are too complex to enter into here. More to the point is the fact that he is recognized as the spiritual and temporal ruler of Tibet. He is regarded as the earthly manifestation of Chenresi, the "Precious Protector," the Tibetan term for Avalokiteshvara, "the Lord who is seen," referred to elsewhere as the "personification of the self-generative, creative cosmic force." Again, in the richness and variety of Buddhist symbology the Dalai Lama represents a Bodhisattva, that is, one who has attained enlightenment yet renounced nirvana in order to help humanity on its pilgrimage. He embodies the "Buddha of Compassion," since love in action guided by wisdom is his aim.

"Homage to the Perfection of Wisdom, the lovely, the holy! Avalokita, the holy Lord and Bodhisattva, was moving in the deep course of the wisdom which has gone beyond (Prajnaparamita) . . . Here, O Sariputra, form is emptiness, and the very emptiness is form . . . It is because of his indifference to any kind of personal attainment that a Bodhisattva, through having relied on the perfection of wisdom, dwells without thought-coverings. In the absence of thought-coverings he has not been made to tremble, he has overcome what can upset, and in the end he attains to Nirvana . . . Therefore one should know the Prajnaparamita as the great spell, the spell of great knowledge, the utmost spell, the unequalled spell, allayer of all suffering, in truth—for what could go wrong? By the Prajnaparamita has this spell been delivered. It runs like this: Gone, Gone, Gone beyond, Gone altogether beyond, O what an awakening, All Hail!" These snatches from *The Heart Sutra*,[61] in praise of the prajnaparamita—that is, the wisdom that leads from samsara to nirvana, or as a Christian might express the thought, from earth to heaven—may convey a brief impression of the "psalmody" to be heard in the monasteries and temples of Tibet and Japan.

A student who cares to investigate such a text as this, one of the best loved in the Buddhist canon, will find in it immeasurably more than a sonorous incantation; it touches the heart of the Buddha's

61. Quoted from Edward Conze, *Buddhist Wisdom Books* (London: George Allen & Unwin, 1958), pp. 77ff. Here will be found Dr. Conze's translation and detailed commentary.

message, as does the following passage from another Sutra, unfolding the role of the Bodhisattva:

All creatures are in pain . . . all suffer from bad and hindering karma . . . so that they cannot see the Buddha or hear the Law of Righteousness or know the Order . . . All that mass of pain and karma I take in my own body . . . I take upon myself the burden of sorrow; I resolve to do so; I endure it all. I do not turn back or run away. I do not tremble . . . I am not afraid . . . nor do I despair. Assuredly I must bear the burden of all beings . . . for I have resolved to save them all. I must set them all free. I must save the whole world from the forest of birth, old age, disease and rebirth, from misfortune and sin, from the round of birth and death . . . For all beings are caught in the net of craving, encompassed by ignorance, held by the desire for existence; they are doomed to destruction, shut in a cage of pain . . . they are ignorant, untrustworthy, full of doubts, always at loggerheads one with another, always prone to see evil; they cannot find a refuge in the ocean of existence; they are all on the edge of the gulf of destruction.

I work to establish the kingdom of perfect wisdom for all beings. I care not at all for my own deliverance. I must save all beings from the torrent of rebirth with the raft of my omniscient mind. I must pull them back from the great precipice. I must free them from all misfortune, ferry them over the stream of rebirth.[62]

For the Christian these words may seem applicable to their suffering Saviour; they will recall the "servant passages" of Isaiah 53:3–12. Buddhists who know something of the Gospel story tend to interpret Jesus in terms of their highest ideal, that of the Bodhisattva.

More than two months were to elapse before I was to return to the congenial company of the Tibetan Buddhists. Back in the area of New Delhi I was able to renew my contacts with Hinduism—this time at the level of actual experience rather than academic discussion. An Indian doctor explained to me some of the techniques of hatha-yoga, and I underwent a mild initiation into processes about which there was nothing occult or mysterious, simply an application of rather more than normal insight into how the psychosomatic system actually works. The word "yoga" means "union"—ultimately with Brahman, or for the Christian, with God. Hatha-yoga has to do with the ordered breathing and physical postures that are calculated

62. Quoted from De Bary, *The Buddhist Tradition*, pp. 84–85.

to facilitate that union, or to assist in bringing about an awareness of it. Among Christians, a modified version of these practices has long been observed in the Eastern Orthodox Church—particularly in relation to the "Jesus Prayer"—and an appreciation of their value is slowly spreading in the West. Here, however, if the dangers of egocentricity and the possibilities of physical and spiritual harm are to be avoided, practice should usually be under the supervision of an experienced adviser. The place held by the guru in the Hindu-Buddhist tradition, though itself open to abuse, has behind it a long and respected tradition.

While in New Delhi, I attended a Hindu service conducted by a famous swami from an ashram near Bombay. His name was Muktananda Paramahamsa ("The Baba"), and he was surrounded by a large and devoted following, including a number of Westerners, both men and women. The service—kirtan, I believe, is its technical name—consisted of a long meditation followed by a hymn with a sensuous, lilting tune, in honor of Govinda ("Rescuer of the Earth"), one of the many incarnations of Vishnu. The swami's personality, though the language barrier prevented any conversation, impressed me greatly. Gentle, friendly, with shrewd, penetrating eyes, his manner combined a reassuring warmth with a hint of serene detachment. As I was leaving the assembly, he pointed me out to his disciples as a dharma acharya—a teacher of the dharma—from the West. They seemed happy enough just to pay their respects to him and then sit quietly in his presence.

The theory behind this in Hindu and Buddhist circles is that the "holy man" does not need to speak. His darshana, his beneficent presence, is enough. From it vibrations or emanations, very salutary to the recipient, are said to go forth. Matter-of-fact Westerners may smile at the idea, forgetful that it was realized in Jesus himself (see Mark 5:30). The thought occurred to me that the practice could be adopted by the Christian Church with advantage. We have our own holy men, sometimes among the highest ecclesiastics. Their frequent appearances in public, to judge by published reports, do not always indicate any compelling need to deliver a verbal message. Among the religiously minded sacred silence, rather than an exhortation or a pronunciamento, is often, to adopt the words of Gerard Manley Hopkins, "the music that I care to hear."

Before flying to the south I was the guest for two or three days of a swami, whose home was at Muzaffarnagar in Uttar Pradesh. Living, even briefly, in a Hindu religious household was a rewarding experience. I saw that elements from astrology and folklore, which I knew of only from books, were mingled with the worship of Ishvara. Evident, too, were the well-known potentialities of Hinduism, at the more popular level, to make the best of all possible worlds. It was a striking contrast to find myself a few days later within sight of the clear, though shark-infested, waters of the Bay of Bengal, at Madras. Here, as has already emerged, I had the pleasure of a long and informative talk with the world-famous scholar, Dr. Sarvepalli Radhakrishnan. In the course of his friendly conversation he alluded to his meetings with the Dalai Lama—"a good man, a gentle soul"—and also Pope Paul, whom he had welcomed at Bombay for the Eucharistic Congress in 1964, being at that time President of the Republic of India.

In Madras I spent the Christmas of 1967 and the opening of the New Year. The opportunity, a relief and greatly to be welcomed, was there to renew contact with the Church, for I had made a point of trying to absorb the Hindu-Buddhist scene as one uninvolved in any Christian missionary endeavor. This procedure, so I had been advised, was indispensable if I was to gain access to those best qualified to speak with authority on Indian religion: persons of learning and integrity for whom Hinduism was as much part of their blood as was Catholicism in my own case. The experience was thus the more heartwarming—to be able to visit the tomb of the Apostle Thomas in the much decorated Cathedral of St. Thomas on his feast day, December 21. The Presentation Sisters have a large convent in Madras, and there I was warmly welcomed to offer Mass in their chapel at Christmas and New Year and the intervening days. The Jesuits have an outstanding establishment, Loyola College, where, too, I was made to feel very much at home by Father Rector and his colleagues. Father Ignatius Hirudayam, S.J., a native of South India, an authority on the Hindu cult of Shiva, proved kindness itself. He was my guide on an excursion south to the Seven Pagodas at Mahabalipuram. From there we turned westward to Kancheepuram with its great temple, center of living Hindu worship. On the return journey we paid a call on Yogi Shuddhananda Shavati, a much respected figure in Madras. Krishnamurti, well known to Western Vedantists, happened to be giving a course of evening lectures, between Christmas and New Year, in an attractive open-air setting. A discovery, so I was informed, of Annie Besant and Madame Blavatsky—founders of the Theosophical Society—he commanded a large audience, mostly Western residents or visitors. His presence and oratorical manner were impressive, but the content of his remarks, no doubt because I was rather travel weary, failed to keep me attentive. My companion and I slipped quietly away under the brightening stars.

Allusion has already been made to my brief but pleasantly memorable sojourn in Ceylon early in 1968. On my return to the mainland from Colombo I had hoped to be able to land at Trivandrum in Kerala and so pay a visit to Father Bede Griffiths. His work in investigating what the Church might accept from and give to Hinduism is well known and widely appreciated. He had visited me when I was living in the United States, and I was anxious to renew our acquaintance—all the more so as an Indian priest had described his as "the only attempt that is being made in India on the part of Catholics to understand and evaluate Hindu meditation and spirituality." Unhappily, the project proved to be impracticable because of the unsettled political and labor conditions in Ceylon. Flights out of Colombo were limited and crowded, and I was advised to take the first one available. This landed me in Bombay some five hundred miles north of Trivandrum, so that a much-looked-forward-to opportunity had, to my great regret, been lost.

The first week in February, 1968, found my companion and me in Calcutta. Armed with the necessary permits from the Indian Government, I had decided to enter Sikkim, on the very border of Chinese-occupied Tibet. The spell of Buddhism, as represented by the Dalai Lama, which captivates so many younger spirits, was hard to resist even at my age. In Calcutta I met Desmond Doigh of *The Statesman* newspaper, a writer and also a painter of distinction, a well-informed, kindly and entertaining personality, to whom I took at once. Together we had lunch with the district commissioner for North Bengal, whose responsibilities extend to the borders of Sikkim, Nepal, Bihar, and Punjab. He was extremely knowledgeable about the Tibetan refugees and had much that was both sad and amusing to tell me. It happened that the Chögyal ("Divine Ruler") of Sikkim was in Calcutta at this time. Better known perhaps in the West as the Maharaja, he and his wife, the Maharanee (an American, the former Hope Cooke), kindly invited me to visit them. He, a Buddhist prince, and she, his princess, a convinced convert to that faith, received me most graciously. Refreshments in the Western fashion and conversation on topics more native to the East blended to make a most agreeable hour together.

On February 9, we flew to Darjeeling, or rather to an airport at the foot of the Himalayas, from which the 7,000-foot ascent to the town was made by car. The district commissioner happened to be on the same plane, and he insisted on my going with him to the flight deck to see the view. The day was cloudless and the sun at midday splendor. He pointed over the pilot's shoulder, away to the left, at a sight I had never expected to see except in photographs. There, distant but with absolute clarity, buttressed by its surrounding peaks, could be seen the 29,000-foot massif of Everest, its wind-blown plume of frozen snow trailing from its summit, like foam breaking from the bows of an enormous ship. Directly ahead of us, perhaps seventy miles away, of only slightly less altitude, was the range of Kangchenjunga, of much greater interest to the states bordering on northeast India.

During my stay at Darjeeling, on days when the sky was clear, the peak of Kangchenjunga could be seen clearly some forty miles distant, floating in the blue sky like a white cloud. For the inhabitants of Nepal, Sikkim, and Bhutan it is holy ground. The sentiment that hilltops and mountain peaks are places where the gods are to be found is common to peoples in many parts of the world. So it was with Moses on Mount Sinai, though subsequent Old Testament writers, anxious either to idealize conditions in the desert, or to centralize worship exclusively at the Temple in Jerusalem, showed little sympathy with this point of view. For the Sikkimese, Kangchenjunga means the "Five Treasuries of the Great Snow"; it is regarded as a god and protector. For this reason, when the British mountaineering expedition set out to climb the peak in 1955, a project successfully achieved, one of the conditions for the Maharajah of Sikkim's acquiescence to the ascent being made was that the summit itself should not be touched. The promise was given and faithfully kept, as the leader of the expedition, Charles Evans, tells us in his book, *Kangchenjunga: the Untrodden Peak.*

Reading the Dalai Lama's autobiography, while comfortably installed at the delightful Windamere Hotel at Darjeeling, I came across what struck me as the following eminently sensible comment on the enthusiasm for mountain climbing: "I have sometimes been asked if we followed the attempts of the British to climb Mount Everest with interest. I cannot say that we did. Most Tibetans have to climb too many mountain passes to have any wish to climb any higher than they must; and the people of Lhasa, who sometimes climbed for pleasure, chose hills of a reasonable size, and, when they came to the top, burned incense, said prayers and had picnics. That is a pleasure which I also enjoy when I have an opportunity."

While in the Darjeeling area and in Sikkim I was surrounded by signs of Tibetan Buddhism. Nearby were a school for refugee children, several monasteries, and prayer flags everywhere. Young lamas, as might be expected, are interested in Western ways. According to sophisticated visitors to the town, you may see almost any afternoon eager tourists on one side of the main street gazing in shop windows at Tibetan than-kas (hieratic paintings, often mandalas) and prayer wheels, while on the other side native Buddhists are absorbed, with no less interest, in the spectacle of typewriters and transistor radios. But traveling around the beautiful town of Darjeeling, visiting one or two monasteries, including the ancient one at Ghoom, I could see nothing of this entertaining human spectacle.

On February 11, I entered Sikkim and reached Gangtok. Such an enterprise, I had often been warned, owing to security precautions on the border abutting Tibet, would prove impracticable. But thanks to the courtesy of Indian and Sikkimese officials, the journey by jeep through rugged Himalayan country was accomplished without mishap. At Gangtok my companion and I were welcomed by a close associate of the Dalai Lama, his official interpreter, whom I had met, together with his wife and charming teen-age daughter, at Dharmsala. He took us on a visit to the nearby Tantric training monastery. Here we had a long discussion with a much respected Rimpoche,[63] belonging to the Nyingma-pa[64] sect.

The next day I visited the Dharma Chakra Centre at Rumtek, near Gangtok. This is one of the largest Tibetan monasteries outside Tibet and houses 150 monks. Its buildings are spacious and of some

63. Pronounced Rimpoch*ay*. Its literal meaning is "Precious One," a title of great honor given to tulkus (to be explained presently) and a few others of high rank and attainment.

64. The oldest of the Tibetan schools of Buddhism; from it emerged the Bardo Thödol, which is used in Tibet as a breviary, better known as The Tibetan Book of the Dead.

splendor. In his almost sumptuous suite of rooms on the top floor, I
was received by the Tibetan equivalent of the abbot, the most genial
and friendly Gyalwa Karma-pa, head of the Karma Kagyu-pa School,
an official ranking not far below the Dalai Lama himself, whose
photograph held an honored place on the wall of the audience cham-
ber (for in its magnificence and general atmosphere it was scarcely
less). In the monastery temple, an all-day ceremony was being conducted—at the request, so I was informed, of the King of Bhutan—
and I watched it for some time. It was an impressive affair: the monks
were divided into two choirs facing each other and they recited their
sutras in much the same way as in a Catholic monastery. Where the
difference lay was in the fact that at about ten-minute intervals the
recitation was punctuated by a long rolling of drums, blowing of
huge conch-shaped trumpets, sounding of enormous gongs, and the
ringing of bells. It was all skillfully synchronized and had a most
telling effect. This was the ceremonial Tantra. Its purpose, I afterward learned, was to speed the process of enlightenment, though I
suspected that it also served another end—that of keeping the monks
awake.

Watching them all from a perfect vantage point on a gallery high
above the temple benches, I could not but compare the scene to a
Benedictine monastic ceremony. Among the seventy or eighty monks
taking part a number were clearly in a state of deep recollection. But
on the whole, the degree of collective discipline and concentration,
the general deportment of those engaged—some of whom admittedly were small boys eager for any distraction—did not strike me
too favorably. The thought occurred, not for the first time, that Buddhism at the level of theoretical exposition is one thing; in actual
practice it is rather different. But this observation, it can hardly be
doubted, is equally applicable to Catholic Christianity.

The term "tulku," mentioned a moment ago, is of some interest,
because the thirteen- or fourteen-year-old girl, daughter of my host
at Gangtok, was recognized as meriting this title. A full explanation
would take us far afield, some of it over ground already covered. The
relevant point in our present context is that a tulku, according to
Tibetan Buddhism, is a reincarnation of some notable and usually
holy (i.e., "enlightened") person who lived in the past. Thus the
Dalai Lama is himself a tulku, being the reincarnation, so it is held,
of his predecessor in office. One who is recognized as an "incarnate,"

a tulku, is treated with some ceremony by the Tibetans. He or she is a "rimpoche," a "precious one." Westerners who tend to be skeptical about the doctrine are usually prepared to admit that there is something "different" once they have met such a personality. Recently I received a letter from a friend, who had visited Dharmsala and been present at a Tibetan drama festival. He writes as follows:

The guest of honor in the big round tent pitched for the occasion, with an altar in the center beneath a photograph of the Dalai Lama—the altar bearing the usual Tibetan articles of ritual offering, symbolizing the entire universe!—was a little incarnate lama aged about ten. He was recognized as the incarnation of a celebrated Abbot whose monks got out of Tibet and were able to take along many scriptures and ritual objects. They have a monastery in Katmandu now, which is flourishing under the abbacy of this little chap. The director of the troupe sat next to the "incarnate," who often asked him questions about the drama. His little playmates, monk and lay, also received his attention. In their case he was very cheerful and humorous. The child's face was rather like Tibetan Buddhist images, very forthright and intelligent as well as serene. The Tibetan whom I talked with during the performance agreed, when I remarked how sophisticated and bright the boy seemed. "Yes," he said, "there's something these high incarnates have in common whereby you can always identify them. Look at this one, for instance, and then look at his playmates: they are swarthy and have undistinguished features in comparison. But it is particularly in their bearing that the high incarnations are distinctive: while fully natural and casual, they exhibit a consciousness of their state and office which gives them dignity. You will also notice the way in which they are approached and treated by the Tibetans. Now that all the monks in exile wear the same habit, including the Dalai Lama, the personal qualities of the child-incarnations are even more obvious."

My little Tibetan girl friend—for so I claim her (though a Buddhist, she was enrolled in a Catholic convent school, spoke perfect English, and we enjoyed some amiable talk together) had been recognized as a reincarnation of a well-known Buddhist nun. Accordingly, she was a "precious one"—and I had not the slightest difficulty in believing it. Having met both her parents, however, of whom she was an only child, I thought it possible that her remarkable though wholly childlike bearing, her bright intelligence, and a quality much deeper than mere charm might well be accounted for by the natural principles of heredity. I sat next to her during a prolonged lunch at a modest restaurant, called the Paradise Hotel in Gangtok. We had been late in arriving and she must have been hungry. The talk went on and on and it could not have held the least interest for her. But she sat patiently, composed and in good humor until at length she leaned over and whispered in her father's ear, clearly asking for some permission. He nodded, and she took out from her bag a sheaf of printed papers. It was a collection of some kind, and keeping it partly under the table, she began unobtrusively to read. My faith was not in the least shaken when at length out of the corner of my eye I saw what it was—a book of comics.

A small incident occurred on our return journey from Gangtok to Darjeeling, with which the present topic may fittingly conclude. It seemed to me to illustrate the close links that exist between cultural upbringing and forms of worship, which are seldom much affected by broadening religious interests. My traveling companion, though a Catholic, was deeply interested in, and indeed influenced by, Tibetan Buddhism. He had acquired for himself a Buddhist rosary, on the beads of which he would quietly recite the well-known mantra— *Om mani padme hum*—as we traveled over the dangerous Himalayan slopes. At one point we were flanked by a deep precipice with a sheer drop of perhaps a thousand feet, the road seeming to narrow as we drove on. As we turned a blind corner, only a few yards off and traveling much too fast, was another jeep coming toward us. A collision was unavoidable; it was simply a question of how sharp the impact would be. Fortunately, it turned out to be slight, and little harm was done to either passengers or vehicles. "When I saw what was going to happen," my friend said to me afterward, "I switched at once to the Hail Mary."

viii. A Note on Sufism

In his learned and interesting work, *The Masks of God: Creative Mythology,* Joseph Campbell alludes to the dominance of the Sanskrit language in the East. "From the yak trails of Tibet to the village markets of Bali, its syllables rose everywhere on the pluming smoke of incense to that void beyond non-being and being that is the destination, ultimately, of all Oriental prayer. And its echoes floated westward too. The influence of Indian thought on the Sufis cannot be doubted. . . ."[65] During one or two of my discussions in India the subject of Sufism came up. I learned of a distinguished Frenchman, impatient of institutional Christianity, who had sought initiation into Hinduism. This he failed to obtain, so he turned instead to Islam and eventually received Sufic initiation. He entered deeply into that tradition which, so I was informed, has similarities with the Hindu Vedanta. "Would you say there's much difference between Sufism and orthodox Brahminism, Hinduism?" I asked a Hindu professor of Sanskrit in Madras. "On the side of practice and daily observances, you have some difference," was the reply. "But the approach and final philosophy are not different."

On my way back to the West I had the opportunity to take at least a passing glance at the Sufism of Iran. It was on March 8, 1968, that I began nearly a month's stay. I was happy to find myself under the kindly and expert care of Dr. Seyyed Hossein Nasr, author of *Ideals and Realities of Islam* and other notable works. From him I learned much about Sufism, considered particularly as manifesting the sanatana dharma, "eternal religion," or at another level of thought, the "perennial philosophy." More than a month later, while staying at Istanbul, I had the good fortune to meet and be much enlightened by another representative of the same tradition, M. Jean-Claude Petit-Pierre.

It was the Persian New Year in Tehran, and I had the opportunity to attend a recital of Sufi poetry, but much of its atmosphere must have escaped me, helped though I was by the ready translations of Dr. Nasr. To linger at the mosques of Isfahan and Shiraz and some weeks later at Sancta Sophia and the Blue Mosque at Istanbul, enabled me to catch something of the flavor of Islam. In Tehran I met and talked with several Muslim theologians, but what knowledge I have of Sufism is still derived chiefly from reading. The most memorable sightseeing event during my stay in Iran took me back to pre-Islamic, indeed pre-Christian, days—to Persepolis, capital of the ancient Persian Empire. Here were the rock-hewn tombs of Cyrus, Darius, and Xerxes, long since despoiled and empty. Here also were the ruins of the palace, much of them splendidly preserved, set on fire by Alexander himself in 331 B.C., prompted, it is said by some, in

65. p. 134.

the course of a night of revelry, by an Athenian courtesan, Thaïs. For the time, at least, we were a long way from Sufism. Or were we quite so far? There are hints in Sufi history, as in the accounts of all religions that strive for a state of ecstasy, that moral fastidiousness was not always required. "Already in some circles the pursuit of the ecstatic state had affected the primitive *dhikr* (liturgy) and introduced into its ritual such adventitious aids as dancing and the rending of garments." [66] But let us consider briefly Sufism at its best, with which I had long felt sympathy. Looking back at an analytical essay published more than thirty years ago, *The Love of God,* I find myself quoting the words of Rabia, the saintly freedwoman of Basra, who used to pray upon the housetop at night: "O my Lord, the stars are shining and the eyes of men are closed, and the kings have shut their doors and every lover is alone with his beloved, and here am I alone with Thee." This now appears to me, though I was unaware of it at that time, as an Islamic version of the Tantra, to which we have already given some attention. Analogous to it is her celebrated prayer, which is perhaps nearer in spirit to the religious tradition of India, than to that of orthodox Christianity:

> O God! if I worship Thee in fear of Hell,
>   burn me in Hell;
> And if I worship Thee in hope of Paradise,
>   exclude me from Paradise;
> But if I worship Thee for Thine own sake,
>   withhold not Thine Everlasting Beauty.[67]

After some debate Islamic scholars seem now to be agreed that the term "sufi" does not derive either from the Arabic word for "purity" or the Greek word for "wisdom" (though Sufism aims at both moral purity and final wisdom) but from the Arabic word meaning "wool." For as R. A. Nicholson has pointed out, "The woolen raiment is the habit of the prophets and the badge of the saints and elect, as appears in many traditions and narratives." It seems doubtful, however, that there was any powerful, creative mind to explain the origins of Sufism like those behind Buddhism, Christianity, and Islam itself at its beginning. The movement was largely

66. H. A. R. Gibb, *Mohammedanism—An Historical Survey* (New York: Oxford University Press, 1962), p. 142.
67. Quoted froom A. J. Arberry, *Sufism* (London: George Allen & Unwin, 1950), p. 42.

derivative, owing much to Christian, Neoplatonic, Zoroastrian and Hindu-Buddhist influences. On the other hand, Sufis can justifiably appeal for sanction to the Prophet Muhammad himself, as is clear from such passages in the Quran as the following: "Everything is perishing except the face (reality) of Allah" (28, 88); "Every one on the earth is passing away, but the glorious and honoured face of thy Lord abides for ever" (55, 26ff.); "Wheresoever you turn, there is the face of Allah" (2, 109).[68]

But these considerations need not detain us. It is the spirit of Sufism that can quicken the religious sense of jaded Westerners in such a paradox, for instance, as the anonymous Sufi aphorism, "When the heart weeps for what it has lost, the spirit laughs for what it has found." "The Sufi," says Jalal-uddin Rumi, "is the son of time present." With what profit could this be taken to heart by the Christian, as St. François de Sales in his own way was later to insist. What an admirable corrective to a mind prone to be absorbed in Biblical history or Christian eschatology. Live in the here and now. Become a child "of time present!" Or this, from Ansari of Herat, which corresponds to the heart of the Gospel, as well as to much that we have heard from India: "Know that when you learn to lose yourself, you will reach the Beloved. There is no other secret to be learnt, and more than this is not known to me."

Sufi virtues, as Seyyed Hossein Nasr has pointed out, are not man-made moral attitudes; they are modes of being, "which transform man's existence in conformity with his inner nature." Again, it may be remarked in passing, this is the concept of ethics that was later to be worked out in detail by St. Thomas Aquinas. Dr. Nasr quotes a text from one of the Sufi masters: "My slave ceases not to draw nigh unto Me through freely given devotion until I love him, and when I love him, I am the hearing with which he hears, and the sight with which he sees, and the hand with which he works, and the foot with which he walks." "Through the mystery that lies at the heart of creation itself, everything is, in essence, identified with God while God infinitely transcends everything. To understand this doctrine intellectually is to possess contemplative intelligence; to realize it fully is to be a saint, who alone sees 'God everywhere.' "

How much does all this, as well as the underlying thought of the

68. Quoted from Reynold A. Nicholson, "Sufis," in *Hastings Encyclopaedia of Religion and Ethics.*

Hindu-Buddhist tradition, amount to pantheism? Pantheism is a word at which orthodox Christian theologians take fright. They forget, it may be, that the authors of the Upanishads, the Bhagavad-Gita, and the Buddhist Sutras, were not professional metaphysicians trying to work out a consistent philosophy. They were attempting to express the inexpressible in words, to indicate by "name and form" that which is nameless and formless. Their aim is not to formulate a creed, to provide an armory of theological concepts, but to lead their readers and hearers to share their experience, to see and hear what they saw and heard. "Pantheism" is merely one theological statement of the age-old problem of "the one and the many." Catholic theologians, so far as I am aware, still cannot get very much further with the question than to say that created beings do not really add anything to God. Given creation, there are more beings but not more Being, more existences but not more Existence.

Does this position throw any greater light on the matter than the following comment by Mr. Christmas Humphreys, an eminent Buddhist scholar? "Buddhism is not a form of pantheism, for it lacks the duality of thought implied in the God-concept and that which the God creates. In Buddhism the One and the All are not different but exist in absolute self-identity." "The 'One and the All,'" to quote a learned authority, "has been forever the laughingstock of fools and the everlasting meditation of the wise." [69] Perhaps we could leave it at that.

69. Campbell, *The Masks of God,* p. 75.

7. Worldly Unworldliness

To pass from Tehran to Jerusalem, from Persia to Israel, brings us back once more to the origins of the Christian religion, and in particular, to its status in the life of humanity today. Institutional Christianity, I believe, has hardly begun to solve the problem of how it is to confront "the world." The root of the difficulty has already been touched on—the Gospel was originally preached in a crisis situation. Since the existing world order was to be radically transformed, there was no necessity to come to terms with it. But the expected transformation did not occur; God's kingdom of self-evident righteousness failed to appear. With the fulfillment of their hopes indefinitely postponed the first Christian communities took up the position that though they were *in* the world they were not *of* it: "Do you not know that friendship with the world is enmity with God? Therefore whoever wishes to be a friend of the world makes himself an enemy of God" (James 4:4). Here we have the evangelical *either/or*, which Kierkegaard was to revive with such relish for the benefit of his nineteenth-century contemporaries: "I who am called 'Either/Or' cannot be at anyone's service with Both-And. I am in possession of a book which is surely all but unknown in this land, and therefore I will cite the title exactly: The New Testament of our Lord and Saviour Jesus Christ. Although I have a perfectly free relationship to that book, and am not, e.g., pledged to it by oath, it nevertheless exercises an enormous influence over me and inspires me with indescribable horror of Both-And."

In practice, however, despite scriptural admonitions to the contrary, most Christians act on the principle of both/and. They have no difficulty in tempering their service of God with a measure, sometimes quite substantial, of deference to mammon. The Biblical message as a whole appears to be that we are to have a love-hate relationship with the world. When God surveyed his creation, according to Genesis, he "saw that it was good" (1:10) and therefore presumably that it was lovable. We are told that the whole redemptive process was set in motion because God himself "so loved the world" (John 3:16). Yet anyone who takes religion seriously will probably admit that worldliness—an inordinate taste for the "things of the world"—is pretty accurately summarized, and justifiably condemned, in such phrases as "the lust of the flesh and the lust of the eyes and the pride of life" (1 John 2:16). These can be interpreted respectively as unbridled sensuality, coveting persons and things for one's own gratification, haughtiness and ostentatious display—all of which militate against that freedom of spirit in which alone God can be duly served and one's true self realized.

As this situation, which I shall now try to elucidate a little, is in the order of practical living rather than ethical theory, it obviously provides a fruitful field for self-deception. Plenty of scope is offered for rationalizing one's own predilections. Returning for a moment to the "personal equation" already discussed (at perhaps too great length), let me admit that, whether as a spectator or occasionally as a participant, I often find the world and its ways rather pleasing. Though well content with the form of monasticism that has fallen to my lot, I now gladly eschew anything in the way of calculated asceticism. An orderly, disciplined existence leading, I like to think, to a moderate degree of self-restraint, has long been for me a congenial part of the pattern of things. Variations on this theme, however, though not exorbitantly sought after, occur fairly frequently. While my monastic brethren agonize over the miseries of the "third world," and the evils of poverty and racism, I have sometimes been elsewhere, enjoying the benefits of the "affluent society." It all leaves me with a faint feeling of guilt. And yet, in a way, there is something not wholly disquieting about the discovery that, after forty years of admittedly not very arduous spiritual struggle, one is no different from the average sensual man. The condition of one who did feel different, though, might be more troubling. Whether it would also be healthier, it is hard to say.

But a word must clearly be said about one's sense of social responsibility. While the desire to raise the general standard of living among the underprivileged peoples, both at home and abroad, is closely linked with true religion, I believe that my modest contribution can only be indirect. Perhaps it could have something to do with the quality of insight among those who are called on directly to help our less fortunate fellow men. If the giver is himself unenlightened, unaware of his own motives or of the situation in which he operates, or without understanding of those he would aid, his gifts may do more harm than good. If, for example, material assistance is given to Africa, Latin America, or India as a basis for future capitalist exploitation, or to prevent the spread of Communism in the fear that the Russians or the Chinese may get there first, and not to benefit these peoples for their own sake, then we are likely to be disseminating the worst rather than the best of what Western civilization has to offer. Sympathetic insight, an absence of self-seeking are obvious prerequisites for bringing genuine relief to suffering humanity. Hence the challenge arises for us to reach if we can, not this or that religion—a varied enterprise causing rivalry and confusion on the mission field— but religion in its essence, at a level beyond which we cannot go. Religion so considered, I submit, must have simultaneously the characteristics of worldliness and unworldliness, a coincidence of seeming opposites.

These thoughts were taking shape in my mind as I landed at Tel Aviv early in April, 1968, having flown westward from Tehran. Two hours later I was in Jerusalem. For all the enriching experiences in Japan, Thailand, India, and Iran, they fell into the background before what was for me, so to speak, my native Holy Land. It held a double fascination: first because of the historic origins of Christianity, then because of the newly formed State of Israel —whose welfare, for reasons easy to explain, had long been close to my heart. How much time will it take before the Arab world can recognize and co-operate with Israel and so bring it about that the injustices inflicted on the followers of the Prophet, instead of being exacerbated, are atoned for and removed? Basically my fellow feeling with Judaism is, I suppose, a response to the fact that it produced Jesus of Nazareth—whose complete Jewishness is being revealed in ever sharpening relief by the findings of modern scholarship.

There are other reasons, too, personal and egoistic. Some of the warmest responses to my writings have come from Jews. My first book, in particular, brought me the friendship of a Jewish lady who had become a Catholic, and her husband, under whose hospitable roof I often enjoyed rest and relaxation. I found my growing interest in the religions of the East to be shared by many of the kindliest and most intelligent Jews. On my fairly frequent visits to New York City, it was a pleasant nonsurprise to discover that in the arts and things of the mind, Hebrews dominated the scene. I even wondered if there might be something in C. P. Snow's verdict that genetically the Jews may be in some way superior to the rest of us. At any rate, it was a pleasure to be in the State of Israel and to encounter, among others, so outstanding a member of the faculty of the Hebrew University as Professor R. J. Zwi Werblowsky. We had a common interest in Zen Buddhism, and he proved informative and enlightening on a variety of topics. A meeting with Professor Hugo Bergman and his wife on the evening of the Sabbath was particularly moving. After a long talk he kindly presented me with one of his books but gently postponed responding to my request for his autograph until the little household ceremony with which the Sabbath ended was performed.

The thought occurs that the distinctive and irreplaceable contribution of Judaism to religion is precisely its "worldliness," that is to say, its insistence that God is to be worshiped and his will carried out *here on this earth*. The Kingdom of God is not a Platonic conception of an ideal society laid up in heaven; it is something to be concretely realized in the world of men and women as we know them. The Old Testament belief that righteousness and material prosperity are not unconnected has been somewhat overshadowed, particularly among Christians, by the later doctrines of personal immortality and the rewarding of virtue hereafter. But the idea persists in Jewry that God wills our physical, not merely our spiritual, well-being. Wearisome and repellent as much of the Old Testament iron-age religion emphatically is—especially to those who have to listen to the inspired, yet decidedly uninspiring, accounts of it read daily in a monastic choir and refectory!—the message that a benign interpretation can extract from the Bible is wholesome and for all time. It is that at the heart of the universe there is goodness, that the stars in their courses are on the side of right, that God is to be regarded as a Father and all men as brothers. We can detect even in the Old Testament the sacred worth of the individual, the importance of personal integrity, and the principle of service to others as the key to happiness. That this is not the whole story of religion has already been rather more than suggested in these pages, but it encourages man with an acceptable view of his place in this world and teaches him how to act in his own best interests.

On my visits to New York I often had occasion to walk past the splendid synagogue on Fifth Avenue overlooking Central Park. Carved on the frieze, plain for all passers-by to see, was the great text, which I felt could never be read too often, from the sixth chapter of the Book of Micah (verse 8): "He has showed you, O man, what is good; and what does the Lord require of you but to do justice, and to love kindness, and to walk humbly with your God?" The quintessence of religion, it seemed and still seems to me, has never been expressed more simply.

But let us return to Jerusalem, where I stayed for the two weeks preceding Passover and Easter. From where I was lodged, out of the main city over the Kidron Valley, it was less than a ten-minute walk to the Garden of Gethsemane. Sometimes I would meditate at the sacred site itself on just what had occurred there at that fateful Passover of 29 or 30 A.D. What had gone on in the tormented soul of Jesus during his agony? Without prejudice to the Church's later understanding of the event, it is permissible to think that we have here one of the chief enigmas of the New Testament. To read into the Gospel accounts the alleged divisions and levels of Christ's knowledge—deduced by the scholastics, including St. Thomas, from the theology of the Incarnation—does not help much. The questions raised by modern scholars cannot easily be answered. If Jesus knew that he was to be arrested that night, why had he troubled to leave the city? Even at this late hour might there not be a cataclysmic intervention by God his Father, thereby establishing the kingdom for the salvation of his own people and the downfall of his enemies? If he was to die, had he perhaps hoped that his disciples would die with him? Whatever these possibilities, it is hard to resist the impression that he who was sent "only to the lost sheep of the house of Israel" (Matthew 15:24; cf. 10:6, 23), according to the early tradition, conceived God's plan as bringing relief and blessedness to his Jewish fellow countrymen here in this world where they were.

For those who live by the post-Resurrection faith these questions are not gravely disturbing, though their implications should be honestly faced, particularly by Christians at the present time. The long-term formulation of this faith took place in the lands bordering the eastern Mediterranean under the dominating influence of Hellenism. Accordingly, it was fitting that shortly after leaving Jerusalem I should find myself in Athens. "What is there in common between Athens and Jerusalem?" asks Tertullian, a second-century Church

Father, in a work titled *De praescriptione haereticorum*. He held severe views about morality, expressed them ably and forcefully and acquired much influence; his was an either/or rather than a both/and type of mind. "What is there in common between the Academy and the Church? What between heretics and Christians? . . . Away with all projects for a 'Stoic,' a 'Platonic' or a 'dialectic' Christianity! After Christ we desire no subtle theories, no acute enquiries after the gospel. . . ." Poor Tertullian! Everything that he here decries was to come into effect, while he himself, to the Church's great loss, was to be regarded as a heretic. Catholicism may be said to owe in part its origins and wholly its survival as a Christian philosophy to a meeting of minds between Jerusalem and Athens.

The Greek element in Christianity is considerable, and it derives from Plato. The Zeus of Aeschylus, pure and lofty as he is, was yet too much the god of the Greek polis to become the God of mankind, just as the God of the Jews could not become also the God of the Gentiles without considerable change. It was Greek philosophy, notably Plato's conception of the absolute, eternal deity, which prepared the world for the reception of a universal religion.[1]

My own sojourn in Greece during the spring of 1968 was pleasant indeed. Contact with the Orthodox Church, which I had long sought, was at last possible. Its ornate ceremonial was on full display in Athens on Good Friday and Easter Day (coming this year a week later than the Roman rites I had witnessed in Jerusalem), with the Greek military government much in evidence. Orthodox theology, so I was to learn, is nowadays professionally expounded by laymen rather than the clergy. Professor Hamilcar S. Alvisatos, much interested in the ecumenical movement, kindly invited me to meet with him—to my great profit. Philip Sherrard—scholar, poet, and internationally famous expert on Byzantium, besides being a most agreeable personality—was good enough to give me much of his time. With him I visited several of the Greek islands and saw something of Orthodox monastic life. Orthodoxy's ceremonial, solemn and impressive though it is, is too long and elaborate for my personal taste. The Orthodox tradition of contemplative prayer appeals to me as of

1. H. D. F. Kitto, *The Greeks* (Harmondsworth: Penguin Books, 1951), pp. 202–3.

much greater interest, though even this may call for a little critical examination before it can be wholeheartedly embraced.

"Whenever human consciousness begins to be alive to the questions Who am I? Whence do I come? Whither do I go? then there arises the possibility of taking and following the narrow, long, blessed path to wisdom." These words, which seem to echo much that we have heard from India, were written at Mount Athos in May, 1951. They appear in the foreword to an English translation from the Russian of *Writings from the "Philokalia" on Prayer of the Heart*.[2] The Philokalia, which means "love of the beautiful, the exalted, the good," aims at leading to that state "above which there is nothing to wish for and beyond which there is nowhere to go." It inculcates spiritual practices that have not escaped criticism within the Greek Church itself, but its central theme, focusing attention on the "Jesus Prayer," must surely appeal to every Christian. In the Philokalia there are many variants of this prayer and much comment upon it. Here is a brief extract from Gregory of Sinai, a fourteenth-century saint of Orthodoxy:

In the morning force your mind to descend from the head to the heart and hold it there, calling ceaselessly in mind and soul: "Lord Jesus Christ, have mercy upon me!" until you are tired. When tired, transfer your mind to the second half, and say: "Jesus, Son of God, have mercy upon me!" Having many times repeated this appeal, pass once more to the first half. But you should not too often alternate these appeals through laziness; for, just as plants do not take root if transplanted too frequently, neither do the movements of prayer in the heart if the words are changed frequently.[3]

The relation between reciting psalms and advancement in personal union with God is touched on by the same authority. His advice should be of interest to all who make use of the Psalter.

Some say one should psalmodise often, others—not often, again others—not at all. But I advise you neither to psalmodise so frequently as to cause unrest, nor to leave it off altogether, lest you fall into weakness and negligence, but to follow the example of those who psalmodise

2. Quoted from *Dobrotolubiye*, trans. E. Kadloubovsky and G. E. H. Palmer (London: Faber and Faber, 1951).
3. *Ibid.*, pp. 84–5. For an easily accessible account of the "Prayer of the Heart" see Timothy Ware, *The Orthodox Church* (Harmondsworth: Penguin Books, 1963, 1964), pp. 74–76, 312–14.

infrequently. For, in the words of simple wisdom, moderation is best in all things. To psalmodise much is good for those who follow active life, since they are ignorant of mental occupations and lead a life of labour. But it is not good for those who practise silence, for whom it is more fitting to abide in God alone, praying in their heart and refraining from thought. . . .

Those too, do right who wholly abstain from psalmody, if they are making progress. Such people have no need of psalmody, but should remain in silence, constant prayer and contemplation, if they have attained enlightenment. For they are united with God and must not tear their mind away from him and plunge it into turmoil, or a crowd of thoughts.[4]

St. Gregory of Sinai, who offers this advice, has a passing comment on those who are merely "wise in words," which moves at the same level of observation as that of Lao Tzu or one of the great Zen Masters: "The sensory and prolix spirit of the wisdom of this age, so rich in words, which create the illusion of great knowledge but actually fill one with the wildest thoughts, has its stronghold in this prolixity, which deprives man of essential wisdom, true contemplation and the knowledge of the one and indivisible."

Yet the extreme otherworldliness of much of the doctrine of the Philokalia needs to be balanced by a sense of the value of God's material creation. Orthodoxy, with its forceful repudiation of "paganism," seems to me to break with, rather than transform fruitfully, the Greek tradition that beauty is to be recognized in every variety of expression, including the most visible and tangible. Perhaps it was only unregenerate human nature that made me feel more at ease when examining a sculptured relief from Eleusis of Demeter with her daughter Persephone, or the magnificent bronze statue of Poseidon (or Zeus)—both in the Athens National Museum—or again, the porch of the maidens in the Erechtheum on the Acropolis, than when standing before the holy icons—windows, it is said, opening on heaven—in the monastery on the island of Paros. And then the Parthenon itself, "in photographs only another Greek temple," as Professor Kitto observes, "but in reality the most thrilling building there is." It is the same worldly taste, I have no doubt, that leads me to find greater satisfaction in the naturalism of Leonardo and Michelangelo than in the stylized restraint of Fra Angelico.

4. *Ibid.*, pp. 76, 88.

Nevertheless, it seems to me that short of an almost completely abstract symbolism (in itself the best of all) the frankly anthropomorphic approach to God is to be preferred to attempts to capture the "formless" in some etherealized sensible form. As early as the sixth century B.C. an Ionian philosopher Xenophanes had observed that if donkeys were religious they would imagine their gods in the form of donkeys. Anthropomorphism, seeing the gods under the aspect of man, is the very soul of myth, and myth, considered as poetic representation, is bound up with all the great religions. As long as we are able to distinguish the myth from what is mythologized, nothing need be lost and much can be gained. It is probable that the Greeks of the sixth and fifth centuries B.C.—with what L. R. Farnell has called "the specially Hellenic theory of the divine character of the artistic and intellectual life"—were better equipped to draw this necessary distinction than were their Hebrew contemporaries.[5] Within its limits the "beautiful idolatry" of the Greeks—exemplified so notably by Pheidias—may have actually effected a sound religious development. It could have weakened the popular faith in the native deities, and when introduced suddenly into Rome, it helped to destroy the old Roman animistic religion.[6] Moreover, that it was possible to embody the authentically Greek artistic spirit within a Christian setting is supported by the following judgment.

Leonardo, Michelangelo and Raphael inherited everything that the questing Renaissance mind and the searching Renaissance technical skill had prepared for them, and yet they succeeded in presenting the Christian case—the fusion of physical beauty with spiritual tensions—with a completeness never achieved before.[7]

To have visited Daphni, Eleusis, and Delphi in succession while in Greece was for me a spiritual as well as a physical experience. At Daphni, a few miles to the west of Athens, are the splendid and

5. Though here a comment from the standpoint of later Talmudic Judaism should be noted. "The anthropomorphic descriptions of God that abound in the Bible have from the earliest times been understood as mere figures of speech employed to impress upon the mind the reality and providence of God and to instruct man in the knowledge of his ways." Quoted from Isidore Epstein, *Judaism: A Historical Presentation* (Harmondsworth: Penguin Books, 1959), p. 137.

6. See Lewis Richard Farnell, *Outline-History of Greek Religion* (London: Duckworth & Co., 1921), p. 103.

7. Eric Newton and William Neil, *Christian Art* (New York: Harper & Row, 1966), p. 140.

largely intact buildings of the monastery of the Dormition of the
Virgin. The name Daphni or Daphneion came from the laurels that
grew around the monastery, a memory of the ancient cult of Apollo.
A temple of this god, situated on the same spot, was destroyed under
the Emperor Theodosius, about 395 A.D. In this we have a reminder
that paganism in the late fourth century was by no means extinct; its
suppression came by much the same methods of harassment as those
to which Christianity had been subjected at an earlier date. At Rome
itself could be seen temples, incense, and sacrifices in full vigor. In
Greece the mysteries of Eleusis and the Olympian games, linked as
they were with the heathen gods, flourished until they were forcibly
suppressed. The emperors Gratian and Theodosius between them
put an end to the popular worship, though the pagan rites still lingered on among the patrician households of Rome. The substance of
a decree, issued by Theodosius, dated November 8, 392, is of considerable interest:

> If any one, by placing incense, venerates either images made by
> mortal labour, or those which are enduring, or if anyone in ridiculous
> fashion forthwith venerates what he has represented, either by a tree
> encircled with garlands or an altar of cut turfs (though the advantage
> of such service is small, the injury to religion is complete), let him, as
> guilty of sacrilege, be punished by the loss of that house or possession in
> which he worshipped according to the heathen superstition. For all places
> which shall smoke with incense, if they shall be proved to belong to
> those who burn incense, shall be confiscated.[8]

Had the Theodosian rule extended to India and the Far East, to say
nothing of the African continent, or if the edict were applicable
today, the result would be a violent onslaught on the religious beliefs
and practices of hundreds of millions of our fellow men.

The philosophical tradition of Greece was later to suffer a similar
fate at the hands of a Christian emperor to that of its worship. In 528
A.D. Justinian issued a constitution forbidding "persons persisting in
the madness of Hellenism to teach any branch of knowledge," thus
striking directly at the Athenian professors. Shortly afterward the
property of the Platonic Academy was confiscated, and the intellectual life of Greece came to an end. Justinian had achieved his purpose, that "no branch of learning be taught by those who labour

8. Quoted from B. J. Kidd, *Documents Illustrative of the History of the
Church,* Vol. 2, (London: S.P.C.K.; New York: Macmillan, 1938), p. 127.

under the insanity of the impious pagans." [9] A further melancholy
fact, touching as it does Christian ecumenism, should be recalled
before we leave the environs of Athens and the monastic church at
Daphni with its superb mosaics still to be seen, dominated by the
resplendent Christ Pantocrator in the cupola. The monastery was
sacked by the Crusaders in 1205—one outrage among the many
offenses committed by these dubious adventurers against Greek Orthodoxy. As they came with the blessing of Rome, their escapades
should be kept in mind, along with other complicating factors, by
those on the Roman side, who seek—with little hope of success, I
would think, within the predictable future—formal reunion with the
Oriental churches.

What exactly were the celebrated "Eleusinian Mysteries"? The
question had fascinated me from the earliest days of my theological
studies. These rites had been performed at Eleusis, some fourteen
miles west of Athens, for centuries before the birth of Christianity.
The "mysteries" of the Catholic liturgy and sacramental system, so I
had been taught, had nothing to do with those of Eleusis other than
a coincidence of names. Be that as it may, the Hellenic mysteries,
which excited the religious interest of the Graeco-Roman world
(every Athenian was obliged to undergo at least a preliminary initiation), were carried out in a sanctuary not much more than thirty
miles from Corinth, where St. Paul had resided for some length of
time, probably 51–52 A.D. Then, as now, one must pass Eleusis when
traveling between Athens and Corinth. When writing to his converts
there, he employs the term "mysteries" on three occasions (1 Corinthians 4:1; 13:2; 14:2) and not elsewhere (in its plural form). Could
its use at the beginning of the hymn to Christian love (agape)—
". . . if I . . . understand all mysteries . . . but have not love, I
am nothing . . ." (13:2)—be an implied reference to Eleusis? At
any rate, I welcomed the opportunity to visit what remains of both
Corinth and Eleusis. But first a few words about the latter.

The town lies to the northwest of Athens. Archaeologists have
worked constructively at the existing ruins, and the plan of the sanctuary of the great goddesses, Demeter and her daughter Persephone,
is now easily discernible. Access to the sanctuary—surrounded by a
high fortified wall, doubled on the entrance side—was forbidden to

9. *Ibid.*, Vol. 3, p. 26.

the uninitiated under pain of death. Those initiated into the Eleusinian mysteries were pledged to die rather than disclose their secret, and that pledge has been extraordinarily well kept. No one to this day can say for certain what precisely was the term of the initiatory rite. A tribal fertility cult may have lain at its origins, but the Homeric hymn to Demeter shows that as early as the sixth century B.C. the myth had made its appeal to the whole Hellenic world. Initiation was open to women and occasionally to slaves. There was much public activity linked with the ceremonies, including a procession from and back to Athens, accompanied by singing and dancing. But just what took place in the initiation room, the Telesterion?

Scholars have concluded that a sacrament of some kind formed part of the preliminary rite: the initiates drank from a sacred cup in which were mystically infused the very life and substance of the kindly Earth Mother, with whom their own being was transcendentally united. But the climax of the rite was a solemn pageant, staged with lighting effects and every device calculated to affect the sensibility, in which certain sacred things fraught with mystic power were shown to the initiated. This was followed by mimetic performances showing the action and passion of a divine drama, portraying the abduction of Persephone, the sorrow and long search of her mother Demeter, and their final reunion and reconciliation. Cicero, in his *de Legibus*, expresses the view that Athens had produced nothing finer than the mysteries of Eleusis, not only with respect to the ordering and civilizing of life, but in regard to the furnishing of a good hope after death. The Church Fathers, as might be expected, regarded these mysteries with suspicion and even horror, but their popularity and influence appear to have waned but little until they were forcibly suppressed by a Christian emperor toward the close of the fourth century.

One other pagan shrine I visited in the course of these worldly-unworldly wanderings before returning home was the sanctuary of Apollo at Delphi. "After the Athenian Acropolis, probably the most impressive sight in Greece," to quote the words of *Hachette's Guide Book*. I had no difficulty in accepting this verdict. "The robust originality of its grandiose and varied scenery 'tortured by the rages of the Shaker of the Earth' [10] contrasts with the calm of the sacred plain,

10. The god Poseidon.

covered with olive groves, and the luminous air of the Gulf of Itea which one sees in the distance." By the sixth century B.C. Delphi had attained pre-eminence among all the Greek holy sites; the oracle was constantly being consulted by inquirers from near and far. The Delphi priests consequently acquired a good deal of information about this and that, not to mention considerable political influence. It was their task to interpret the ecstatic and often incoherent utterances of the Pythian prophetess; and as the questions put to her were required to be fairly specific—e.g., the proper moment to plan a voyage, the place where a colony should be founded, the chances of success in war or marriage or business—no supernatural revelation was required to provide a reasonably satisfying answer. General questions about one's personal destiny were discouraged as being offensive to Zeus.

The sacred buildings at Delphi were several times destroyed and several times rebuilt, so ready were the Greeks to contribute to the maintenance of their central shrine in its heyday. The sayings of the Seven Sages inscribed on the walls of the Temple of Apollo, so a classicist friend assures me, probably made no more impact than the average message on a wayside pulpit today; but their content strikes me as rather more luminous—"Know yourself," "Nothing in excess." Inevitably the glories of Delphi were to pass, even before they were finally extinguished by the Theodosian decree already mentioned. The oracle came to be ridiculed by the more sophisticated, among them the poet Lucian, who flourished in the reign of Marcus Aurelius. The Christian emperors, led by Constantine, robbed the Apollonian temple of its treasures to beautify the new city of Constantinople. By this date Eleusis held undisputed pre-eminence as the site for the celebration of the pre-Christian forms of worship.

But now, what of the relevance of all this for today? Have I been digressing from, while trying to illustrate, a point which seems worth making—that religion, if it is to be genuine, must be both unworldly and worldly at the same time? It is significant that the Greeks use the same word for both goodness and beauty. The emphasis is thus thrown on what is appropriate to the time and place in human action; conduct is to be judged by its fittingness, its suitability to the occasion. The Hebrew prophets with their stress on "righteousness" in terms of compliance with the will of a transcendent God would doubtless be unhappy with such a point of view. The religions of

India would, I imagine, find it rather superficial, since the Hindu-Buddhist tradition is concerned with "realization" as an aspect of ultimate truth. Nevertheless, there is much to be said in matters of religion for holding together in harmony the ancient triad—the true, the good, and the beautiful.

Worldly unworldliness implies a capacity "to care and not to care," to be fully involved with other people, with the community, with what one has to do, and yet paradoxically, while mind and heart are responding to the full, to be quietly aware that from the nature of things every individual commitment short of the ultimate one has its limits. These limits do not arise from self-preoccupation or ungenerosity but from the situation itself, of which we must be fully aware. One of the central doctrines of the Bhagavad-Gita stresses the importance of working with nonattachment. What is implied is not any neglect of the work itself; we ought to be fully engaged with it. The requirement is that we should have a nonpossessive attitude toward its results. "Perform every action with your heart fixed on the supreme Lord. Renounce attachment to the fruits. Be even-tempered in success or failure." We are responsible for what we do; but the results depend on factors beyond our control. Therefore we should not be weighed down with a sense of responsibility for them. The work itself requires us to be worldly, for it is in the world that it is to be done. The nonattachment to results cannot be achieved without a sense of unworldliness. The point was made by St. Paul to the church at Corinth: "Those who deal with the world" are to act "as though they had no dealings with it" (1 Corinthians 7:31). Although the context shows that his advice is given in the expectation that "the appointed time has grown very short" (verse 29), it remains true by any reckoning that the human condition is bound up with impermanence: "For the form of this world is passing away."

At the end of April, 1968, I was able to spend several hours amid the ruins of the city to whose tiny Christian community these words were first addressed. St. Paul had been at Corinth in 51–52 A.D. to preach the new religion of Christianity to the most frivolous and dissolute society in the pagan world. It was here that as a tentmaker he had lived in the tentmaking household of Aquila and Priscilla, earning a living by his trade so that he should not be financially beholden to those to whom he brought the "good news." They were to be reminded, in what is still the earliest written record known to us (1 Corinthians 11:23–26), of what sharing in the Holy Eucharist implied. Egoistic individualism must yield place to a living sense of community: "The cup of blessing which we bless, is it not a participation in the blood of Christ? The bread which we break, is it not a participation in the body of Christ? Because there is one bread, we who are many are one body, for we all partake of the one bread" (10:16–17).

Paul himself may fittingly have the last word on what I have called "worldly unworldliness." For all his preoccupation with God's kingdom and the cross of Christ, his attitude to the whole realm of human values is open-minded and generous. Anything worthwhile in the world we live in can be thought about and accepted. "Finally, brethren, whatever is true, whatever is honourable, whatever is just, whatever is pure, whatever is lovely, whatever is gracious, if there is any excellence, if there is anything worthy of praise, think about these things" (Philippians 4:8).

8. Toward Realizing Religion

i. Suggestions

By way of emphasizing the tentative nature of this and the following chapters, and indeed of all that has so far been said, the author's standpoint should perhaps again be made clear. As a Catholic I gladly accept whatever the Church authoritatively teaches; I respect its officials when acting within their rights, and I would not wish to say or do anything harmful to the Church's genuine interests. However, this loyalty and affection, for it is nothing less, spring from a sense of gratitude to the institution in which I was brought up and by which I have been so greatly helped, rather than from any conviction that the Church as yet presents religion in its totality. The troubles through which the ecclesiastical establishment is now passing, even while they elicit the sympathy of thoughtful onlookers, are not hard to account for. Nor, unhappily, are they likely to grow less. Here G. K. Chesterton's lines may well apply.

> I tell you naught for your comfort,
> Yea, naught for your desire,
> Save that the sky grows darker yet
> And the sea rises higher.

No one, it seems to me, is particularly to blame for the situation that now confronts us: one of confusion and uncertainty. The disparity between the official Church's claims on its own behalf and what the world in general, including many Catholics, is prepared to concede is the real question at issue. The Second Vatican Council was a symptom, not a cause or a possible solvent, of the unrest that lay behind the apparently monolithic façade. The Council's participants were habituated to exercising the Church's regulative functions, not to examining with scrupulous reference to the original Christian proclamation what their limitations might be. Hence they failed, for all their good intentions, to achieve much that was calculated to bring lasting satisfaction. They did what they could: they put out a great many documents, some of them quite liberal in tone and content, and they changed the liturgy, which proved a highly controversial step. As a result, there is a greater sense of freedom among the faithful, an increased awareness that the structure of the Church is not so much hierarchical as communal, but little evidence of any deepening of its interior life. Encouragement has been given from the highest quarters to the practice of traditional asceticism; what has been lacking is an indication that humanity's present condition is well understood. There have been many encounters, an abundance of dialogue, and much discussion, but few signs of "renewal" with regard to ways and means directed to raising the general level of mutual understanding and compassion.

At its present stage the ecumenical movement appears to be no more than a pointer in this direction. Dialogue on controversial matters and interdenominational worship, though attracting sections of the clergy and their supporters, do not always have the intended results. During a recent church-unity week in a large northern city an observer remarked that he could detect only two religions in effective operation; one was anti-Catholicism and the other anti-Protestantism. If ecumenism is to be taken as anything more serious than an amiable "togetherness," it should be working from the bottom upward rather than from the top downward. Essentially it is a long-term educational process beginning, I should have thought, in the schoolroom and home rather than in churches and assembly halls. Such a program would involve ultimately the study of *religion* rather than religions (are Christian ecumenists really prepared to face this prospect?), thus promoting friendship and mutual respect at the most impressionable age. Courteous exchanges between representative members of the clergy, each highly conscious of his position, are hardly a substitute for the intercommunion of everyday life, sharing experiences at the basically human level.

Before an education in ecumenism has been achieved, the policy of conducting interdenominational services and exchange of pulpits seems to me of questionable wisdom. The outward structure in which religion is preserved and by which it is manifested is of immense psychological value—as the Roman Church until recently has shown itself keenly aware. The traditional practices of each of the

Christian churches have had a formative influence on their members: to abandon or change such distinctive ways of worship, or to mingle them with others hitherto regarded as strange and unacceptable, is to suggest that they are to be treated as of small importance. From the ultimate standpoint this may be the enlightened attitude, but it is surely better that it should develop unforced in each individual rather than be organized from above in the form of mass demonstrations. An ecumenism of the spirit, which is the point and purpose of the search for Christian unity, does not easily lend itself to portrayal before press photographers and television cameras.

The same principles apply to what has been called "the larger ecumenism"—the approach of the Church to the religions of the East. One of the aims of the present essay is to suggest that institutional Christianity, when conducting its long overdue self-examination, should avail itself of certain insights from India. What is emphatically not intended is any attempt at mingling the essentials of Christian and non-Christian worship, or ignoring the ideological differences between East and West. The cultural roots of Catholicism on the one hand, and of Hinduism and Buddhism on the other, lie far too deep to be reached by any ecumenical "dialogue." Only through a form of spiritual practice enabling the individual to attain a level deeper than that of cultural roots can any progress in this direction be made.

The eventual detaching of religion from its setting in a specific culture, so that it floats free of every cultural context and yet can be embodied in any—an enterprise not so far achieved, hardly even attempted, in the history of the human race—is surely the goal to which a radical ecumenism invites us. If Christianity is to become a genuine world religion—and not merely worldwide, as an adjunct of Western imperialism, commercial expansion, industry, science, and technology—then it may have to practice corporately what it preaches to the individual: ". . . unless a grain of wheat falls into the earth and dies, it remains alone; but if it dies, it bears much fruit" (John 12:24). Thus, for example, much of the suffering in the Church today is caused, not by stupidity or ill-will, as is sometimes supposed, but by a decision-making process that stems from the arbitrary rule of Byzantium, a superficially Romanized form of Oriental despotism, having little to do with either the freedom of the Gospel or the natural rights of the individual.

The currently developing concept that Church authority should be exercised with the consent of those affected and that even the appearance of autocratic rule is undesirable is not a notion derived from modern secular democracy. Its origin is to be found in the Greece of classical times, to which Western civilization owes so much. "Arbitrary government offended the Greek in his very soul," writes Professor Kitto. "That he was not a god, he knew; but he was at least a man. He knew that the gods were quick to strike down without mercy the man who aped divinity, and that of all human qualities they most approved modesty and reverence." Yet the fact remains that "the Oriental custom of obeisance struck the Greek as not 'eleutheron' (= free-spirited); in his eyes it was an affront to human dignity. Even to the gods the Greek prayed like a man, erect; though he knew as well as any the difference between the human and the divine." [1]

The thought occurs that the Church might most of all be helped if the attention of the faithful, and not the faithful only, were drawn with fresh emphasis and in a new way to Christianity's central proclamation—its message concerning God and its manner of presenting Christ. No abandonment of traditional teaching is here being proposed; we shall be concerned only with a question of emphasis, supported by what is to be found in the New Testament revelation. A fact that has often been noted in the history of religion is that the mass of mankind find it more natural to be polytheistic than monotheistic, to have many gods instead of just one. The mythologies of India and Greece rejoice in a multiplicity of gods; the Semitic religions, Judaism and Islam, are more restrained, but even there deviations from strict monotheism—the divinization of angels, for example—are to be found. Orthodox Christianity has combined monotheism with trinitarianism, and the Catholic Church has substituted its throngs of saints for the pantheons of Greece and Rome.

The honor paid to the Blessed Virgin Mary is noteworthy in this connection. Merely Biblical Christianity is heavily weighted in favor of the male of our species. Consequently, many New Testament scholars, particularly those who dismiss the first two chapters of Luke as literary invention, are reluctant to accept Catholicism's insistence on the unique form of worship to be paid to the Mother of Jesus. We have already noted how in Hinduism the gods were not

1. Kitto, *The Greeks*, pp. 9, 10.

left without their female consorts. A comparable situation existed in the Graeco-Roman world at the time Christianity was born. Demeter, the mother-goddess, one of the great divinities of Greece, was the central figure of the Eleusinian mysteries. Her Egyptian counterpart was Isis, whose worship was introduced into Rome toward the end of the Republic and became very popular. The early Christians, many of whom were to be martyred, must have seen the splendid temple to Isis in the Campus Martius. "The Isis cult in particular seems to have produced a really living and spiritual type of piety. Isis becomes the sum of all deity, the Queen of Heaven. She is also the Mother goddess, who, like the Christian Madonna in later times, nurses the holy child in her bosom." [2] It is hardly to be wondered at that as the centuries passed the Mother of Jesus should be accorded a place of supreme honor.

Mary's role as mediatrix, along with her Son as the "one mediator," demonstrates in itself that men are not happy with an almighty God who so infinitely transcends them as to seem totally inaccessible. That God is not actually "up there," that he is, as the theologians express it, immanent as well as transcendent, is a truism familiar theoretically to every Christian schoolchild. Nevertheless, God's exaltation above man as his Ruler and Lord is the aspect of the divine that dominates the Church's liturgy and theology, and it is this which needs to be complemented by an appreciation of God's nearness. At least three factors conspired together at the birth of Christianity to place a veritable chasm between God and man. First, we have the Judaic emphasis precisely on the divine transcendence, the horror of even the appearance of divinizing nature, and the prophetic emphasis that man is subordinate to God as the earth to the heavens (Isaiah 55:9). Secondly, the heroic Christian resistance to emperor worship—"divine" Caesar actually being accorded the titles *dominus* and *deus*—a blasphemy denounced in the New Testament apocalyptic book Revelation (13:1), which stresses the exaltation of "the Lamb" above any power on earth (5: 11–14). Finally, the linking of the Christian revelation with the Platonic-Aristotelian philosophical tradition, so that God comes to be conceptualized as the Absolute, the "supreme good" of Plato, the "pure act" of Aristotle.

The validity of all this is not here being questioned, but the sublimity needs to be counterbalanced, as in fact it is in St. Paul's speech

2. Bultmann, *Primitive Christianity*, p. 159.

in the Areopagus, by the truth that God is also indescribably close to us. The author of the Acts of Apostles, deeply concerned to commend Christianity to the pagan world, reports Paul as quoting with approval the words of the poet Aratus of Soli, who flourished about 270 B.C., to the effect that man is born of God: "For we are indeed his offspring" (Acts 17:28). Obviously, this says more than the familiar Judaic teaching that God is omnipresent (cf. Psalm 139). Linked with the words, "In him we live and move and have our being," there emerges a position that could have been endorsed by the Stoics, as was no doubt intended. For the Stoics held that God is with man and within him and would have understood the statement pantheistically.[3] Both the substance and the manner of this approach to a world yet to be converted clearly has relevance today, when believers and unbelievers alike are looking for an explanation of human life less remote than that provided by a power outside the system, a God beyond the sky.

Nor is the seeming remoteness of God entirely overcome by focusing attention on the orthodox doctrine of the Incarnation, though a good deal of devotional writing takes little account of this fact. We have already noted [4] that the official Church, as long ago as the fifth century, took care to maintain the nonidentity of the human and divine natures even in Christ. Moreover, the traditional view is that Christ's union with God is unique; no other human being could be said to be personally divine. Here we have what is perhaps the Church's least acceptable dogma from the standpoint of the non-Christian world. In Mahayana Buddhism, for example, it is believed that everyone has the potential to become as fully enlightened as was Gautama; but a Christian is not encouraged to believe that he can become in a literal sense another Christ. When St. Paul claimed to be living with the very life of Christ (Galatians 2:20), he was pointing to a goal that cannot be adequately expressed in any orthodox formula. The livelier minds in the Church today show a sound instinct in stressing the New Testament witness instead of the abstractions of the old-time theologians. Yet again, the titles given to Jesus, used frequently by his followers as the Church was making its difficult way within the hostile Roman Empire, need to be balanced by others, no less scriptural but more in keeping with the sentiment of the world we live in today. Lord, Son of God, Saviour should have

3. On pantheism, see p. 200.   4. See pp. 76–77.

for their complement servant (Mark 10:45; Philippians 2:7), brother (Romans 8:29), friend (John 15:14–15). Perhaps as the Church's worship comes more and more into contact with life as it actually is, we shall hear from the lips of the chief celebrant at Mass some such supplication as the following.

O God, whose offspring we are, in whom we live and move and have our being, teach us always to act in the spirit of your Son, so that now and hereafter we may keep company with him, the first born among us his family, Jesus Christ our Lord.

ii. Prayer

All true prayer, whether expressed in the first person singular or plural, is an act of community, since we are members one of another. The individualism of private prayer and meditation should be in appearance only; if an increase of fellow feeling toward others fails to result, something is wrong. Negatively, it is not possible to compose oneself alone in prayer of any depth and earnestness and to be at the same time out of charity with anyone. Positively, prayer is robbed of its fruit if it does not issue in genuine friendliness, combined with generous and constructive action toward those who have claims upon us and even to those who do not. Physically we may be isolated when at prayer; but spiritual isolation, to be without openness toward and concern for those around us, is merely self-defeating. In that condition we cannot truly pray.

Nevertheless, there is a difference between public and private prayer. When worshiping together, we are witnessing as a corporate group and should feel ourselves to be such. Within much less than a lifetime the hieratic, stylized worship of past ages—linked historically with kingly despotism—has given place to a much less formal, more intimate, liturgical manner, better suited to a democratic society. We are still in the midst of this transition, which like all seemingly drastic changes, is painful to many. Yet no sensible person can doubt that the future of popular worship lies in this direction. But once this is admitted, private, personal prayer, or rather prayerfulness, is still, I think, the heart of the matter. Speaking autobiographically, I am sometimes accused of underestimating the importance of corporate worship, and this may be fair enough. But it seems to me that you can best attain the needful concentration—the "one-pointedness," as it has been called—when one is silent and alone, or with a small group engaged in a similar effort. Jesus taught us to say the Our Father, which is a communal prayer; but perhaps he indicated that its informing spirit can best be captured when we observe the proviso: "But when you pray, go into your room and shut the door and pray to your Father who is in secret; and your Father who sees in secret will reward you" (Matthew 6:6).

Only exceptionally are we able, when alone and meditative, to recite with conviction a prayer composed by another person. Where other people's prayers can sometimes be helpful, however, as a Benedictine abbot recently pointed out to me, is by way of what in monastic circles is known as *lectio divina,* "holy reading." Certain texts, calculated to lift the mind above the daily routine and to elicit a fruitful response, are considered, which the reader then reflects on, accepting or discarding the message as his insight dictates. Thus the hypothetical Collect printed above[5] could be recited sincerely by me, but possibly by no one else; yet its underlying thought might prove to be of more than personal interest.

Psychologically, it goes without saying, prayers are minor revelations of the character, the limitations and needs of the person who prays: "Jesus gentle and lowly in heart, make my heart like unto yours." "O Sacred Heart of Jesus, I put all my trust in you." "Blessed be the holy and undivided Trinity now and for ever." "O Mary conceived without sin, pray for us who have recourse to you." "O Lord Jesus Christ, Son of God, have mercy on me." "Blessed be God for ever." "Jesus." "God be blessed." "God be praised." "God, God . . ." Such aspirations as these, familiar to every Catholic, most of them learned in childhood, still break into the mind whenever I try, not very successfully, to pray.

By way of celebrating my religious profession—that is, taking monastic vows—in 1931, a kind friend gave me a small edition of the

---

5. *The Collect,* as is well explained in the Cambridgeshire Syllabus of Religious Teaching for Schools (1939), is a "highly developed form of great beauty and with a full and unified content. A 'regular' Collect consists of five parts: (1) The address to God; expanded (2) by a relative clause indicating the special grounds on which we approach him; (3) the petition; (4) the purpose of our petition; (5) the ending." Quoted from *Daily Prayer,* ed. Eric Milner-White and G. W. Briggs (Harmondsworth: Penguin Books, 1959), p. 200.

Roman missal. Sadly out of date nowadays, it still remains on my shelf. Shortly after receiving it, I wrote out on the flyleaf a prayer composed by St. Thomas Aquinas. Its manner is medieval, but I used to recite it daily throughout my student and teaching years. It may retain a little interest, at least for those engaged in the business of study and imparting knowledge to others:

Ineffable Creator, who out of the treasures of your wisdom has appointed three hierarchies of angels and set them in admirable array high above the heavens, disposing also the various parts of the universe in such marvelous array: You are the true source of light and the supreme principle of wisdom. Be pleased, therefore, to cast a beam of your radiance on the darkness of my mind, and dispel from me the double darkness of sin and ignorance in which I was born.

You who make eloquent the tongues of little children, fashion my words and pour upon my lips the grace of your benediction. Grant me penetration to understand, capacity to retain, method and facility in study, subtlety in interpretation and abundant grace of expression.

Order the beginning, direct the progress and perfect achievement of my work, you who are true God and true man, living and reigning for ever and ever.

One of the duties of Benedictines is to recite or sing together in community the Psalms. The practice might well be studied afresh with a view to revision. Inspired, so we are taught, by the Holy Spirit, these Hebrew poems appear, for the most part, as very much bound up with a time and place that are simply not ours. Frequently self-righteous in sentiment and rancorous in tone, they are an odd form of address to a God whose essence, according to Christian belief, is love. The best of them (I think especially of Psalms 8, 19, 23, 34, 51, 84, 90, 91, 103 and 139)[6] can hardly be surpassed in any form of worship, but they cannot, for all their solemn impact, extinguish the critical spirit. Even the touching 23rd Psalm "The Lord is my shepherd, I shall not want," is marred for me by our being notified that the Lord's banquet is prepared—derisively, one presumes—"in the presence of my enemies" (verse 5). We are here at some remove, or so I feel, from the worship due to a God who "makes his sun rise on the evil and on the good, and sends rain on the just and on the unjust" (Matthew 5:45). And yet it is pleasant to engage in psalm-

---

6. The numeration here follows the Hebrew Bible, i.e., the nonbracketed numbering of the Psalms in the Catholic edition of the Revised Standard Version.

ody with one's monastic brethren in the early morning hours or at evening. Being at worship with those to whom one is linked by so many communal ties turns the rhythmic chanting into an agreeable lullaby, soothing one through, unnoticed, when need be, the not so agreeable words.

Finally, not long ago I was asked to compose a series of twenty short prayers, suitable for use by youngsters while at school. The following petitions reflect, though without explicit reference, both the theological and moral virtues of Christianity and the Buddha's "noble eightfold path." Again, if they have any value, it is probably to be found more in their being read privately than publicly recited.

Twenty Prayers—of Possible Interest to Young People

O God, since you often seem unreal and far away, please make yourself real and near to me, so that I may be what you would have me be and act as you would have me act.

O God, please give me clarity of mind, so that seeing other people and every situation as they are, and not as confused by my own hopes and fears, I may act according to your truth.

O God, teach me as soon as possible to discover my true self and how to shape my life; for it is only in the light of that knowledge that I can be close to you and live happily in this world.

O God, help me to think before I speak or act, so as to relate my speech and actions to an end that is worthy and pleasing to you.

O God, grant me light and strength to hold in check the pursuit of my own interests; preserve me from riding roughshod over anyone, and help me always to be fair in my dealings with other people.

O God, make me brave and able to stand the strain: teach me to understand that courage does not lie so much in aggressiveness, as in being patient—patient with myself, with other people, and with the disagreeable situations that duty requires me to face.

O God, teach me to steer a middle course between excess and defect, between being overenthusiastic and apathetic, between developing a character that is too hard or too soft, between being a puritan kill-joy or a sensual hedonist: for the good life in this material world consists in holding the balance between extremes.

O God, enlighten my faith and strengthen my trust in you; for it is only when I commit myself to you who are unseen that I can do your will amid the anxieties and troubles of daily life.

O God, make me a loving person: so that I may respond to you who are Love itself and to the lovableness, often hidden by my own blindness, in everyone I meet.

O God, teach me not just to turn on the charm, but to be truly friendly; not merely to those I like but to those to whom I feel indifferent or even hostile.

O God, help me to understand how I must lose self in order to find self, for only then can I really sympathize with those who have a right to my compassion: all who are suffering or in trouble.

O God, teach me the secret of true joy: give me the grace to live in the present, not to be overanxious about the future, to regard those around me cheerfully but with affectionate concern, and not to take myself too seriously.

O God, give me the grace not to be thrown off balance, or to get overexcited about things that disturb me. Help me to understand that there are other points of view besides mine, and in all emergencies grant me calm of mind.

O God, guard me against the evils of hatred, aversion, and resentment. As long as I harbor these, all peace is gone; so help me to turn my mind away from these deadly darkeners of the heart.

O God, give me a true understanding, wisdom rather than cleverness. Let me not become dull and stupid and lacking in common sense simply because I fail to pay careful attention to people and the situations with which I have to deal.

O God, take care of me particularly when I have lustful thoughts and desires, when my imagination is full of sensual fantasies. Grant that you, who understand human nature perfectly, will help me not to fall—and when I do, may I quickly return, not too burdened with a sense of guilt, to serve you afresh.

O God, give me strength of resolve. Let me see clearly what is true and right, where my duty lies, and then resolutely carry out, despite all difficulties, what I know should be done.

O God, give me the grace to be truthful and tactful in speech. Let me not tell lies, so as to deceive others, or say anything that is indiscreet or hurtful.

O God, help me to concentrate my mind, particularly in matters of study, so as to eliminate daydreaming and distractions, focusing my attention precisely on what has to be done.

O God, strengthen and perfect my memory. Guard me against forgetting things that don't happen to interest me. Above all, never let me be forgetful of you.

These petitions are open to criticism as being too self-regarding. It should be remembered, however, that selfless sentiments verbally expressed do not necessarily leave us any the less self-centered. Prayer can be sheer praise, an end in itself, and this, they say, is the highest form of worship. Nevertheless, I think that prayer is intended in the long run to have a transforming effect, a transformation that can take place only in us, not in God. The prayer of petition should instruct as well as plead, making explicit what are our true needs. About these we are sometimes, particularly when young, unclear. Therefore, we could be helped by having put upon our lips, or at least reviewing in our minds, sentences and sentiments that embody a wisdom long tried and tested. To attain that wisdom, the masters of the spiritual life are agreed, we shall have to pass beyond any form of words. But in general it is well for us to remember that prayer is basically an effort to bring our consciousness into a condition where we can hear what God has to say to us. Prayer is not a method of influencing God but of being influenced by him.

iii. Meditation

Books on specifically Christian meditation abound. Their message, needless to say, will not here be overlooked; though we shall be chiefly concerned with meditation in all its generality,[7]

7. For those who might be interested in a specifically Buddhist form of meditation, as it emerges from Japan, *The Way of Zazen* by Rindo Fujimoto Roshi, may be warmly recommended. This brief and illuminating essay is published in pamphlet form by the Cambridge Buddhist Association, Cambridge, Massachussetts, 1961. Translated by Tetsuya Inoue and Yoshihiko Tanigawa,

which might be summed up in the term "mindfulness." Commonly
we think of meditating on or about something. We have a theme for
our meditation. This makes sense as giving a focus to our minds. But
whatever theme we choose, even the highest, we usually find that it
turns out to be rather banal and cannot hold our attention. So we
become distracted, our minds wander, we daydream, which is a form
of wishful thinking, and meditation becomes as frustrating as, perhaps more frustrating than, any of our normal everyday activities.
Here I would suggest that the fine point of meditation is not to think
about something, however edifying, but just to *be* something—in
this case our true selves. Whenever we are doing anything that requires external action—necessary as it is that we should be concerned with external activity almost all day long—we are never quite
our true selves. We are actors, doers, assuming some necessary role
or other, though it could be a highly virtuous, even a heroic role.

Yet at times we need just to be ourselves—for it is only when a
man's actions flow out, so to speak, from his true being that they
make acceptable sense. It is commonly admitted, I think, that we
are our best selves when we are wide awake and aware. Not self-
consciously aware, in an egoistic self-preoccupied sense, but in so far
as our consciousness is actualized—existentially (to use a current
phrase)—so that in some indefinable way our being and our knowledge merge. Momentarily freed from distractions—we just *are*. To
achieve this condition implies not that we should think about something but rather that we should think about *nothing* (no-thing).
However, our minds being what they are, this seems almost impossible. As soon as we strive to think about *nothing*, that too becomes a
thing (perhaps an image of a circle, or an empty hole), and we are
as badly off as ever. What we can do, though, if we are sufficiently
alert, is not to cling to any thought—to let all thoughts flow by, detach ourselves from them, so allowing them to fade away into nothingness from lack of attention. For anyone tempted to ask what all
this has to do with God, it should be remembered that we cannot,
strictly speaking, think about God. We can only think about an idea
of God in our minds, or a picture of God in our imagination—and
neither the idea nor the image is God, or even a remotely adequate

---

with an Introduction by Elsie P. Mitchell. For an authoritative exposition of
Zen Buddhism according to the Soto tradition by Fujimoto Roshi, see my *Conversations: Christian and Buddhist*, pp. 88–112.

representation of God. "What God actually is always remains hidden from us," writes St. Thomas Aquinas in his *De Veritate*. "And this is the highest knowledge we can have of God in the present life, that we know him to be beyond every thought we are able to think of him."

What is now to be said is intended to be practical and deliberately to avoid theory. The aim is to describe a technique of meditation that I have observed in the East and to suggest how it might be applied in a Western context. We shall be involved in nothing occult or mysterious, only with a concentration and perhaps an expansion of natural consciousness. The aim is not to meditate about anything or anyone in particular but to attain a meditative state—mindfulness.

Usually the best time to meditate is in the early morning, though for many people this is not practicable, and for them probably the most suitable time is not too late (so as to avoid undue tiredness) in the evening. A reasonable degree of quiet and a room not too brightly lit are the first prerequisites. Bodily posture is important. Young people can usually learn fairly quickly to sit cross-legged, supported by a cushion or thick rug, Eastern fashion, on the floor. This is the most helpful position, being the one, as long experience has shown, most conducive to mental calm. It has a number of variants; one of these should be learned and if possible adhered to until, after some practice, it can be maintained without difficulty. The best situation, at least to begin with, is to have a small group of meditants presided over by an experienced instructor. To be seated on a chair or bench in the normal Western manner is only a minor disadvantage. A much greater one is to be kneeling with one's shoulders slumped forward and one's face more or less covered, or reclining backward as if in an armchair, since the former attitude impedes breathing as well as, like the latter, tending to induce sleepiness. The spine should be erect, the eyelids lowered but not closed completely, the hands gently in contact with each other at the center of one's body. The immediate object in view is to achieve a balanced physical posture in which the mind is calm yet fully awake. Physically, one is neither relaxed nor under strain, achieving attention without tension.

Breathing should next be attended to. This must not be forced artificially in any way; the important thing is that it be *noticed*. Normally we breathe without being aware that we do. In the early stages of practice, at the beginning of meditation though not throughout its course, we should make the quite considerable effort of concentration required to observe each one of our intakes and outputs of breath. (Try to count the inhalations and exhalations; the chances are that you will lose count before reaching ten!) Let the breathing be as slow and regular as possible without any special expenditure of effort. Gradually you should experience calm.

Within the mind itself what are called "distractions" do not matter, provided two conditions are observed: first, that we are not engaged in planned thinking, for example, reviewing the work to be done or the problems to be solved in the near future; secondly, that we are not conceptualizing, that is, forming ideas or images, presenting some kind of mental spectacle, large or small, to ourselves. If these two nonmeditative activities are avoided, then the seemingly continuous flow of conscious imagery need not disturb us. We shall find that for a time at least we can withdraw our minds completely from our internal moving-picture show with the result that we are in a state of full awareness without the external senses being activated by, or the mind fixed on, anything in particular. To designate this condition of "mindfulness"—that is, the mind being actualized in complete consciousness—which is not the preserve of any one religion, the Hindu-Buddhist tradition uses the term samadhi.[8] Westerners have applied to it Milton's strikingly apt phrase, describing his experience of music: "Such sober certainty of waking bliss."

In this state of alert calm we are very near to the heart of reality. As a consequence, the Christian will often find his religious emotions deeply stirred. He may feel himself pervaded by a sense of his own emptiness and of God's fullness. This in turn will probably evoke certain devout aspirations that can be inwardly vocalized. These will almost invariably take the form of pure praise, rejoicing in the fact that God is. If his mercy is asked for, as in this condition it often is, the request will not have for its motive fear or spiritual self-seeking; it will be prompted by the awareness that without God we are nothing.

There is a variant of this form of meditation that can be recommended to those who despite what has just been said find themselves overwhelmed by distractions and extraneous thoughts. Take one of the verbal paradoxes in which the New Testament abounds and use

8. See pp. 155–156.

it as a focus for concentration. Here are some obvious examples: "Many that are first will be last, and the last first." "Whoever will save his life will lose it." "Why do you call me good? No one is good but God alone." "It is no longer I who live, but Christ who lives in me." Other examples will also occur to the reader. It will be noticed that I have not supplied the references for these texts. The reason is that for meditation purposes they need not be looked up and studied according to their context. In themselves they are enough; they are arresting, they cut across the normal processes of logic, and they could force us, if sufficiently concentrated on, to a kind of personal breakthrough. The term of such a meditation is not to enable us to state what these paradoxical statements *mean*. They are not to be reasoned or argued about, for then we should merely be providing ourselves with another set of concepts and words. These scriptural sayings may properly reduce us to mental, as well as verbal, silence. At the same time, they could occasion a flash of insight into the Christian realities comparable to the Zen satori (enlightenment) experience. As a result, for a period at least, Christ and his message would not simply be the object of our contemplation; we should be identified with them.

Finally, there is another form of basically the same meditative effort, which we can adopt (and adapt) from the style of Buddhism prevailing in Ceylon, Burma, and Thailand. The preliminaries are the same: the achievement, as far as possible, of mental calm and the withdrawal from distractions. Then we begin a meditation on, or rather an exercise in, *friendliness*. Its precondition, as always, is the highest attainable degree of awareness; we must be fully awake. Consciousness is in the first place directed to ourselves—and with affection. What we are concerned with is not specifically an exercise in self-love, but the elimination of those elements of self-hatred and self-disgust that plague the majority of people. Inevitably such self-disapproval is projected upon others, so that in some degree we hate and disapprove of them. An appreciation of oneself—which, if truly enlightened, is at the opposite pole from self-complacency—is the basis of our love for others, since neighborly love is impossible unless we are amiably disposed toward ourselves. However, this phase of the meditation should not be lingered on unduly. Having established a mood of amiability, our affection is to be consciously directed outwards—first to those physically nearest to us, should we be meditat-

ing in a group. This is the time for the removal of aversion, perhaps a
secret distaste for this or that individual, and replacing it with an
active compassion. Thereafter the scope of this affective meditation
can be progressively widened, all the time holding its objects in consciousness—to our family or community group, to our friends and
enemies, to our country, to humanity at large, to nature itself and the
animal world (for which the Judaeo-Christian tradition has shown so
little regard). This manner of meditating, it will at once be apparent,
is in the clearest harmony with the belief that we are "members one
of another" (Ephesians 4:25), the doctrine of the Body of Christ. It
is in harmony, too, with the conviction, now being forced upon us,
that man must come to friendly terms with his natural environment
or suffer the consequences.

Insofar as these forms of meditation have any end in view, it
consists in bridging three notable gaps: the gap between our superficial, empirical ego (which can give ourselves and others so much
trouble) and our true, underlying, self; the gap between ourselves
and God; the gap between us and the whole created order, animate
and inanimate. Experience shows that Christians can habituate
themselves to meditating in these ways without much trouble. Both
in the United States and England I have conducted, at their own
request, small meditation sessions of this kind with groups of teen-
agers, and found them serious and persevering. Knowing a little of
their everyday lives, I can testify that they were not notably virtuous
or particularly addicted to churchgoing; but they seem to have found
in some indescribable way "sitting quietly, doing nothing" definitely
worthwhile. Relieved by quietness, their minds lay open, ready to
respond to a simple yet ageless wisdom:

> Teach us to care and not to care
> Teach us to sit still.

Perhaps this sort of thing should be more generally encouraged
among "the people of God."

9. A Miscellany of Thoughts

*When planning these "explorations," I began to keep a note-
book in which to jot down not so much factual information as a
series of reflections. Some of these are elaborated in the main text of
the book; others have either not been developed at all or were dis-
carded as irrelevant. The following selection, being more or less related to the general theme, may have some slight interest on its own
account. A number of these "thoughts" are mere truisms; others
could provide pointers for discussion, illuminate a little, or provoke
constructive disagreement. None is offered as a confident pronouncement; their intent is to open, not to settle, questions. They are unsys-
tematized and follow no particular order but are numbered for the
sake of convenience.*

1

When anyone mentions Vatican II or Church "renewal," I find it
hard to respond with more than a flicker of interest. This reaction, I
suspect, is shared by quite a few.

2

Is religion basically a means of salvation from our present state, a
transformation of our lives so that we can live in another mode of
existence? Or is it fundamentally a means of enlightenment, so that
we can become adjusted to life as it actually is (whatever that may
mean) and live in the world of today? To say, as it is easy to say, that
religion is a bit of both seems to me to evade the issue. We have here
an ineluctable either/or. Religion is either an escape from this
world, or a living more or less happily in it and with it.

   Now it appears that Christianity has never fully resolved this
difficulty. To begin with, it was completely a system of salvation, a
looking to the imminent coming of Jesus and the establishment of

the Kingdom of God. "He who testifies to these things says, 'Surely I
am coming soon.' Amen. Come, Lord Jesus!" (Revelation 22:20).
But these expectations were not realized. Has the Church ever really
faced the implications of this fact? In part, perhaps, but only in part.
Ultimate salvation still lies in some remote future. Meanwhile, with
the help of God's grace and a more or less natural system of ethics,
we must strive to live appropriately in the world as it is. But the
unresolved problem remains, and this perhaps accounts for Christianity's failure to hold many of our contemporaries. The more
thoughtful among them sense an incoherence in the Church's proclamation.

Jesus and his first followers found the world situation in which
they lived intolerable, and they sought release from it. But today we
have a world that a large minority do not find intolerable at all. They
live in a state of well-being—material, intellectual, aesthetic, moral,
perhaps even spiritual—which they have no desire to exchange for a
problematical state of future bliss, "where congregations ne'er depart
and sabbaths never end." Moreover, the vast majority of the world's
population—the poor, the uneducated, the undernourished, the
underprivileged generally—do not appear to be looking for it either
—"pie in the sky when we die." They want to cease being "have-
nots" and become "haves," like the fortunate minority.

Any religious approaches that ignore this situation are a waste of
time and a betrayal—all the more so when they are put forward by
those who are themselves among the affluent. There is thus a great
deal to be said for the secularization of Christianity, especially when
we remember that "the only secular thing on earth is the secular
heart of man."

3

Authority. When one who holds a position of authority is faced by
conflicting opinions among his subordinates, it is usually more grati-
fying to his ego to take sides and polarize the situation than to com-
promise and choose the middle way. For the first course will at least
win approval from those who receive support, whereas the second
will displease everybody. Nevertheless, it is almost always the second that should be chosen.

4

The Bible.   The world's most overrated book. It is regarded conventionally by many as the *fons et origo* of true religion, yet it carries no simple and self-evident message directly and powerfully relevant to our everyday lives. It is made up, for the most part, of historical or supposedly historical documents, extravagant denunciations, and exclusivist devotions, requiring long and deep research before they can be properly understood. Parts of the Old Testament, the Gospels, and the Pauline Epistles abound in memorable, heart-touching sayings; but most of them call for careful elucidation before they can be correctly grasped and appropriately applied.

5

Belief.   Not to know the origin of one's own belief is not to know oneself. . . . What affects most religious minds is not what is true but what is believed to be true. If a belief proves satisfactory as an ideal or source of inspiration, its historic or rational foundations are of so little importance that they need not be investigated.

6

I seem to discern four religious types:

The "gnostic"   —concerned with responding to Ultimate Reality (however that is regarded) and stating or analyzing the appropriate response for the benefit of others (e.g., the Buddha).

The "prophetic" —believing themselves to be emissaries of God and proclaimers of his message of salvation (e.g., Jesus, Muhammad).

These are world-shaking types

The "devotional"—those who link religion with dogmas, observances, and prayers.

The "moralistic" —those who more or less identify religion with morality and good conduct.

These are not world-shaking types

There are doubtless others, and the above overlap somewhat and could be subdivided indefinitely. Still, this "insight" seems to me pretty valid.

7

Could the following be the stages of advance toward religious maturity? (1) Uncritical acceptance; (2) religion regarded as a moral support; (3) religion as a refuge and consolation; (4) faith striving to understand; (5) not a rejection of but an insight into the limitations of creeds and dogmas; (6) a withdrawal from ecclesiastical group thinking; (7) a nonattachment to certainty as conceived intellectually, but an identification with selflessness as realized, each in his distinctive way, by Jesus and the Buddha.

8

Christianity, despite itself, was associated at its outset with an unholy trinity of bitter controversy, bloody violence, and exclusivist intolerance.

9

Christianity originated against a background of crisis. If it is to survive, it must be reinterpreted to meet a situation in which the originating crisis is no longer believed to be relevant.

10

The Weakness of Vatican II. The Church tried to examine its relations to the world without first radically examining itself.[1]

11

Ecumenism. For me Christian ecumenism has lost much of its interest since it became official. The movement of the Spirit bringing men closer together in mutual understanding and love has become entangled in elements of a power struggle concerning how much of its traditional positions the ancient Church is able to retain and how much it can be forced to yield. The churches are too much caught up

1. This note appears to be corroborated by Cardinal Suenens. "At the council we remained too much on the surface. . . . Our theology was still too clerical. . . . We must remember that the Holy Spirit is not bound by our juridical laws and that 'He breathes where he will.' " *The Tablet,* May 16, 1970, p. 469.

in vested interests, their own ecclesiastical structures and traditional formulas to do much more than scratch the surface of the problem of Christian unity. Besides, they are in need of radical self-examination, each on its own account, before they can hope to get together with one another. The required dimension lies much deeper than doctrine and liturgy, about which agreement might be reached without anything of real importance being achieved.

12

Conversion. When this is from one ecclesiastical jurisdiction to another, it raises a question mark—except perhaps in adolescence, when it can be the equivalent of a true change of heart, metanoia. Ecclesiastical conversions are often allegedly based on a concern for historic truth (which is a problem in itself), but converts mostly have a taste for authoritarianism and appear to have little enthusiasm for the pursuit of truth for its own sake. Their search is for a secure religious framework, to be rid of uncertainty. And why not? But what is to be said of Albert Camus's entry in his diary: "An atheist when he was a perfect husband, he became a convert when he started to commit adultery"?

13

What needs to be sorted out is how much of official Christian teaching affirms ontological truth, how much historic fact, how much no more than a creedal position.

14

Christ. The main sources for the orthodox doctrine about Jesus are the God experiences of the authors of the Pauline Epistles and the Fourth Gospel, expressed against the background of the Hellenistic world.

15

Christianity. As a result of the nonrealization of the expected eschatological Kingdom of God, the nature of Christianity was changed from looking forward to the second coming of Christ in the near future to an adjustment to the realities of the Graeco-Roman world. In many ways this was a considerable improvement.

16

If institutional Christianity is to transform itself into a truly world religion, it must drop its implicit claim to be *the* world religion. That is to say, it must practice what it preaches—die in order to be born again.

17

Cosmic Consciousness. A not very satisfactory term, sometimes applied to the enlightenment experiences of the Buddha, Jesus, and Paul. What is important in such experiences, if they are to profit others as well as oneself—as in the Mahayana Bodhisattva ideal or the Christian Apostolate—is that they should not bring about a complete break with one's former unenlightened life. This may have happened in the case of the Buddha, Paul, and Augustine, with the result that they have passed on to those influenced by them elements of an inhuman asceticism. The enlightened man should always consciously preserve some of the actuality of his former unenlightened state. If he is to be fully human he must be in sympathy and sometimes in deed a sinner as well as a saint—or rather, he must resolve in his own person the antithesis between the two.

18

Disillusionment. This is part of the life process: the clearing away of ignorance and in particular the ignorance of the one who *thinks* he has no illusions. The result should be wisdom, not cynicism, which is merely the acquiring of another set of illusions. Here we may recall the splendid observation of Confucius: "Wisdom is rooted in watching with affection the way people grow."

19

Death. I believe that most people might prefer to entertain the prospect of complete extinction at death rather than to live under traditional Christianity's alternatives: either eternal beatitude in heaven or unending torment in hell. But the question remains: Would such a preference affect the situation?

20

Demythologizing. Rudolf Bultmann's theory of demythologizing, as explained in his *Jesus Christ and Mythology* and elsewhere, is in principle sound and illuminating. It is applied in his works generally with immense erudition and mental power. Nevertheless, his Lutheran piety prevents him from working out the logic of his theory in the range and depth of which he is intellectually capable. Is this because he conceives the nature of Christian faith too narrowly? The answer to the questions he raises lies with John rather than Paul, as he partly sees. But John does not have the whole answer, either. The conclusion of Bultmann's procedures, which he never tries to reach, is that the *existential self-understanding that arises from responding to the proclaimed word of God* (for Bultmann, the heart of the matter), could come as much from responding to the words of the Buddha, or Confucius, or Socrates, as from responding to the words of the historic Jesus of Nazareth.

21

Eschatology. The aspect of the Christian proclamation around which there is the largest question mark.

22

Egoism. We are all egoists; what matters is the quality of our egoism and how clearly we perceive its nature. Self-restraint and self-effacement need be no more than a decorous, necessary, and widely acceptable method of handling the problem of the obtrusive ego. The worship of God "for his own sake" may be an illusion—at least if God is worshiped by me as the source of my being, which is egoism at its deepest if least spectacular level. Perhaps the ultimately sound approach is to distinguish the self-conscious, empirical ego from the true *self*—which is the same in all men. As man's prayer can do nothing for God, its aim should be, while praising God, to dispel the illusion of the empirical ego and *realize* the true self. In this state we must necessarily be in a relationship of compassion with all other men.

23

Faith. I believe that Protestantism with Luther may have a truer understanding of the Pauline and Johannine conception of faith than Catholicism with Thomas Aquinas. But Catholicism, with or without St. Thomas, still remains better equipped to conduct the search for true religion.

24

Generalization. It may be the result of a true intuition into the nature of things, or it may be the objectification of a purely individual notion.

25

God. He is reached by subjectivity yielding to objectivity, in spite of what Kierkegaard may say. When the mind—in a flash, or as the term of a profound meditation—transcends itself so that egoistic self-awareness disappears, then we are in the realm of objectivity. When this confronts us not as a field of multiplicity, of innumerable "things," but as pure existence, happy-making and inexpressible, how does this differ from what mystics call the "ground of being," the Hindus "Brahman," the Buddhists "Sunyata," the Sufis "the Beloved," and we Christians "God"?

26

The modification of the early Old Testament concept of God by Greek philosophy in the Hellenistic period was providential. It was the beginning of the end of the angry magician Sky God still lingering behind much of so-called biblical theology. It set a term to the bloody narrative of the God of history. A vision is made possible of a salvation which, although it may be neither temporal nor timeless, is certainly not bound to the wheel of historical events.

27

God, so runs the time-worn cliché, is both immanent and transcendent. But how? Scientific humanism and secularism, when they are religious (which, unconsciously at least, their exponents often are), stress the divine immanence; Protestant Christianity stresses the divine transcendence. Catholicism has attempted without much success a synthesis of the two. This may have been realized in practice more impressively in the religious tradition stemming from India: Hinduism and Buddhism.

28

A more important question than belief in the existence of God is what kind of God you believe him to be. Thus the critics of the

Homeric gods were right in ridiculing them not on the grounds of their nonexistence but inasmuch as they were defective as ideals and founts of inspiration. A god without a history or whose history is of no importance, who can yet be a focus of worship and source of inspiration—as, for example, Rama and Krishna—may have a greater religious value than a god whose alleged interventions in history have sometimes appeared arbitrary, despotic, and cruel.

29

We are nearer to salvation in *realizing* that there is a share of the divine in every man and woman, including ourselves, than by seeking to be saved by a God who is "out there."

30

History. Much of the mental confusion and uncertainty among Christians today arises from the current fashion of attaching a profound religious importance to history. Yet the only tangible link with world history in the early creeds is that Jesus was "crucified under Pontius Pilate." The point made by Adolf Deissmann in his book on Paul remains valid. "Many among us have become cult-blind through a modern cult, the cult of the historical. And accordingly they try with historical means either to give Christianity a sure foundation, or to explode it into the air as a troublesome ruin. But Christianity, if it is reacting Christ-cult, cannot be exploded and requires no historical justification. Its foundations are good. It stands today on the same basis on which it stood originally, that is, it reveals the ever present God in the ever present Saviour."

31

Hindu-Buddhist tradition: based on a mythology rather than history, considered as one event happening after another at a known place and time; offering a way of life (an ethic) and an experience rather than an all-embracing ideology.

32

Incarnation. To what extent was the theology of the Incarnation a direct inference from primitive Christian data? To what extent was it a product of the Greek mind equating the good, the true, and the beautiful—and therefore a harmonious construct?

33

Vanity and Pride.   Vanity consists in attaching weight, by reason of one's own interest, to what is intrinsically empty or unimportant. When this is done consciously and with no wish to be taken seriously, with an eye to diverting others, as is often the case, then it can be amusing and even agreeable. Pride is an overweening preoccupation with one's own ego; it can take many forms, none of them agreeable. Thus a dedicated ascetic might achieve a higher degree of pride than an uncalculating voluptuary. Socrates touched on this point, when he observed to his Stoic friend: "Through the rent in your garment, Cleanthes, vanity peeps out."

34

My position as a Catholic is that I accept everything that the Church teaches in the sense in which it is true. But how far in each case or in what sense it is true I do not profess to know.

35

Jesus.   The correct antithesis is not between the Jesus of history and the Christ of faith but between the observed Jesus and the idealized Christ.

36

Jesus never broke with Pharisaic Judaism (Klausner convincing on this); his "universalism" is to be thought of not in terms of an all-embracing world religion (though that is not excluded) but as reflecting the vision of a limitless God.

37

Christianity can only remain a vital religion by our reaching behind Jesus to God. That would be to return to his own teaching—theocentric rather than Christocentric. This point is well made by C. K. Barrett in his *Jesus and the Gospel Tradition:* "It is true that the gospels (and the New Testament at large) are Christocentric, but Christ himself is theocentric; or, in the simpler and better language of Paul, 'You belong to Christ, and Christ belongs to God' (1 Corinthians 3:23). More simply still, 'He that has seen me has seen the Father' (John 14:9); only, as the context of these words shows, it is possible to study the history of Jesus at some length without even perceiving that the issue involved in it is the truth about God. It is to this truth that Jesus himself directs us."

38

When I study Jesus as disclosed in the New Testament, I am persuaded that this is the Church's or the gospel writers' presentation of Jesus, rather than a disclosure of just what he would have been like to meet face to face. How little we really know about that. Why was he at times so harsh, e.g., to the Syrophoenician woman (Mark 7:27)? Why, theological presuppositions apart, did he go to Jerusalem for that fatal Passover? What really happened at the cleansing of the Temple, in Gethsemane (why were some of the disciples armed?), at his condemnation and death? Yet the genuineness of the Resurrection experiences among the disciples is certain. Further, Paul was a Christ-intoxicated man.

For me Jesus has always been and remains the center of my devotional life. Without the thought of him I would not have such goodness as I have. But this is not simply the Christ I read about in the New Testament, whom I don't find wholly appealing—perhaps not as much as the Buddha or Socrates. What is the solution to this problem? Perhaps in regarding Christ as objectively *the archetypal man*, and subjectively as Paul's Christ, or Mark's, or John's, and therefore also as *my* Christ, i.e., the archetype of what I am meant to be, whatever that is.

39

Liturgy. An interest in liturgy for its own sake indicates a concern for religion of the second order. Jesus the Son of God and Gautama the Buddha agreed on this point, as on many others.

40

In transforming the Latin liturgy into the vernacular the Church authorities chose to sacrifice the numinous quality of a language hallowed by long usage in worship—the same quality as is to be found in the recitation of the Quran by Muslims who do not understand Arabic—for the sake of immediate intelligibility. This was a considerable gamble. How much more attractive did it make the service of God to regular churchgoers? How many nonchurchgoers did it bring back to the fold? The change has also exposed the weakness as well as the strength of what is said and sung in church.

41

Love. It is not hard for professing Christians to love others for Christ's sake; it is much harder to love them for their own sake.

42

The proclamation that the love of God above all things and one's neighbor as oneself is the heart of religion was not an original discovery of Jesus. It is to be found in Judaism before him and with varying terminology in the great world religions—Hinduism, Buddhism, and Islam, as well as Christianity. The important questions only arise after this statement has been made: Who is God? What is love? How is the nexus between the two to be *realized?*

43

Man. The approach of the West is to ask what man *is*. Answers: a being made up of a material body and a spiritual soul, or an individual substance of a rational nature, or a creature made in the image of God. Here we are concerned with something *static* (as expressed in nouns).

The approach of the East is to ask: What must man *do*, or how must he *live* to become his own best self? Answers: he must attain the ideal of the sage (Confucius); he must act in harmony with the cosmos, become a co-creator, act in congruence with the ways of the great *tao*, adapting himself to any circumstance of life in the flux of change (Lao Tzu); he must so live as to realize the identity or close affinity of his own self with the supreme Self (Hinduism); he must be rid of the illusion of his conscious ego in order to attain boundless wisdom and compassion (Buddhism). Here we are concerned with something *dynamic* (as expressed in verbs).

44

QUESTIONS

Jesus—Progress in Love.
Buddha—Liberation through Enlightenment.
Muhammad—Surrender to the will of Allah.
Are these three one?

45

Has Christ worship been substituted for becoming Christlike?

46

If by some miracle we could know the full content of other people's private lives, both past and present, they also knowing ours, would the world be a better place to live in? Given the human condition as it is today, the answer is emphatically no. But if our insight and compassion—the Buddhist prajna and karuna—were realized to the full, the world would be transformed into paradise.

47

How is the symbolic, sacramental rebirth signified (in what sense is it actually brought about?) by Christian baptism transformed into a realistic second birth so that we become existentially authentic?

48

To what extent are we led to salvation by our nature being frustrated, our inclinations rejected? To what extent by our deepest desires being fulfilled?

49

Why did Jesus bring on (provoke?) the climax of his life so soon? Why did he not wait patiently like the Buddha for another forty years? Why the hurry? Why the impatience for his "baptism?" The answer is easy, given the situation in which he lived and worked, to say nothing of the later theological explanations. But it makes one think all the same.

50

From a certain point of view, according to St. Thomas Aquinas, even the most carefully elaborated doctrinal formulations appear worth no more than straw. The question is: From what point of view?

51

Optimism and pessimism are equally unsatisfactory, though they are commonly found in the everyday world of untruth. The truth lies with realism, not in the sense of *Realpolitik*, but in seeing life steadily and seeing it whole.

52

Person. The two qualities most to be valued in a person are character and sound judgment. By character I mean the product of moral training by which an individual becomes and remains reliable where a duty needs to be fulfilled. By sound judgment I mean a capacity to envisage a situation with detachment in all its aspects and then articulate the appropriate response.

Nevertheless these robust qualities need a gentle, civilized setting. Intelligence, learning, humor, wit, sensitivity, friendliness, compassion, even a certain easy sensuousness—these I like to see combined, as they can be (though rarely), with character and sound judgment.

53

Pronouncements. The pronouncements of professional churchmen, when they affront the intelligence of the enlightened faithful as misguided or untimely, need not be publicly opposed or even criticized; they have merely to be understood.

54

Publication. As soon as one decides on publication, one is involved in self-advertisement. This makes one vulnerable to the criticism, and also the jealousy, of others. There is no remedy except to observe truthfully the self that is advertised and the manner in which it is done.

55

Religion. Religion should be shown to be directly and powerfully relevant to the course of our everyday lives. Christ's message was precisely so to his contemporaries.

56

Jesus did not reveal anything hitherto unknown. What he proclaimed was directed to action rather than reflective thought, to a way, not a theory, of living. His proclamation presupposed the acceptance of the best Jewish teaching of his day. He did not discuss this, as if it could in any way be called in question; he brought home its urgency, its imperative quality with unprecedented force.

57

True religion has for its purpose the elimination of fear and the bringing to birth of freedom.

58

The fundamental aspects of religion have often been classified as the "three C's": creed, code, and cult, representing respectively a system of belief, a form of ethical conduct, and an order of worship. But there is a fourth aspect—the empirical, the element of *experience*, that is to say, what religion yields in terms of self-authenticating emotional and intellectual satisfaction, or more accurately, as personal fulfillment. "O taste and see that the Lord is good!" (Psalm 34:8). But what if a religion offers little that is agreeable to the modern taste, hardly anything that our contemporaries find worth seeing?

59

All interest in religion, especially a deep and sustained interest, is the search for a solution to a personal problem. It is the need to feel oneself loved, that one's life is significant to others and worthwhile in itself. We should not allow our attempts at selflessness to blind us to this fact.

60

All men have a religious need, understood as a search for a deeper satisfaction than that of the empirical self. But this need cannot be met by a glorification of our Judaeo-Christian heritage from the past, or the promise of eschatological hopes to be fulfilled in the future. What is called for is the experience of the joy of truth—Augustine's *gaudium de veritate*—now.

61

The publicity surrounding religious activities is usually in inverse ratio to their intrinsic importance.

62

In religion "conservative" or "progressive" are irrelevant categories. The categories that really apply are "radical" or "superficial." All the charismatic religious personalities of history, e.g., Jesus and the Buddha, were radicals, not in the sense of being revolutionaries but in the basic meaning of the word radical: reaching to the roots. Compared with them, their followers are inevitably superficial—and from this point of view it doesn't much matter whether they happen to be "progressive" or "conservative." The important thing is that they should strive to achieve according to their own insight, experientially rather than theoretically, the reaching-to-the-roots point of view.

N.B. The majority of the discussions at the Vatican Council were, within the above terminology, "superficial." So have been most of the subsequent elaborations of Vatican themes—necessarily. But what the younger generation, and many of the older, are seeking today is a restatement of the radical approach to religion in living examples. These not being forthcoming, and the churches impeded by their own structures, there result confusion and bewilderment among the "progressives" and complacency mixed with fear among the "conservatives."

63

The religious need today is not for the prophet but for the *catalyst*. By this I mean not the professor of comparative religion, who can exchange ideas about various religious ideologies, or the negotiator who can find the formula for uniting religious institutions, but the man who has become experientially so enlightened that he enters the very heart of religion itself, and so is in a position to manifest to others, beyond the level of mere controversy or ecumenical dialogue, in precise relation to their own religious traditions, what religion truly is.

64

Revelation means unveiling; it is a relative process. What needs to be revealed to one may be self-evident to another. The attainment of truth is seldom by a swift and positive intuition; rather it is by the slow and careful process of removing error. At least this is the case when truth is to be communicated intelligibly to others.

65

It is better to be a moderate sensualist than a puritan ascetic.

66

St. Thomas Aquinas. He was true to all the light available to him from external sources at the age he lived in. Finally, because external sources are always inadequate, he became true only to his own enlightenment experience.

67

When the ablest and most gifted Western theologian was invited to an Ecumenical Council in 1274, he seemingly found the prospect so distasteful that he died on the way there.

68

Supernatural. The word does not occur in the New Testament. Hence a possible question arises: Did theological "supernaturalism" replace the existential being "born again" (St. John), or becoming a "new creature" (St. Paul), of early Christianity?

69

Vocation. It has happened in the past that young men in their teens could enter a monastery or religious order and preserve their naïve adolescent pieties, undisturbed by serious reflective thought, until old age. This is no longer possible, and it is better so.

70

Truth. Is a disinterested search for truth possible? Apparently not. Because in some sense one is already committed to a view of the truth one is seeking; otherwise how would one know if one had found it? In scientific and perhaps also in historical inquiry objectivity can at least be aimed at. But one is self-deceived if one thinks one is being objective about religion or ethics, because here the personal equation always enters in. What you discover will either confirm opinions already held or change them. Either way, you are involved in subjectivity. Thus no atheist, agnostic, Jew, Muslim, or, least of all, Christian churchman, can conduct an objective inquiry into the significance, i.e., the personality, life work, and message of Jesus of Nazareth.

10. Ultimate Religion

It will long have been clear to the reader that the sense in which "end" is used in the title of this book is not with reference to the disappearance from the scene of any given religious institution. The viewpoint is teleological rather than chronological: the concern is with what religion really amounts to, its heart, its purpose, the terminal state beyond which there is nowhere further to go. This, I believe, remains constant amid the outdatings and updatings of the churches, the transformations of the great world faiths. Again, we are to consider what religion could be now, as embodied in the individual, not religion's future prospects, some "omega point," in Teilhard de Chardin's phrase, toward which society as a whole might be thought to be moving. Individual and society are inextricably linked, and for this reason something must first be said about the present state of the Church. However, the signs seem unmistakable that the area for personal decision, whether or not it be welcomed, is being enlarged, while that of corporate authoritarian leadership conspicuously diminishes.

The Church was able to hold its own as an institution when it was linked with a traditional culture, or when it controlled the education of the faithful or could insulate its dogma and discipline from hostile criticism. But none of these conditions now obtains. It seems true to say that science and technology have dissolved most of the cultural horizons, so that no separate civilization is likely to appear again. Education as dominated by the clergy is already a thing of the past. The Church's dogma and discipline can no longer be privately administered; mass communications media promptly make public the initiatives of churchmen, together with the popular reactions to them. These pressures may in time effect an almost complete restructuring of religion in its traditional form. Religion does not die, though it may disappear underground—including in that term the recesses of the individual unconscious—or assume another guise. Marxist atheism, for example, simply substituted the vision of the classless society for that of the Kingdom of God. As for the sophisticated few who are or at least claim to be tone-deaf to the appeal of religion, when they are civilized, talented, and generous human beings, as is often the case, then demonstrably religious values can usually be discerned in their lives. Taking religion as it is generally understood—the embodiment of a creed, an ethic, and a mode of worship—I believe it to be bound up in one form or another with the human condition. If, or when, the nuclear conflict is let loose, what is left of the race will crawl out of the rubble and start the religious process over again.

Meanwhile the Church within its limits is very much alive. It is not so much the Church's life, since that depends on God, that today requires anxious examination as the Church's limits—particularly the limits of its self-understanding and authority. What calls for wider recognition is that the Church's central doctrines—the incarnation, the life work of Christ, the atonement, the nature of God himself—have not once and for all been encapsulated in words. They can be understood in a variety of ways. To anyone who has had the opportunity to enter sympathetically into the viewpoints of Hinduism, Buddhism, or Islam, the question is bound to present itself: To what extent and in what way is Christianity "truer" than these religions? Or is this perhaps an improper question, concealing so many assumptions that it cannot be answered and therefore should not be asked? Consider the "world" to which the Gospel was first preached; the world as it was envisaged by St. Paul had little relation to the planet as we now know it. The world he knew comprised the Roman Empire with the portions of Asia and Africa more or less under its sway. When, for example, we read that "all the world" was to be enrolled (Luke 2:1), no one outside the Empire could have been included. When, therefore, the Gospel writers and the first missionaries thought and spoke of Jesus as the "Saviour of the world" (John 4:42), they could not have had in mind, since they did not know of their existence, those large areas of the earth's surface where Hinduism and Buddhism were at that time flourishing religions. Accordingly, it can be said "that grace and revelation are not *exclusively* opened to men in the Christ-event, but that other events may have served as bearers of God's truth as well." [1]

It has for a long time been pointed out by scholars that such

1. John Macquarrie, *Studies in Christian Existentialism* (Montreal: McGill University Press, 1965), p. 166.

references as those that appear in the New Testament to the "whole world" (Luke 2:1; Acts 11:28), are mere "popular hyperbole." The setting for the "world" of the early Church was diminutive indeed.

The Christ-cult was in the time of Paul a secret affair of humble unknown people in the back streets of the great Mediterranean cities. When Paul chanced to write that the faith of a Christian church was known "throughout the whole world" (Romans 1:8), he of course means in the amiable hyperbole, dear to the ancient Oriental, the microcosmos of the Christian "world" (1 Thessalonians 1:8; 2 Thessalonians 1:4), not the great official world. And when, as reported by Luke, he emphatically states that the facts of his Christian life did not take place "in a corner" (Acts 26:26), the apologetically satisfying expression does not contradict the statement that the new cult and its leading personalities still remained as good as unknown to the world at large, and that we may look in vain to find any reflection of the man Paul either in contemporary literature or in the art of that day.[2]

Christians have high authority to look to the rock from which they were hewn and the quarry from which they were "digged" (cf. Isaiah 51:1). There are signs that even the official Church is taking a rather more modest view of its proper functions. Any movement in this direction, I would think, is greatly to be encouraged. Obviously, there is no better way than by the study of Jesus himself. The kind of evidence that is leading New Testament scholars to adopt the view that what Jesus thought and taught about himself is in possible contrast with some of the presentations of him in circulation among the early Christian communities cannot be ignored indefinitely. These investigations are now public property, taught to college students and available in innumerable paperbacks; their fruits may help to account for the diminishing impact of crudely stated orthodox positions on the minds of even fervent believers.

If it could be shown convincingly, for example, that Jesus took a less imposing view of his historic role than that which the Church later assigned to him, Christianity as a world religion might gain rather than lose by such an admission. The more the Church is disentangled from the now defunct Graeco-Roman culture that providentially saw its birth, the more clearly Jesus is seen as one with God in terms of a uniquely dedicated service, the more likely he is to win the allegiance of the as yet unconverted. This raises the interesting

2. Deissmann, *Paul—A Study in Social and Religious History*, pp. 56–57.

question of the acceptability of the Gospel in relation to its truth. Are we to say that a trinity of Father, Son, and Holy Spirit is as "true" for a Brahmin in Banaras as that of Brahma, Vishnu, and Shiva? Is the Lord Buddha any less "true" than the Lord Jesus in Ceylon, Thailand, and Tibet? I find it hard to think so. From this emerges the problem facing any missionary effort, especially where the prevailing culture has a long-established religious tradition of its own—as in India, Thailand, and Japan. It was pointed out in one of our discussions in South India[3] that where a conversion takes place and the Church's teaching is nominally accepted, it will promptly be reinterpreted in accordance with the prevailing habits of thought.

In my travels I found missionaries depressed at the seeming ineffectiveness of their efforts. The Church is welcomed for its schools, its medical and social services, even for its liturgical ceremonies. But its distinctive doctrines concerning God and man's salvation show little signs of replacing beliefs already held, some of which we have touched on in my encounters in Thailand and India. Could the right approach be not trying to convert but aiming at sharing truth together? Consider a key New Testament text: ". . . God our Saviour, who desires all men to be saved and to come to the knowledge of the truth" (1 Timothy 2:3–4). The four non-Christian faiths we have met with—Hinduism, Buddhism, Judaism, and Islam—would, I believe, willingly assent to this proposition, but they would understand it each in its own characteristic way. Does orthodox Christianity have the right to set limits to its meaning? Clearly our task is to reach beyond external cults and verbal expressions of belief to the underlying realities. And this is what I want to try to do, hesitantly but with some care, by way of bringing these reflections to a close.

Let me end as I began, on a limiting autobiographical note, the better to avoid any pretense of impersonal objectivity. When I was young, a theologian once told me that the good and happy life consisted in an ideal conceived in youth and lived out to old age. He was French, a doctrinaire, an ideologue, but he had a point. It made its impact, though now I am distrustful of such pronouncements and tend to value sound instincts above high ideals. At any rate, here I am at the moment, sitting in a monastery "cell" (adequately, in fact comfortably, furnished) thinking about the essence of religion. When I look out of the window, I see one of the most beautiful vales

3. See p. 138.

in Yorkshire. On it, dotted about here and there from time to time, are schoolboys playing games. They have come to the school, in part at least, for the purpose of learning about religion—*their* religion, the Catholic faith. What are they to be told? I am glad not to have to decide, since they should be taught in such a way as not to have to unlearn anything later on. Besides, the essence of religion—though perhaps we should speak of its *dynamism,* as we may discover that it has no "essence"—is caught rather than taught, which, being only a half-truth, need do no more than provoke a thought. Slowly, step by step, and still only at the verbal level, can I find my way to the heart of religion.

Now in my sixties, all, or nearly all, passion spent, I join my monastic brethren shortly after 5:00 A.M. each day at a service consisting chiefly of psalms and Bible readings (on the limitations of which I have commented on an earlier page). Then, a meditation, which, thanks to the retired life I am so kindly allowed to lead, can be taken up again at intervals throughout the day. Thereafter, the daily concelebration of the "sacred mysteries," [4] which is the central and most acceptable feature of the revived liturgy. The rich significance of this ritual—now emphasizing the existential intercommunion of all who are present—needs no description; the historic link with Jesus himself could not be more movingly portrayed. For me the daily round of public worship ends with the Church's songs at evening, vespers, still chanted in Latin with the ancient rhythms. This Benedictine routine has somehow never proved boring; it still appears as worthwhile as when it had the freshness of novelty forty years ago.

The law of prayer, so it is said, is the law of belief, which is one of those memorable simplifications: for prayer, or at least meditation, can reach far beyond the regions of explicit belief. For my part, I accept in my own way (in the final analysis, this is all that any Catholic can do) whatever the Church authoritatively teaches—right down to "infallibility," though I have long regarded the operative phrase in this particular doctrine as effectively removing any possible embarrassment. Nothing more is in question than "that infallibility with which the Divine Redeemer willed his Church to be endowed"

---

4. The phrase, with its inevitable reminiscence of matters already touched on (see pp. 211 ff.), is now prescribed in the opening rite of the new liturgy of the Mass.

(*ea infallibilitate pollere, qua divinus Redemptor Ecclesiam suam . . . instructam esse voluit*), a mystery within a mystery, which recent events affecting the Church have not made any the less inscrutable. The challenge arising from the present ecclesiastical disarray is not to rebellion or disloyalty, but to achieve personal *authenticity*. Less and less can Catholics depend on authority figures to do their religious thinking for them, on external directives pointing to what is right and what is wrong. Willy-nilly the alternatives present themselves: achieve spiritual maturity and under God a certain autonomy, or remain an inauthentic person, practicing religion at second hand, obeying the rules and conforming to the conventions as if they themselves were self-authenticating.

It is worth recalling that there is no record of the words "religion" or "religious" coming from the lips of Jesus. Perhaps one inference is that the more we talk about religion, or strive consciously to be religious, the greater the danger of the reality escaping us. My own conclusion is that religion is not so much concerned with a comprehensive world view as with an attitude to life, an attitude that could be largely independent of an ideology or doctrinal framework. Though religion in practice is communal rather than individualistic, it can best be studied as it operates within the individual. This fact needs emphasizing at a time when Christian thinking has become impregnated with sociology. Eloquent descriptions of the Church and its significance, though providing the believer with some reassurance, do not give him much guidance on what he is actually meant to become here in this life largely by his own insight and effort, for which God's grace is an assistance but not a substitute. For the Christian, to belong to Christ is to be a member of his body and therefore to be bound to the other members in the unity of the Church. But each person stands before God, in the first place at any rate, in utter loneliness, extricated from every natural tie. This individualizing of man's relation to God, as Bultmann has pointed out, "has it roots in the psalms and Wisdom literature, and above all in Jeremiah. But its full implications were never realized until the time of Paul with his radical conception of the grace of God." [5] With regard to the actual message of Jesus, not as it was later interpreted but within its historic context, so far as this can be ascertained, I am again persuaded by Bultmann's view: "Unlike the prophets' preach-

5. Bultmann, *Primitive Christianity*, p. 188.

ing, his preaching is directed not primarily to the people as a whole, but _to individuals_ [italics in original]." [6] For Jesus the focus of concern is not the nation but each single man and woman. His God is "precisely that God, who stands aloof from the history of nations, meets each man in his own little history, his everyday life with its daily gift and demand; de-historicized man (i.e., naked of his supposed security within his historical group) is guided into his concrete encounter with his neighbour, in which he finds his true history."

As has already been shown, one of the recurring themes in our discussions of religion in India was the need for the individual to undergo an "enlightenment," so transforming in its effects that it might be described as a "second birth," being born again. That Jesus underwent an experience at his baptism not necessarily identical with but parallel to that of the Buddha under the Bo tree I find it hard to doubt. Jesus the man felt himself to be filled with the divine spirit, and so identified with the very ground of his being, so lost to any merely egoistic, self-centered concern that he heard the approving voice of God his Father declaring him to be uniquely his Son (see Mark 1: 10–11). Later, the Church was to understand this event as the moment from which the sacrament of baptism took its origin. When the Fourth Gospel reports Jesus as requiring of his followers a new birth by "water and the Spirit" (John 3:5), something of greater personal consequence is implied in terms of a life attitude than what results from pouring baptismal water over the head of a newborn infant. Jesus is speaking to a grown man, Nicodemus, who is himself "a teacher of Israel" (John 3:10); it is he who needs to undergo a second birth, not merely in sacramental symbolism, but in terms of a total outlook on life. This, it seems to me, is still the basic religious requirement—not just believing but in some way observing by experience that we have been born again. What can be said of this regeneration, a second birth, other than affirming its necessity and citing texts—as it is easy to do, not only from Christian but from Hindu, Buddhist, and Islamic sources—in support of the view that here we reach the heart of the matter?

Consider the situation in its most commonplace aspects. To be lifted out of our everyday, routine, mundane selves is what all of us

6. Rudolf Bultmann, _Theology of the New Testament_, Vol. 1 (London: S.C.M. Press, 1952), p. 25.

are seeking. That is why people imbibe intoxicants or take drugs—to achieve, at least for a time, a sense of newness. The very expression, so common among the young, "getting high," implies the need to rise somehow or other above our normal condition. The urge to cut loose, to "break set," points to the fact that a conventional life of bourgeois respectability, the virtues of right-thinking people, are somehow not enough. The need here being indicated is that of becoming our true selves, as distinct from the image we and perhaps other people have of us, to become authentic—as the existentialists put it—rather than remain inauthentic. "I was not myself when I did that" is an expression we sometimes hear. What is the "I" and what the "myself" in such a context? The implication obviously is that our true "self" is in some way distinct from the busy, unreflective "I." But precisely in what way?

So far as the West is concerned existentialist thinkers have reached, I believe, closest to the roots of the problem. Existentialism lays stress not on man as a substantial being, fundamentally static, able perhaps by a contemplative effort of the mind to reach a timeless state, to see the world in the Platonic manner as "the moving image of eternity." What has to be recognized is the temporal structure of existence itself, so that future, present, and what has been are held together in their unity. This constitutes the authentic present, the "moment" in existentialist terminology from Kierkegaard to Heidegger. Here are disclosed the three dimensions of temporality, by contrast with the inauthentic present, which dwells in the present alone. In view of what has been said earlier of the importance of living in the here and now, being a "child of time present," [7] the difference between the inauthentic and authentic present should be well understood.

Touching briefly on Heidegger's "three ekstases of temporality"— meaning, roughly, our relation to the past and the future from the standpoint of the present—we may note that living inauthentically in the present is to take life as a succession of "nows," hopping, so to speak, from one moment or situation to the next without regard to the past or future. Reacting merely at the level of sense observation, this is what we are all too apt to do, regarding life as merely "one damned thing after another." Authentic existence, on the other hand, our "being there," holds within itself an openness to what has been

7. See p. 199.

and to what is to come in such a way that these are somehow brought into the present. What we have to avoid is the inauthenticity of a life made up of switching from one immediate concern to the next, from one "now" to another. We must look before and after, while at the same time being fully aware of where we are now. To be conscious of what we have learned from the past, both factually and as a distillation of its wisdom, combined with a resolute grip upon the future to the extent that we are open to all its possibilities constitutes the authentic present.

An inauthentic, unregenerate way of life lies in a preoccupation with the present that pays no heed to what has been or what may be, the past and the future, and so in effect ignores the temporal dimensions of existence. Both past and future can be effectively made present, not by prodigious feats of memory on the one hand or by efforts at intelligent anticipation on the other, but by a profound *openness*. This possibility is excluded by an unrealistic attitude either to what has happened or what could be. Dwelling in the past by surrounding oneself with the security of familiar routines and rituals, taking care not to expose oneself to future possibilities in the form of novelty and radical change precludes an authentic living in the present. So does the irresoluteness of wishful thinking, any form of utopianism, and in general the failure to co-ordinate contemplated future possibilities both with what actually is and what has been. Viewing the past as it was and the future as it could be in such a manner that what we see is incorporated in the "moment" we call the present is what makes a truly human existence possible.

So far, I believe the existentialist position to be unchallengeable. Our actions should be based on the simultaneous fusion of the experience of what has been, the vision of future possibilities, and the challenge of where we are. Stimulus to action comes from the voice of conscience, which may be described as the call of the authentic, that is, unified self to the empirical self, scattered in its inauthentic immediate concerns. On the other hand, the existentialist attitude to the future and its possibilities appears open to question. The "master possibility," in Heidegger's phrase, is death—which can hardly be denied. But just how in realistic terms is this possibility to be faced? By resoluteness, by commitment, by making decision after decision simply from the standpoint of the position into which life has "thrown" us, say the existentialists. But this does not appear to be enough; or, rather, it is too much. We are in danger of foreclosing the openness that is the condition, according to existentialism itself, of authenticity.

At this point let me recall the fundamental concept of religion suggested earlier in these pages (p. 18): an attitude or life style based on the conviction that one's individual ego needs to undergo a transformation, whereby we become our authentic selves by being brought into harmony with pure Existence. By "pure" in this context, as has been remarked earlier, I mean *unconditioned* existence. The term is intended to have its maximal content, so that we might say quintessential existence, though that, too, is unsatisfactory since it suggests an ultimate reality that is static. However, the opposition between that which is supposedly static and what is dynamic, of which so much is made in contemporary religious discussions, is to some extent illusory. Unfortunately it has been made the basis for drawing sharp and unnecessary distinctions between so called "essentialist" and "existentialist" thinking, between the Greek and the modern approach to philosophy, between what is held to be timeless and that which is clearly involved in time. Consider for a moment the word "being," first as a noun, then as a verb, e.g., you as a human being, then as your being in the world where you are. After that, subtract yourself from the picture, so that you are left with the undifferentiated concept of *being* (very difficult, though not impossible, to hold in mind, I admit). It was to this idea of "being" that philosophers like Plato and Aristotle gave so much attention. Nowadays they are apt to be dismissed as only thinking of being as if it were a noun, statically. This may have been true of Plato but not, I would say, of Aristotle, whose philosophy showed the dynamism of his own biological interests. But whatever the merits of this criticism, it seems to me that the only notion of *being* that is now acceptable is one that transcends the antithesis between the static and dynamic, and therefore includes both. Thus when St. Thomas states that God is "subsistent being" (*ipsum esse subsistens*), I believe that this admittedly inadequate description (though immensely significant, if we can concentrate our minds enough really to think about it) is still tenable, provided the suggestion, which is not Aquinas's, of God as a fixed substance ("subsistent") is merged in the concept of "being," understood in its full existential dynamism.

All this can easily be linked to God's revelation of his character to

Moses, as recorded in Exodus 3:14: "I am who I am." Interpreters generally now agree that notions derived from Greek metaphysics are inapplicable here. God is to be regarded as existing not as an eternal absolute but concretely in time. "It is the God himself who unfolds his name as the one who is and will be present, not merely some time and some where but in every now and in every here." [8] The question nevertheless remains whether *being*, as conceived existentially, is a reality each man creates for himself out of nothing by a series of personal decisions or whether it is that to which, having a validity of its own, we respond by our actions. The former view eliminates any transcendent dimension; the latter places man in subordination to Being. A thinker, in Heidegger's striking phrase, must be "obedient to the voice of Being." He goes even further. Differentiating his own position from that of the French atheistic school, he declares that "man is not the lord of what is. Man is the shepherd of Being." As a perceptive theologian has pointed out, "The 'shepherd of Being' is the one to whom Being has entrusted itself and made itself open, and the phrase is reminiscent of St. Paul's expression 'stewards of the mysteries of God' (1 Corinthians 4:1)." [9]

According to my basic way-of-being-in-the-world, Being offers itself to me in proportion to the degree of my openness to receive it. Being, which is the same as transcendence, is beyond man and not at his disposal; it can therefore be considered as grace. Grace, as thus understood, is the drawing near of the divine Being. When my openness and the gift of Being coalesce, there results the transformation, the "rebirth," whereby I become my authentic self. Here we do not have a meeting of two substances. The key concept is that of "openness"—the unrestricted openness of Being in giving, the elimination of my closedness in receiving. It should be added that we are not at this point entering the realm of "mysticism," of something hidden from common observation. That a sustained authenticity can actually be achieved demands faith, but in itself it is a matter of experience, answering to the familiar test that a tree can be known by its fruits. When I try to think of other ways of speaking of Being, or what I have called "pure Existence," God is the easiest. For the Hindu it might be Brahman, for the Muslim, Allah, but for the Christian it will always be God and in particular God as existentially realized in Christ.

8. *Peake's Commentary on the Bible* (London: Thomas Nelson, 1962), p. 213.   9. Macquarrie, *Studies in Christian Existentialism*, p. 135.

What of the attitude or life style best adapted to bringing ourselves into harmony with Being, or Existence, as so considered? It will be generated less by an ideology, an indoctrination of a so-called world view, even when this is regarded as divinely revealed, than by letting in light on the wellsprings of conduct. To be persuaded in the first place ourselves and thus to persuade those who may be influenced by us of the value of acting with forethought and consideration, to be convinced of the necessity always to be fair to others, to bring fully to life our latent capacity to tackle and be patient under difficulties, to realize that our well-being and that of those we make contact with largely depend on our acting with self-restraint and moderation—all this, summing up aspects of the good life that go back to ancient Greece—reaches the foundations of morality far more effectively than the bald prescriptions of the decalogue.

Nevertheless, worship in forms suitable to the mentality and circumstances of the worshipers holds first place, since this is the condition of "openness," of our being brought into harmony with the supremely existent, God. Whether explicitly in a communal act, as in the Eucharist, or implicitly so, as in meditation, the end in view is the same—to make our relationship with God more conscious and so intensify devotion. As long as it remains at this level—that of bhakti, as it is called in the Hindu-Buddhist tradition—it will usually be focused on God as manifested, Christ. From this will result an increasing desire to surrender to the "Lord of what is" and a deepening conviction that despite its problems, its horror and suffering, human existence is meaningful and worthwhile—which I take to be a substantial element in religious faith.

If I were asked for the impossible, to sum up what I mean by ultimate religion in a phrase, I would say that it consisted in *enlightened openness*. But what, it may be asked, of love, which Jesus himself exemplified and insisted on so often? The answer is that love is not so much a challenge or a goal, something we can achieve and practice, helped by divine grace; it is a profound psychological problem. The love that Jesus advocated was *selfless*. And that brings us into a different world—precisely that of rebirth, authenticity, realization, enlightenment, salvation, whichever term we prefer. It is significant that in the prayer that Jesus taught his disciples the word "love" does not occur. The stress is on openness to God—"Thy kingdom come, Thy will be done"—and similarly with man, the removal of all barriers—"Forgive us our debts as we forgive . . ." Unselfless love, the best that most of us have to offer most of the time, is always flawed, however imperceptibly, by self-interest; it easily falls away into some form of paternalism or mere "do-goodism." Awareness that this is so lies behind the song often sung by blacks in America.

> Too much love,
> Too much love,
> Nothing kills a nigger like
> Too much love.

The Buddhist "compassion," it seems to me, has richer implications than all but the supreme form of Christian love. Christianity at the level of practice only rarely overcomes its theoretical dualism between man and God, between man and man. Here we may note in passing that "sin," a very Christian concept, has the same derivation as "sunder," and means *separation*. Sin is what separates us from God and from man, and it may well be, as the ecologists are insistently pointing out, from nature itself. Though here we could have been led astray by an influential guide to conduct already referred to, the Old Testament.

Behind the environment crisis in the U.S. are a few deeply ingrained assumptions. One is that nature exists primarily for man to conquer. Many thinkers have traced the notion back to early Judaism and Christianity. Genesis 1:26 is explicit on the point that God gave man "dominion over the fish of the sea, and over the birds of the air, and over the cattle, and over all the earth." The ecological truth is quite different. The great early civilizations—Babylonian, Sumerian, Assyrian, Chinese, Indian and perhaps Mayan exploited the basic resources of the land. In the end, says LaMont Cole, "they just farmed themselves out of business." [10]

It seems likely that Buddhists, as they would readily admit, often fall as far below their own teaching on the nature of compassion as Christians reach beyond the individualistic dualism latent in much of their theology. The adherents of both faiths when at their best will readily endorse Walt Whitman's declaration.

10. "Fighting to Save the Earth from Man," *Time*, February 2, 1970, p. 46. True to the principles of biblical theology, the compilers of the new Catholic liturgy show themselves as innocent of the findings of the ecologists as the author of Genesis. One of the Eucharistic prayers clearly echoing the text just cited runs as follows: "Father . . . You formed man in your own likeness and *set him over the whole world* to serve you, his creator, and *to rule over all creatures* [italics inserted]."

I am the man, I suffer'd, I was there.

. . . .

I do not ask the wounded person how he feels, I myself become the wounded person. . . .

Perhaps the Buddhist and Christian ways of loving can meet if the emphasis is thrown on enlightened understanding rather than on benevolence. Such understanding is not a matter of forming correct ideas about another person; it means becoming existentially one with him. This can only happen at the level of *being*—not my being in relation to his being, but being at its ground, or in its "suchness." To love another person is to sit down in front of him, so to speak, without any preconceptions, to lose one's self-centered awareness, to drop thoughts about any interpersonal relationship, because attention is then impeded by being focused on action and reaction between self and the other. When understanding passes from a mental activity to full realization, there is neither self nor other, only that which really is. Love is selfless in the sense that it is the attainment of the basic harmony of being, which is both obscured and revealed by the distinctive surface egocentricities of those who love.

The distinguished psychiatrist Thomas Hora has pointed out that a person who truly loves "is concerned with participating in existence as a beneficial presence. Such love is neither personal, nor interpersonal, nor impersonal—it is trans-personal." Here we reach the level of the existentialist "openness," which seems to me to be only another word for the Buddhist "emptiness," sunyata. We are removed from any form of idolatry (which is the essence of sin), that is to say, making an idol of the self, or of the other, or of what seems to be, or of what we think should be. The concern is not with egocentric self-realization but only with the realization of that which is, unqualified, unconditional Existence.

Religion in the ultimate sense lies in man's responding to the Existence in virtue of which he himself exists. Nothing lies outside existence; therefore existence is "nondual," as the Eastern philosophers say. This is the basic meaning to be attached to that admirable Christian word "atonement"—"at-one-ment." Openness is all—openness to the play of existence, whether it is manifested as God, as man, as animals or the world of nature; not openness as mere passivity but as the response of enlightened understanding, which will often lead to vigorous and sustained activity. Such openness enables us to realize that individual selfhood—the ego closed in on itself—is illusory. Only in piercing through this illusion, which is a function belonging not to the will but to the mind, can I become a loving person—as distinct from a man of good will, whose genuine affections are restricted to a comparatively small circle of relatives, friends, and acquaintances. When we love our neighbor in the New Testament sense, the focus of love is not his personality or character structure but his being. Similarly, the conventional forms of religious devotion, ritualism and liturgy, for all their importance, are not enough. The ultimate concern is with holiness understood as wholeness within the conditions of our own mode of being-in-the-world and centered on existential fulfillment. Whenever we think or act self-centeredly, holiness is precluded because we are involved in a "cognitive deficiency." Our view is partial and fragmented; we are no longer fully open to reality in all its possibilities. In order to achieve the final authenticity and be brought into harmony with "pure Existence" we need to enlarge our consciousness to the point of attaining an existential perspective that is without limits. Hence the importance of prayer and meditation, particularly some such form of the latter as was described on an earlier page. By thus enlarging and purifying our consciousness, we learn to see life from the standpoint of total existence and accordingly to know the truth that makes us free.

When we try to think of the all-important "openness" to existence, as practiced within the Christian framework, certain difficulties arise that are more apparent than real. Dogma, legalism, purposeful virtue have all to be understood in the light of the Johannine primacy of truth and the Pauline emphasis on freedom. Nevertheless, Christian moral training would lose nothing if—alongside its ethical virtues of prudence, justice, courage, and moderation—it incorporated the Buddhist counterparts, all of which center upon openness: friendliness, compassion, joy, and equanimity. A classical Buddhist text on "right mindfulness" runs as follows: "Develop the state of mind of friendliness, for as you do so, ill-will will grow less; and of compassion, for thus vexation will grow less; and of joy, for thus aversion will grow less; and of equanimity, for thus repugnance will grow less." [11]

God is open to us in proportion to our openness to him. God,

11. De Bary, *The Buddhist Tradition*, p. 27.

simply without qualification, *is*. He is not masculine, feminine, or neuter; yet he could just as well be said to be all three. He is not abstract, for he cannot be thought; he is not concrete, for he cannot be touched; he is not a subject, for he does not underly anything; he is not an object, for he is not at anyone's disposal; he is "all in all" (1 Corinthians 15:28). God's fullness has for its complement our emptiness, that is to say, our being empty of self. To understand this situation, to *realize* it, is to transpose emptiness into love—love here signifying not the dualism of a subject-object, I-thou relationship but the non-dualism of compassionate identification with what exists, or rather with existence itself. "I do not ask the wounded person how he feels, I myself become the wounded person."

Translated in terms of everyday, practical living—since it is impossible for the individual to enter into the particularities of the whole world's troubles—what is called for is that I should become a loving person at the existential level, that is to say, love creatively the being in everyone and everything. The attainment of this condition is what I understand by rebirth, enlightenment, being harmonized with pure Existence—an impossibility unless initiated and sustained by Existence itself in that actualization we call grace. Loving in this manner, we worship God as he should be worshiped, for we are liberated from any idolatry, which is nothing else but being fixated on some particular manifestation of being, while at the same time we are left free to pay due reverence to every embodiment of existence —to the Buddha, for example, as well as Jesus. On the supreme value of existential selflessness, that is, responding with compassionate insight to every aspect of being, I believe, with proper acknowledgment to all the orthodoxies, that the higher religions speak with one voice. Names may be different, but the actuality is the same. It is the "realization" of Hinduism, the "liberation" of Buddhism, the "walking with God" of Judaism, the "love" of Christianity, and the "surrender," which is the very meaning of Islam. At the greatest crisis of his life it was expressed in full measure in the agonized prayer of Jesus: "Not what I will, but what thou wilt" (Mark 14:36).

God is neither "up there" nor "down here." He is existential Being (Exodus 3:14) and he is Love (1 John 4:8). Therefore the ultimate form of the worship of God, it seems to me, is to become a loving person, or to love being loving. Perhaps this is the point of entry for those impatient of established rituals, who hanker after a religion of no religion—to love being loving, for we tend to become what we love. "If we love one another, God abides in us" (1 John 4:12). In the ancient Latin of the Maundy Thursday liturgy the point is strikingly made: *Ubi caritas et amor, Deus ibi est* ("Wherever charity and love are found, God is there"). Worship at the popular level cannot exist without external forms and creeds, which, if they always to some extent conceal, can also powerfully reveal the realities they represent. Let these autobiographical explorations end then, as befits a Catholic, with a profession of belief in the Holy Trinity[12]—the "Father of lights" (James 1:17), the Son who was so often "moved with compassion" (Mark 1:41; 6:34), the "Spirit of life," which "has set me free" (Romans 8:2). May the triune God be worshiped more widely, as *realized* in our authentic existence, being manifested in the divine-human trinity—enlightenment, compassion, freedom. And these three are one.

12. At the level of religious experience, within the Catholic tradition, compare the opening of Chapter 44 of the *Revelations of Divine Love* by Mother Julian of Norwich: "Of the properties of the Trinity, and how a creature has the same properties, doing that which it was made for, seeing, beholding and marvelling at his God, so that he seems to himself as nothing."

Appendix

A Note on Chapter Six: *"Promptings from India"*

Below are the names of those who were kind enough to give me the benefit of their expert knowledge while I was in India and Thailand from October, 1967, to early March, 1968. Though these learned exponents of the Hindu-Buddhist tradition generously co-operated to the full, and every care has been taken to ensure an accurate version of what was tape-recorded—a transcript of the appropriate dialogue having been forwarded respectively to each of the participants—final responsibility for the text as it appears can only be mine. The names are listed alphabetically, followed by the contraction (in parentheses) used in each dialogue.

MR. JOHN BLOFELD (J. B.): United Nations, Bangkok, Thailand

DR. LOKESH CHANDRA (DR. C.): International Academy of Indian Culture, New Delhi, India

DR. ROBERT EXELL (DR. R. E.): Chulalongkorn University, Bangkok, Thailand

REVEREND S. KAPPEN (JESUIT): Lumen Institute, Cochin, India

PHRA KHANTIPALO BHIKKHU (BHIKKHU): Wat Bovoranives Vihara, Bangkok, Thailand

DR. R. S. MISRA (DR. M.): Banaras Hindu University University, Varanasi, India

DR. T. R. V. MURTI (DR. T. M.): Banaras Hindu University, Varanasi, India (Since September, 1970, Professor of Religion, McMaster University, Hamilton, Ontario, Canada)

DR. S. RADHAKRISHNAN (DR. S. R.): Former President of the Republic of India, Madras, India

DR. VENKATARAMA RAGHAVAN (DR. R.): University of Madras, Madras, India (Professor of Sanskrit at the University of Madras at the time of our meeting, now retired with a Jawaharlal Nehru Fellowship)

The warmest thanks are due to the above named, each of whom, by the kindly welcome extended to me, witnessed in his own person to the religious tradition he so notably represents. With them should be linked the name of my friend Harold Talbott, who accompanied me throughout the journey and gladly undertook the work of recording these encounters. To them all, for their contribution toward greater mutual understanding between East and West, I wish to express my deep appreciation and gratitude.

A. G.

Index

Aaron, 90
Abbot, at Ampleforth, x, 51, 52, 59; a Benedictine, 223; a Chinese, 162; at Portsmouth, R. I., 66; a Tibetan, 194; a ten-year-old, 195
Absolute, the, 106, 109, 112, 113, 116, 118, 152, 166, 174, 175, 220; the Hegelian, 130; the Platonic, as basis of universal religion, 206
Absolution, priestly, 35
Absolutism, 92
Academy, the Platonic, 206, 210
Acquaintances, 264
Acropolis, the, 208, 212
Action, religious path of, 138
Activity, 263
Acton, John (Lord), 12
Acts of Apostles, 72, 94, 96, 221
Adam, 135, 136
Adamantine Vehicle, 167
Adibuddhas (primordial Buddhas), 166
Adolescence, 34, 237
Adolescents, 27, 33, 48. *See also* Young, the
Adoration, 79
Adultery, 237
Advaita (nondualism), 109, 113, 119, 121, 127, 174
Advaitin(s) (adherents of Advaita), 113, 128
Aeon (a power), 87
Aeschylus, 206
Affection, 231, 238
Affluent, the, 202, 234
Africa, 142, 148, 203, 210, 251
Agapé (divine love), 211
Aggressiveness, 28
Agnostic, 160, 161, 249
Agnosticism, 109, 144, 160, 161
Agricultural society, 180

Alcibiades, 55
Alcohol, 44
Alexander the Great, 83, 198
Alexandria, 84, 98
Allah, 199, 244, 260
Allahabad, 23
Alvisatos, Hamilcar S., 206
Amdo, Tibet, 186
Amenhotep IV (Egyptian king), 46
America, 48, 58, 60, 61, 66, 67, 107, 149. *See also* Latin America; North America; United States
Amiability, 163, 231
Ampleforth Abbey, x, 30, 51, 52, 54, 56, 57, 61, 67, 103, 145; Abbot of, x, 51, 52, 59
Ampleforth Journal, 101
Anatta (non-ego, doctrine of Buddhism), 154
Andrews, C. F., 142
Angels, 86, 219, 224
Anger, 27, 136
Anglicanism, 50, 155
Animals, 232, 263; sacrifice of, 89, 145
Annihilation, 144, 156, 157
Ansari of Herat, 199
Anthropomorphism, 119, 159, 209
Anti-Catholicism, 217
Antifeminism, 180
Antigua, 45
Antinomianism, 177
Antioch, 84, 88, 96
Anti-Protestantism, 217
Anti-Semitism, 73
Apocalyptic beliefs, 42, 85, 94, 99
Apologia Pro Vita Sua (John Henry Newman), 1
Apollo, 210, 212
Apostles, 79
Apostolate, 238
Appreciation, 231, 268